Bloom's Major Literary Characters

Sir John Falstaff

Edited and with an introduction by
Harold Bloom
Sterling Professor of the Humanities
Yale University

CHELSEA HOUSE
PUBLISHERS
A Haights Cross Communications ◆ Company
Philadelphia

©2004 by Chelsea House Publishers, a subsidiary of
Haights Cross Communications.

A Haights Cross Communications Company

Introduction © 2004 by Harold Bloom.

Printed and bound in the United States of America.

10 9 8 7 6 5 4 3 2 1

Library of Congress Cataloging-in-Publication Data

Sir John Falstaff / edited and with an introduction by Harold Bloom.
        p. cm .— (Bloom's Major Literary Characters)
Includes bibliographical references and index.
  ISBN 0-7910-7666-0 HC   0-7910-7982-1 PB
Shakespeare, William, 1564–1616—Characters—Falstaff. 2. Shakespeare,
William, 1564–1616. King Henry IV. Part 1. 3. Shakespeare, William,
1564–1616. King Henry IV. Part 2. 4. Shakespeare, William, 1564–1616.
Henry V. 5. Falstaff, John, Sir (Fictitious character) 6. Soldiers in
literature. I. Bloom, Harold. II. Major literary characters III.
  PR2993.F2S53 2003
  822.3'.—dc22

                                                      20030168954

Contributing editor: Pamela Loos

Cover design by Keith Trego

Cover: © Hulton-Deutsch Collection/CORBIS

Layout by EJB Publishing Services

Chelsea House Publishers
1974 Sproul Road, Suite 400
Broomall, PA 19008-0914

www.chelseahouse.com

Contents

HAROLD BLOOM

The Analysis of Character

"Character," according to our dictionaries, still has as a primary meaning a graphic symbol, such as a letter of the alphabet. This meaning reflects the word's apparent origin in the ancient Greek character, a sharp stylus. *Charactēr* also meant the mark of the stylus' incisions. Recent fashions in literary criticism have reduced "character" in literature to a matter of marks upon a page. But our word "character" also has a very different meaning, matching that of the ancient Greek *ēthos*, "habitual way of life." Shall we say then that literary character is an imitation of human character, or is it just a grouping of marks? The issue is between a critic like Dr. Samuel Johnson, for whom words were as much like people as like things, and a critic like the late Roland Barthes, who told us that "the fact can only exist linguistically, as a term of discourse." Who is closer to our experience of reading literature, Johnson or Barthes? What difference does it make, if we side with one critic rather than the other?

Barthes is famous, like Foucault and other recent French theorists, for having added to Nietzsche's proclamation of the death of God a subsidiary demise, that of the literary author. If there are no authors, then there are no fictional personages, presumably because literature does not refer to a world outside language. Words indeed necessarily refer to other words in the first place, but the impact of words ultimately is drawn from a universe of fact. Stories, poems, and plays are recognizable as such because they are human utterances within traditions of utterances, and traditions, by achieving authority, become a kind of fact, or at least the sense of a fact. Our sense that literary characters, within the context of a fictive cosmos, indeed are fictional personages is also a kind of fact. The meaning and value of every character in a successful work of literary representation depend upon our ideas of persons in the factual reality of our lives.

Literary character is always an invention, and inventions generally are indebted to prior inventions. Shakespeare is the inventor of literary character as we know it; he reformed the universal human expectations for the verbal imitation of personality, and the reformation appears now to be permanent and uncannily inevitable. Remarkable as the Bible and Homer are at representing personages, their characters are relatively unchanging. They age within their stories, but their habitual modes of being do not develop. Jacob and Achilles unfold before us, but without metamorphoses. Lear and Macbeth, Hamlet and Othello severely modify themselves not only by their actions, but by their utterances, and most of all through *overhearing themselves*, whether they speak to themselves or to others. Pondering what they themselves have said, they will to change, and actually do change, sometimes extravagantly yet always persuasively. Or else they suffer change, without willing it, but in reaction not so much to their language as to their relation to that language.

I do not think it useful to say that Shakespeare successfully imitated elements in our characters. Rather, it could be argued that he compelled aspects of character to appear that previously were concealed, or not available to representation. This is not to say that Shakespeare is God, but to remind us that language is not God either. The mimesis of character in Shakespeare's dramas now seems to us normative, and indeed became the accepted mode almost immediately, as Ben Jonson shrewdly and somewhat grudgingly implied. And yet, Shakespearean representation has surprisingly little in common with the imitation of reality in Jonson or in Christopher Marlowe. The origins of Shakespeare's originality in the portrayal of men and women are to be found in the *Canterbury Tales* of Geoffrey Chaucer, insofar as they can be located anywhere before Shakespeare himself, Chaucer's savage and superb Pardoner overhears his own tale-telling, as well as his mocking rehearsal of his own spiel, and through this overhearing he is emboldened to forget himself, and enthusiastically urges all his fellow-pilgrims to come forward to be fleeced by him. His self-awareness, and apocalyptically rancid sense of spiritual fall, are preludes to the even grander abysses of the perverted will in Iago and in Edmund. What might be called the character trait of a negative charisma may be Chaucer's invention, but came to its perfection in Shakespearean mimesis.

The analysis of character is as much Shakespeare's invention as the representation of character is, since Iago and Edmund are adepts at analyzing both themselves and their victims. Hamlet, whose overwhelming charisma has many negative components, is certainly the most comprehensive of all literary characters, and so necessarily prophesies the labyrinthine complexities of the will in Iago and Edmund. Charisma, according to Max Weber, its first codifier, is primarily a natural endowment, and implies a primordial and idiosyncratic power over nature, and so finally over death. Hamlet's uncanniness is at its most suggestive in the scene of his long dying, where the audience, through the mediation of Horatio, itself is compelled to meditate upon suicide, if only because outliving the prince of Denmark scarcely seems an option.

Shakespearean representation has usurped not only our sense of literary character, but our sense of ourselves as characters, with Hamlet playing the part of the largest of these usurpations. Insofar as we have an idea of human disinterestedness, we tend to derive it from the Hamlet of Act V, whose quietism has about it a ghostly authority. Oscar Wilde, in his profound and profoundly witty dialogue, "The Decay of Lying," expressed a permanent insight when he insisted that art shaped every era, far more than any age formed art. Life imitates art, we imitate Shakespeare, because without Shakespeare we would perish for lack of images. Wilde's grandest audacity demystifies Shakespearean mimesis with a Shakespearean vivaciousness: "This unfortunate aphorism about art holding the mirror up to Nature is deliberately said by Hamlet in order to convince the bystanders of his absolute insanity in all art-matters." Of *Hamlet's* influence upon the ages Wilde remarked that: "The world has grown sad because a puppet was once melancholy." "Puppet" is Wilde's own deconstruction, a brilliant reminder that Shakespeare's artistry of illusion has so mastered reality as to have changed reality, evidently forever.

The analysis of character, as a critical pursuit, seems to me as much a Shakespearean invention as literary character was, since much of what we know about how to analyze character necessarily follows Shakespearean procedures. His hero-villains, from Richard III through Iago, Edmund, and Macbeth, are shrewd and endless questers into their own self-motivations. If we could bear to see Hamlet, in his unwearied negations, as another hero-villain, then we would judge him the supreme analyst of the darker recalcitrances in the selfhood. Freud followed the pre-Socratic Empedocles, in arguing that character is fate, a frightening doctrine that maintains the fear that there are no accidents, that overdetermination rules us all of our lives. Hamlet assumes the same, yet adds to this argument the terrible passivity he manifests in Act V. Throughout Shakespeare's tragedies, the most interesting personages seem doom-eager, reminding us again that a Shakespearean reading of Freud would be more illuminating than a Freudian exegesis of

Shakespeare. We learn more when we discover Hamlet in the Freudian Death Drive, than when we read *Beyond the Pleasure Principle* into *Hamlet*.

In Shakespearean comedy, character achieves its true literary apotheosis, which is the representation of the inner freedom that can be created by great wit alone. Rosalind and Falstaff, perhaps alone among Shakespeare's personages, match Hamlet in wit, though hardly in the metaphysics of consciousness. Whether in the comic or the modern mode, Shakespeare has set the standard of measurement in the balance between character and passion.

In Shakespeare the self is more dramatized than theatricalized, which is why a Shakespearean reading of Freud works out so well. Character-formation after the passing of the Oedipal stage takes the place of fetishistic fragmentings of the self. Critics who now call literary character into question, and who proclaim also the death of the author, invariably also regard all notions, literary and human, of a stable character as being mere reductions of deeper pre-Oedipal desires. It becomes clear that the fortunes of literary character rise and fall with the prestige of normative conceptions of the ego. Shakespeare's Iago, who wars against being, may be the first deconstructionist of the self, with his proclamation of "I am not what I am." This constitutes the necessary prologue to any view that would regard a fixed ego as a virtual abnormality. But deconstructions of the self are no more modern than Modernism is. Like literary modernism, the decentered ego came out of the Hellenistic culture of ancient Alexandria. The Gnostic heretics believed that the psyche, like the body, was a fallen entity, mechanically fashioned by the Demiurge or false creator. They held however that each of us possessed also a spark or pneuma, which was a fragment of the original Abyss or true, alien God. The soul or psyche within every one of us was thus at war with the self or pneuma, and only that sparklike self could be saved.

Shakespeare, following after Chaucer in this respect, was the first and remains still the greatest master of representing character both as a stable soul and a wavering self. There is a substance that endures in Shakespeare's figures, and there is also a quicksilver rendition of the unsettling sparks. Racine and Tolstoy, Balzac and Dickens, follow in Shakespeare's wake by giving us some sense of pre-Oedipal sparks or drives, and considerably more sense of post-Oedipal character and personality, stabilizations or sublimations of the fetish-seeking drives. Critics like Leo Bersani and René Girard argue eloquently against our taking this mimesis as the only proper work of literature. I would suggest that strong fictions of the self, from the Bible through Samuel Beckett, necessarily participate in both modes, the sublimation of desire, and the persistence of a primordial desire. The mystery of Hamlet or of Lear is intimately invested in the tangled mixture of the two modes of representation.

Psychic mobility is proposed by Bersani as the ideal to which deconstructions of the literary self may yet guide us. The ideal has its pathos, but the realities of literary representation seem to me very different, perhaps destructively so. When a novelist like D. H. Lawrence sought to reduce his characters to Eros and the Death Drive, he still had to persuade us of his authority at mimesis by lavishing upon the figures of *The Rainbow* and *Women in Love* all of the vivid stigmata of normative personality. Birkin and Ursula may represent antithetical and uncanny drives, but they develop and change as characters pondering their own pronouncements and reactions to self and others. The cost of a non-Shakespearean representation is enormous. Pynchon, in *The Crying of Lot 49* and *Gravity's Rainbow*, evades the burden of the normative by resorting to something like Christopher Marlowe's art of caricature in *The Jew of Malta*. Marlowe's Barabas is a marvelous rhetorician, yet he is a cartoon alongside the troublingly equivocal Shylock. Pynchon's personages are deliberate cartoons also, as flat as comic strips. Marlowe's achievement, and Pynchon's, are beyond dispute, yet they are like the prelude and the postlude to Shakespearean reality. They do not wish to engage with our hunger for the empirical world and so they enter the problematic cosmos of literary fantasy.

No writer, not even Shakespeare or Proust, alters the available stock that we agree to call reality, but Shakespeare, more than any other, does show us how much of reality we could encounter if only we retained adequate desire. The strong literary representation of character is already an analysis of character, and is part of the healing work of a literary culture, which implicitly seeks to cure violence through a normative mimesis of ego, *as if it were stable*, whether in actuality it is or is not. I do not believe that this is a social quest taken on by literary culture, but rather that we confront here the aesthetic essence of what makes a culture *literary*, rather than metaphysical or ethical or religious. A culture becomes literary when its conceptual modes have failed it, which means when religion, philosophy, and science have begun to lose their authority. If they cannot heal violence, then literature attempts to do so, which may be only a turning inside out of the critical arguments of Girard and Bersani.

I conclude by offering a particular instance or special case as a paradigm for the healing enterprise that is at once the representation and the analysis of literary character. Let us call it the aesthetics of being outraged, or rather of successfully representing the state of being outraged. W. C. Fields was one modern master of such representation, and Nathanael West was another, as was Faulkner before him. Here also the greatest master remains Shakespeare, whose Macbeth, himself a bloody outrage, yet retains our imaginative sympathy precisely because he grows increasingly outraged as he experiences the equivocation of the fiend that lies like truth. The double-natured promises and the prophecies of the weird sisters finally induce in Macbeth an apocalyptic version of the stage actor's anxiety at missing cues, the horror of a phantasmagoric stage fright of missing one's time, of always reacting too late. Macbeth, a veritable monster of solipsistic inwardness but no intellectual, counters his dilemma by fresh murders, that prolong him in time yet provoke him only to a perpetually freshened sense of being outraged, as all his expectations become still worse confounded. We are moved by Macbeth, however estrangedly, because his terrible inwardness is a paradigm for our own solipsism, but also because none of us can resist a strong and successful representation of the human in a state of being outraged.

The ultimate outrage is the necessity of dying, an outrage concealed in a multitude of masks, including the tyrannical ambitions of Macbeth. I suspect that our outrage at being outraged is the most difficult of all our affects for us to represent to ourselves, which is why we are so inclined to imaginative sympathy for a character who strongly conveys that affect to us. The Shrike of West's *Miss Lonelyhearts* or Faulkner's Joe Christmas of *Light in August* are crucial modern instances, but such figures can be located in many other works, since the ability to represent this extreme emotion is one of the tests that strong writers are driven to set for themselves.

However a reader seeks to reduce literary character to a question of marks on a page, she will come at last to the impasse constituted by the thought of death, her death, and before that to all the stations of being outraged that memorialize her own drive towards death. In reading, she quests for evidences that are strong representations, whether of her desire or her despair. Such questings constitute the necessary basis for the analysis of literary character, an enterprise that always will survive every vagary of critical fashion.

Editor's Note

The visionary center of this gathering is the cover photograph of Sir Ralph Richardson playing Falstaff in 1946, an event that made me a lifelong Falstaffian.

My introduction sketches my defense of Falstaff against his moralizing detractors.

The great Romantic critic William Hazlitt and the important late Nineteenth Century Shakespearean interpreter, A.C. Bradley, join in their preference for Falstaff over his rejecting pupil, Prince Hal who becomes King Henry V.

Harold C. Goddard, to me the most humane of Twentieth Century Shakespeareans, warmly appreciates the immortal Falstaff, after which Kenneth Tynan praises Ralph Richardson's apotheosis in that role.

In a sensitive, dialectical response to the rejection of Falstaff, Leo Salingar emphasizes that critics will never agree about the rights and wrongs of King Henry V's brutal action.

E. Talbot Donaldson, fiercely Chaucerian, shows us the likely influence of the Wife of Bath upon Falstaff, while Northrop Frye, the great Canadian Magus, observes that Falstaff stands against the movement of history.

William Empson, always brilliant, contrasts Falstaff's vitalism to Henry V's deathliness, after which Paul M. Cubeta studies Falstaff's death-scene, as narrated by Mistress Quickly in *Henry V*.

The vexed issue of morality in the Falstaff plays is analyzed by Edward Tomarken, in the wake of Dr. Samuel Johnson, who both moralized against Falstaff yet loved him.

François Laroque strongly observes that Falstaff's excess argues for life at the expense of tragic sacrifice.

HAROLD BLOOM

Introduction

In an earlier study (*Ruin the Sacred Truths*, 1989) I ventured the judgment that Shakespeare's Falstaff was a successful representation of what Freud thought impossible, a human being without a superego. Nietzsche, I remarked, had attempted just such a representation in his Zarathustra, and rather conspicuously had failed. What I forgot then, or more likely repressed, was that Freud had commented upon Falstaff in his *Jokes and Their Relation to the Unconscious* (1905). As a fierce Falstaffian, and a rather ambivalent Freudian, I rather dislike Freud on Falstaff, and I quote it here with some distaste:

> The grandiose humorous effect of a figure like that of the fat knight Sir John Falstaff rests on an economy in contempt and indignation. We recognize him as an undeserving gormandizer and swindler, but our condemnation is disarmed by a whole number of factors. We can see that he knows himself as well as we do; he impresses us by his wit, and, besides this, his physical misproportion has the effect of encouraging us to take a comic view of him instead of a serious one, as though the demands of morality and honor must rebound from so fat a stomach. His doings are on the whole harmless, and are almost excused by the common baseness of the people he cheats. We admit that the poor fellow has a right to try to live and enjoy himself like anyone else, and we almost pity him because in the chief situations we

1

find him a plaything in the hands of someone far his superior. So we cannot feel angry with him and we add all that we economize in indignation with him to the comic pleasure which he affords us apart from this. Sir John's own humor arises in fact from the superiority of an ego which neither his physical nor his moral defects can rob of its cheerfulness and assurance.

Freud's economics of the psyche certainly are not Shakespeare's, and I am reminded again how much we need a Shakespearean reading of Freud and how little use is a Freudian reading of Shakespeare. The cheerfulness and assurance of the greatest wit in all literature do not stem from the superiority of his ego but from his freedom, specifically freedom of his ego from the superego. It is dangerous to condescend to Falstaff (as Freud does) because there is no greater wit in a literary representation than Shakespeare invested in Falstaff, the Falstaff of the *Henry IV* plays. Fundamentally, Freud thought that the comic spirit could flourish only when the superego mitigated its severities towards the battered ego. But what of the comedy that rises where there simply is no superego, no overdetermined need for punishment, no turning of the ego against itself? Where is the superego in the magnificent Falstaff? Is there any other literary character whatsoever who seems so free, free to play, free to mock the state, free to evade time? With a few honorable exceptions, Shakespeare's critics simply seem incapable of hearing what Falstaff says, and how he says it. Not even Hamlet is endowed by Shakespeare with more wit and intellect than Falstaff. It is Falstaff's cognitive strength that should astonish us. Nearly everything he says demands subsequent meditation on our part, and rewards our reveries with fresh insights that expand our understanding of far more than Falstaff himself. I am suggesting that the disreputable Falstaff—glutton, boozer, womanizer—is a teacher of wisdom, a hilarious teacher. When I was fifteen, I saw Ralph Richardson play Falstaff (with Laurence Olivier as Hotspur), and I have carried the image of Richardson's exuberant and inventive Falstaff in my head for forty-five years now, and find the image informing the text every time I reread or teach the *Henry* IV plays. Richardson's Falstaff was neither an adorable roisterer nor a kind of counter-courtier, eager for possibilities of power. Rather, he was a veteran warrior who had seen through warfare, discarded its honor and glory as pernicious illusions, and had decided that true life was play, both as we play on stage or in games, and as we play when we are children. Falstaff, wicked and old, has become a wise child again, which is the meaning of the magnificent apologia delivered by him to the Lord Chief justice, when that embodiment of the state's sagacity reproves him for pretending to be young:

My lord, I was born about three of the clock in the afternoon, with a white head and something a round belly. For my voice, I have lost it with hallowing and singing of anthems. To approve my youth further, I will not. The truth is, I am only old in judgment and understanding; and he that will caper with me for a thousand marks, let him lend me the money, and have at him!

Falstaff is of the company both of the heroic wits, Rosalind and Hamlet, and of the heroic vitalists, the Wife of Bath and the Panurge of Falstaffian Rabelais. He could also ride into the world of Sancho Panza and the Don, because in some sense he is their synthesis, fusing Sancho's ribald realism and the Don's faith in his own imagination and in the order of play. The Don's chivalric madness is shared by Hotspur, and not at all by Falstaff, but Cervantes is perhaps the only author except Chaucer, and Shakespeare himself, who could have imagined Sir John Falstaff. Hazlitt charmingly remarked that the Fat Knight "is perhaps the most substantial comic character that ever was invented," and certainly Falstaff is the patron of all fat men forever. There is a great deal more to him psychically than his wit, and yet wit is more central to him than to Rosalind or Hamlet. The formidable Rosalind has a gentleness that tempers her exuberance, while Hamlet, in his bewildering complexity, has in him a savagery nearly as strong as his skepticism. Falstaff's exuberance is primal and unstoppable, while he has nothing of Hamlet's savagery, or of Hal's. If there is a mystery to Falstaff, it is in his vexed relationship to Hal, which is hardly to be understood if we refuse to imagine its prehistory. L. C. Knights and other Formalists long ago shamed most critics out of considering the long foregrounds of Shakespearean protagonists, but I am no more a Formalist than I am an Historicist, and I am happy to puzzle out how the given has been constituted each time I start on one of the plays.

Hal's ambivalence towards Falstaff evidently passed into an exasperated negativity, almost a murderousness, long before the first part of *Henry IV* opens. A Formalist or an Historicist would say there was no such "long before," but no start is an authentic genesis after Genesis itself, and Shakespeare is much the greatest master of implied foregrounds that we ever will know. When we first encounter Falstaff and Hal, their dialogue is already the death's duel it rarely ceases to be, with the Prince of Wales almost perpetually attacking, and Sir John defending with deftness and a teacher's dignity, since he is aware that the rhetoric used against him by Hal remains always his own invention. The character of the future Henry V is fortunately hardly my concern here, since this cold opportunist, so admired by scholars, is precisely what Harold Goddard termed him: a hypocritical and ambitious politician, caring only for glory and for power, his father's true son. Hal is best categorized by his own despicable couplet:

> I'll so offend, to make offence a skill;
> Redeeming time when men think least I will.

Redemption of time is not exactly the Falstaffian project, as Hotspur tells us, when he asks if Hal and Falstaff's gang are coming to the battle:

> Where is his son,
> The nimble-footed madcap Prince of Wales,
> And his comrades, that daffed the world aside
> And bid it pass?

Thrusting the world aside, and telling it to pass, indeed is pure Falstaff, when one translates "the world" as Hotspur's exaltation of battle. However one wants to interpret Hal's Falstaffian phrase, it is difficult to improve upon Dr. Johnson's analysis of the relationship between Falstaff and Hal:

> Yet the man thus corrupt, thus despicable, makes himself necessary to the Prince that despises him, by the most pleasing of all qualities, perpetual gaiety, by an unfailing power of exciting laughter, which is the more freely indulged as his wit is not of the splendid or ambitious kind but consists in easy escapes and sallies of levity, which make sport but raise no envy. It must be observed that he is stained with no enormous or sanguinary crimes, so that his licentiousness is not so offensive but that it may be borne for his mirth.

Johnson's ambivalence towards Falstaff only superficially resembles Hal's. Both despise Falstaff, on conventional grounds, but Johnson, afflicted by a vile melancholy, forgives Falstaff everything for his perpetual gaiety, which the great doctor so desperately sought in his companions. Hal, no melancholic, found something else in Falstaff, a teacher of wit and wisdom, but a teacher he no longer cares to need. We, the audience, find more in Falstaff, because Falstaff—more than any other character in Shakespeare, indeed in all literature—bears the Blessing, in the original Yahwistic sense of more life. Falstaff, in himself, is one of the enlargements of life, one of the intimations of a time without boundaries, of a desire that cannot be beggared by fulfillment.

It is another critical commonplace to assert that Falstaff undergoes a degeneration in moral sensibility in Part Two of *Henry IV*. His humor may be a touch coarser, I might admit, but his exuberance does not falter, and his intelligence remains triumphant. What a teacher instructs us in is at last himself, and the more attractive qualities manifested by the protagonist of *Henry V* are subtly traceable to the lesson of the master. Falstaff is more than equal to every event and to every antagonist. Hamlet's intellect has faith neither in language nor in itself; Falstaff's intellect molds language precisely to its ends, and retains a perfect confidence in the mind's triumph over every danger. Hal's obsessive need to prove Falstaff a coward tells us nothing about Falstaff, and almost too much about Hal.

Falstaff's rivals in Shakespeare are not many: Hamlet, Rosalind, and Cleopatra would complete the list unless we admit the intellectual villains, Iago and Edmund. All six of these have the rhetorical genius to overcome any disputant. Yet Falstaff stands apart from the others, because he is older than all of them, and younger than all of them, younger and older even than Cleopatra, who ends in absolute transcendence, whereas Falstaff ends in rejection and grief. The great wit has violated Freud's admonition, which is not to invest too much affection in any single person. Falstaff's tragedy (what else can we call it?) is one of misplaced love, but Shakespeare does not allow that to be our final sense of his grandest comic creation. Instead, we are given the great vision of the death of Falstaff in *Henry V*, which assures us that "he's in Arthur's bosom, if ever man went to Arthur's bosom. A' made a finer end and went away an it had been any christom child." Playing with flowers, and smiling upon his fingers' end, Sir John dies as a child, reminding us again of his total lack of hypocrisy, of what after all makes us love him, of what doubtless first drew the Machiavellian Hal to him. Freedom from the superego, authentic freedom, is the liberty to play, even as a child plays, in the very act of dying.

WILLIAM HAZLITT

Henry IV: *In Two Parts*

If Shakespeare's fondness for the ludicrous sometimes led to faults in his tragedies (which was not often the case), he has made us amends by the character of Falstaff. This is perhaps the most substantial comic character that ever was invented. Sir John carries a most portly presence in the mind's eye; and in him; not to speak it profanely, 'we behold the fullness of the spirit of wit and humour bodily'. We are as well acquainted with his person as his mind, and his jokes come upon us with double force and relish from the quantity of flesh through which they make their way, as he shakes his fat sides with laughter, or 'lards the lean earth as he walks along'. Other comic characters seem, if we approach and handle them, to resolve themselves into air, 'into thin air'; but this is embodied and palpable to the grossest apprehension: it lies 'three fingers deep upon the ribs', it plays about the lungs and the diaphragm with all the force of animal enjoyment. His body is like a good estate to his mind, from which he receives rents and revenues of profit and pleasure in kind, according to its extent, and the richness of the soil. Wit is often a meagre substitute for pleasurable sensation; an effusion of spleen and petty spite at the comforts of others, from feeling none in itself. Falstaff's wit is an emanation of a fine constitution; an exuberance of good-humour and good-nature; an overflowing of his love of laughter, and good-fellowship; a giving vent to his heart's ease and over-contentment with himself and others. He would not be in character, if he were not so fat as he

From *Characters of Shakespeare's Plays*. © 1916, 1975 by Oxford University Press.

is; for there is the greatest keeping in the boundless luxury of his imagination and the pampered self-indulgence of his physical appetites. He manures and nourishes his mind with jests, as he does his body with sack and sugar. He carves out his jokes, as he would a capon, or a haunch of venison, where there is *cut and come again*; and pours out upon them the oil of gladness. His tongue drops fatness, and in the chambers of his brain 'it snows of meat and drink'. He keeps up perpetual holiday and open house, and we live with him in a round of invitations to a rump and dozen.—Yet we are not to suppose that he was a mere sensualist. All this is as much in imagination as in reality. His sensuality does not engross and stupify his other faculties, but 'ascends me into the brain, clears away all the dull, crude vapours that environ it, and makes it full of nimble, fiery, and delectable shapes'. His imagination keeps up the ball after his senses have done with it. He seems to have even a greater enjoyment of the freedom from restraint, of good cheer, of his ease, of his vanity, in the ideal exaggerated descriptions which he gives of them, than in fact. He never fails to enrich his discourse with allusions to eating and drinking, but we never see him at table. He carries his own larder about with him, and he is himself 'a tun of man'. His pulling out the bottle in the field of battle is a joke to show his contempt for glory accompanied with danger, his systematic adherence to his Epicurean philosophy in the most trying circumstances. Again, such is his deliberate exaggeration of his own vices, that it does not seem quite certain whether the account of his hostess's bill, found in his pocket, with such an out-of-the-way charge for capons and sack with only one halfpenny-worth of bread, was not put there by himself as a trick to humour the jest upon his favourite propensities, and as a conscious caricature of himself. He is represented as a liar, a braggart, a coward, a glutton, &c., and yet we are not offended but delighted with him; for he is all these as much to amuse others as to gratify himself. He openly assumes all these characters to show the humorous part of them. The unrestrained indulgence of his own ease, appetites, and convenience, has neither malice nor hypocrisy in it. In a word, he is an actor in himself almost as much as upon the stage, and we no more object to the character of Falstaff in a moral point of view than we should think of bringing an excellent comedian, who should represent him to the life, before one of the police offices. We only consider the number of pleasant lights in which he puts certain foibles (the more pleasant as they are opposed to the received rules and necessary restraints of society) and do not trouble ourselves about the consequences resulting from them, for no mischievous consequences do result. Sir John is old as well as fat, which gives a melancholy retrospective tinge to the character; and by the disparity between his inclinations and his capacity for enjoyment, makes it still more ludicrous and fantastical.

The secret of Falstaff's wit is for the most part a masterly presence of mind, an absolute self-possession, which nothing can disturb. His repartees are involuntary suggestions of his self-love; instinctive evasions of everything that threatens to interrupt the career of his triumphant jollity and self-complacency. His very size floats him out of all his difficulties in a sea of rich conceits; and he turns round on the pivot of his convenience, with every occasion and at a moment's warning. His natural repugnance to every unpleasant thought or circumstance of itself makes light of objections, and provokes the most extravagant and licentious answers in his own justification. His indifference to truth puts no check upon his invention, and the more improbable and unexpected his contrivances are, the more happily does he seem to be delivered of them, the anticipation of their effect acting as a stimulus to the gaiety of his fancy. The success of one adventurous sally gives him spirits to undertake another: he deals always in round numbers, and his exaggerations and excuses are 'open, palpable, monstrous as the father that begets them'. His dissolute carelessness of what he says discovers itself in the first dialogue with the Prince.

> *Falstaff.* By the lord, thou say'st true, lad; and is not mine
> hostess of the tavern a most sweet wench?
> *P. Henry.* As the honey of Hibla, my. old lad of the castle; and
> is not a buff-jerkin a most sweet robe of durance?
> *Falstaff.* How now, how now, mad wag, what in thy quips and
> thy quiddities? what a plague have I to do with a buff-jerkin?
> *P. Henry.* Why, what a pox have I to do with mine hostess of
> the tavern?

In the same scene he afterwards affects melancholy, from pure satisfaction of heart, and professes reform, because it is the farthest thing in the world from his thoughts. He has no qualms of conscience, and therefore would as soon talk of them as of anything else when the humour takes him.

> *Falstaff.* But Hal, I pr'ythee trouble me no more with vanity. I
> would to God thou and I knew where a commodity of good
> names were to be bought: an old lord of council rated me the
> other day in the street about you, sir; but I mark'd him not, and
> yet he talked very wisely, and in the street too.
> *P. Henry.* Thou didst well, for wisdom cries out in the street,
> and no man regards it.
> *Falstaff.* O, thou hast damnable iteration, and art indeed able
> to corrupt a saint. Thou hast done much harm unto me, Hal;

God forgive thee for it. Before I knew thee, Hal, I knew nothing, and now I am, if a man should speak truly, little better than one of the wicked. I must give over this life, and I will give it over, by the lord; an I do not, I am a villain. I'll be damn'd for never a king's son in Christendom.

P. Henry. Where shall we take a purse to-morrow, Jack?

Falstaff. Where thou wilt, lad, I'll make one; an I do not, call me villain, and baffle me.

P. Henry. I see good amendment of life in thee, from praying to purse-taking.

Falstaff. Why, Hal, 'tis my vocation, Hal. 'Tis no sin for a man to labour in his vocation.

Of the other prominent passages, his account of his pretended resistance to the robbers, 'who grew from four men in buckram into eleven' as the imagination of his own valour increased with his relating it, his getting off when the truth is discovered by pretending he knew the Prince, the scene in which in the person of the old king he lectures the prince and gives himself a good character, the soliloquy on honour, and description of his new-raised recruits, his meeting with the chief justice, his abuse of the Prince and Poins, who overhear him, to Doll Tearsheet, his reconciliation with Mrs. Quickly who has arrested him for an old debt, and whom he persuades to pawn her plate to lend him ten pounds more, and the scenes with Shallow and Silence, are all inimitable. Of all of them, the scene in which Falstaff plays the part, first, of the King, and then of Prince Henry, is the one that has been the most often quoted. We must quote it once more in illustration of our remarks.

Falstaff. Harry, I do not only marvel where thou spendest thy time, but also how thou art accompanied: for though the camomile, the more it is trodden on, the faster it grows, yet youth, the more it is wasted, the sooner it wears. That thou art my son, I have partly thy mother's word, partly my own opinion; but chiefly, a villainous trick of thine eye, and a foolish hanging of thy nether lip, that doth warrant me. If then thou be son to me, here lies the point;—Why, being son to me, art thou so pointed at? Shall the blessed sun of heaven prove a micher, and eat blackberries? A question not to be ask'd. Shall the son of England prove a thief, and take purses? a question not to be ask'd. There is a thing, Harry, which thou hast often heard of, and it is known to many in our land by the name of pitch: this pitch, as ancient writers do report, doth defile; so doth the company thou keepest: for, Harry, now I do not speak to thee in drink, but in tears; not in pleasure, but in passion; not in words only, but in woes also:— and yet there is a virtuous man, whom I have often noted in thy company, but I know not his name.

P. Henry. What manner of man, an it like your majesty?

Falstaff. A goodly portly man, i'faith, and a corpulent; of a cheerful look, a pleasing eye, and a most noble carriage; and, as I think, his age some fifty, or, by'r-lady, inclining to threescore; and now I do remember me, his name is Falstaff: if that man should be lewdly given, he deceiveth me; for, Harry, I see virtue in his looks. If then the fruit may be known by the tree, as the tree by the fruit, then peremptorily I speak it, there is virtue in that Falstaff: him keep with, the rest banish. And tell me now, thou naughty varlet, tell me, where hast thou been this month?

P. Henry. Dost thou speak like a king? Do thou stand for me; and I'll play my father.

Falstaff. Depose me? If thou dost it half so gravely, so majestically, both in word and matter, hang me up by the heels for a rabbit-sucker, or a poulterer's hare.

P. Henry. Well, here I am set.

Falstaff. And here I stand:—judge, my masters.

P. Henry. Now, Harry, whence come you?

Falstaff. My noble lord, from Eastcheap.

P. Henry. The complaints I hear of thee are grievous.

Falstaff. S'blood, my lord, they are false:—nay, I'll tickle ye for a young prince, i'faith.

P. Henry. Swearest thou, ungracious boy? henceforth ne'er look on me. Thou art violently carried away from grace: there is a devil haunts thee, in the likeness of a fat old man; a tun of man is thy companion. Why dost thou converse with that trunk of humours, that bolting-hutch of beastliness, that swoln parcel of dropsies, that huge bombard of sack, that stuft cloak-bag of guts, that roasted Manningtree ox with the pudding in his belly, that reverend vice, that grey iniquity, that father ruffian, that vanity in years? wherein is he good, but to taste sack and drink it? wherein neat and cleanly, but to carve a capon and eat it? wherein cunning, but in craft? wherein crafty, but in villainy? wherein villainous, but in all things? wherein worthy, but in nothing?

Falstaff. I would, your grace would take me with you: whom means your grace?

P. Henry. That villainous, abominable misleader of youth, Falstaff, that old white-bearded Satan.

Falstaff. My lord, the man I know.

P. Henry. I know thou dost.

Falstaff. But to say, I know more harm in him than in myself, were to say more than I know. That he is old (the more the pity) his white hairs do witness it: but that he is (saving your reverence) a whore-master, that I utterly deny. If sack and sugar be a fault, God help the wicked! if to be old and merry be a sin, then many an old host that I know is damned: if to be fat be to be hated, then Pharaoh's lean kine are to be loved. No, my good lord; banish Peto, banish Bardolph, banish Poins; but for sweet Jack Falstaff, kind Jack Falstaff, true Jack Falstaff, valiant Jack Falstaff, and therefore more valiant, being as he is, old Jack Falstaff, banish not him thy Harry's company; banish plump Jack, and banish all the world.

P. Henry. I do, I will.

> [*Knocking; and Hostess and Bardolph go out.*
> *Re-enter* BARDOLPH, *running.*]

Bardolph. O, my lord, my lord; the sheriff, with a most monstrous watch, is at the door.

Falstaff. Out, you rogue! play out the play: I have much to say in the behalf of that Falstaff.

One of the most characteristic descriptions of Sir John is that which Mrs. Quickly gives of him when he asks her, 'What is the gross sum that I owe thee?'

Hostess. Marry, if thou wert an honest man, thyself, and the money too. Thou didst swear to me upon a parcel-gilt goblet, sitting in my Dolphin-chamber, at the round table, by a sea-coal fire on Wednesday in Whitsunweek, when the prince broke thy head for likening his father to a singing man of Windsor; thou didst swear to me then, as I was washing thy wound, to marry me, and make me my lady thy wife. Canst thou deny it? Did not goodwife Keech, the butcher's wife, come in then, and call me gossip Quickly? coming in to borrow a mess of vinegar; telling us, she had a good dish of prawns; whereby thou didst desire to eat some; whereby I told thee, they were ill for a green wound? And didst thou not, when she was gone down stairs, desire me to be no more so familiarity with such poor people; saying, that ere long they should call me madam? And didst thou not kiss me, and bid me fetch thee thirty shillings? I put thee now to thy book-oath; deny it, if thou canst.

This scene is to us the most convincing proof of Falstaff's power of gaining over the goodwill of those he was familiar with, except indeed Bardolph's somewhat profane exclamation on hearing the account of his death, 'Would I were with him, wheresoe'er he is, whether in heaven or hell.' One of the topics of exulting superiority over others most common in Sir John's mouth is his corpulence and the exterior marks of good living which he carries about him, thus 'turning his vices into commodity'. He accounts for the friendship between the Prince and Poins, from 'their legs being both of a bigness'; and compares Justice Shallow to 'a man made after supper of a cheese-paring'. There cannot be a more striking gradation of character than that between Falstaff and Shallow, and Shallow and Silence. It seems difficult at first to fall lower than the squire; but this fool, great as he is, finds an admirer and humble foil in his cousin Silence. Vain of his acquaintance with Sir John, who makes a butt of him, he exclaims, 'Would, cousin Silence, that thou had'st seen that which this knight and I have seen!'—'Aye, Master Shallow, we have heard the chimes at midnight,' says Sir John. To Falstaff's observation, 'I did not think Master Silence had been a man of this mettle', Silence answers, 'Who, I? I have been merry twice and once ere now.' What an idea is here conveyed of a prodigality of living? What good husbandry and economical self-denial in his pleasures? What a stock of lively recollections? It is curious that Shakespeare has ridiculed in Justice Shallow, who was 'in some authority under the king', that disposition to unmeaning tautology which is the regal infirmity of later times, and which, it may be supposed, he acquired from talking to his cousin Silence, and receiving no answers.

> *Falstaff.* You have here a goodly dwelling, and a rich.
> *Shallow.* Barren, barren, barren; beggars all, beggars all, Sir John: marry, good air. Spread Davy, spread Davy. Well said Davy.
> *Falstaff.* This Davy serves you for good uses.
> *Shallow.* A good varlet, a good varlet, a very good varlet. By the mass, I have drank too much sack at supper. A good varlet. Now sit down, now sit down. Come, cousin.

The true spirit of humanity, the thorough knowledge of the stuff we are made of, the practical wisdom with the seeming fooleries in the whole of the garden-scene at Shallow's country-seat, and just before in the exquisite dialogue between him and Silence on the death of old Double, have no parallel anywhere else. In one point of view, they are laughable in the extreme; in another they are equally affecting, if it is affecting to show *what a little thing is human life*, what a poor forked creature man is!

The heroic and serious part of these two plays founded on the story of Henry IV is not inferior to the comic and farcical. The characters of Hotspur and Prince Henry are two of the most beautiful and dramatic, both in themselves and from contrast, that ever were drawn. They are the essence of chivalry. We like Hotspur the best upon the whole, perhaps because he was unfortunate.—The characters of their fathers, Henry IV and old Northumberland, are kept up equally well. Henry naturally succeeds by his prudence and caution in keeping what he has got; Northumberland fails in his enterprise from an excess of the same quality; and is caught in the web of his own cold, dilatory policy. Owen Glendower is a masterly character. It is as bold and original as it is intelligible and thoroughly natural. The disputes between him and Hotspur are managed with infinite address and insight into nature. We cannot help pointing out here some very beautiful lines, where Hotspur describes the fight between Glendower and Mortimer.

> ——When on the gentle Severn's sedgy bank,
> In single opposition hand to hand,
> He did confound the best part of an hour
> In changing hardiment with great Glendower:
> Three times they breath'd, and three times did they drink,
> Upon agreement, of swift Severn's flood;
> Who then affrighted with their bloody looks,
> Ran fearfully among the trembling reeds,
> And hid his crisp head in the hollow bank,
> Blood-stained with these valiant combatants.

The peculiarity and the excellence of Shakespeare's poetry is, that it seems as if he made his imagination the hand-maid of nature, and nature the plaything of his imagination. He appears to have been all the characters, and in all the situations he describes. It is as if either he had had all their feelings, or had lent them all his genius to express themselves. There cannot be stronger instances of this than Hotspur's rage when Henry IV forbids him to speak of Mortimer, his insensibility to all that his father and uncle urge to calm him, and his fine abstracted apostrophe to honour, 'By heaven methinks it were an easy leap to pluck bright honour from the moon,' &c. After all, notwithstanding the gallantry, generosity, good temper, and idle freaks of the mad-cap Prince of Wales, we should not have been sorry if Northumberland's force had come up in time to decide the fate of the battle at Shrewsbury; at least, we always heartily sympathize with Lady Percy's grief when she exclaims:

> Had my sweet Harry had but half their numbers,
> To-day might I (hanging on Hotspur's neck)
> Have talked of Monmouth's grave.

The truth is, that we never could forgive the Prince's treatment of Falstaff; though perhaps Shakespeare knew what was best, according to the history, the nature of the times, and of the man. We speak only as dramatic critics. Whatever terror the French in those days might have of Henry V, yet to the readers of poetry at present, Falstaff is the better man of the two. We think of him and quote him oftener.

A.C. BRADLEY

The Rejection of Falstaff [1]

Of the two persons principally concerned in the rejection of Falstaff, Henry, both as Prince and as King, has received, on the whole, full justice from readers and critics. Falstaff, on the other hand, has been in one respect the most unfortunate of Shakespeare's famous characters. All of them, in passing from the mind of their creator into other minds, suffer change; they tend to lose their harmony through the disproportionate attention bestowed on some one feature, or to lose their uniqueness by being conventionalised into types already familiar. But Falstaff was degraded by Shakespeare himself. The original character is to be found alive in the two parts of *Henry IV.*, dead in *Henry V.*, and nowhere else. But not very long after these plays were composed, Shakespeare wrote, and he afterwards revised, the very entertaining piece called *The Merry Wives of Windsor*. Perhaps his company wanted a new play on a sudden; or perhaps, as one would rather believe, the tradition may be true that Queen Elizabeth, delighted with the Falstaff scenes of *Henry IV.*, expressed a wish to see the hero of them again, and to see him in love. Now it was no more possible for Shakespeare to show his own Falstaff in love than to turn twice two into five. But he could write in haste—the tradition says, in a fortnight—a comedy or farce differing from all his other plays in this, that its scene is laid in English middle-class life, and that it is prosaic almost to the end. And among the characters he could

From *Oxford Lectures on Poetry*. ©1909 by Macmillan and Co., Ltd.

introduce a disreputable fat old knight with attendants, and could call them Falstaff, Bardolph, Pistol, and Nym. And he could represent this knight assailing, for financial purposes, the virtue of two matrons, and in the event baffled, duped, treated like dirty linen, beaten, burnt, pricked, mocked, insulted, and, worst of all, repentant and didactic. It is horrible. It is almost enough to convince one that Shakespeare himself could sanction the parody of Ophelia in the *Two Noble Kinsmen*. But it no more touches the real Falstaff than Ophelia is degraded by that parody. To picture the real Falstaff befooled like the Falstaff of the *Merry Wives* is like imagining Iago the gull of Roderigo, or Becky Sharp the dupe of Amelia Osborne. Before he had been served the least of these tricks he would have had his brains taken out and buttered, and have given them to a dog for a New Year's gift. I quote the words of the impostor, for after all Shakespeare made him and gave to him a few sentences worthy of Falstaff himself. But they are only a few—one side of a sheet of notepaper would contain them. And yet critics have solemnly debated at what period in his life Sir John endured the gibes of Master Ford, and whether we should put this comedy between the two parts of *Henry IV.*, or between the second of them and *Henry V*. And the Falstaff of the general reader, it is to be feared, is an impossible conglomerate of two distinct characters, while the Falstaff of the mere playgoer is certainly much more like the impostor than the true man.

The separation of these two has long ago been effected by criticism, and is insisted on in almost all competent estimates of the character of Falstaff. I do not propose to attempt a full account either of this character or of that of Prince Henry, but shall connect the remarks I have to make on them with a question which does not appear to have been satisfactorily discussed—the question of the rejection of Falstaff by the Prince on his accession to the throne. What do we feel, and what are we meant to feel, as we witness this rejection? And what does our feeling imply as to the characters of Falstaff and the new King?

I.

Sir John, you remember, is in Gloucestershire, engaged in borrowing a thousand pounds from Justice Shallow; and here Pistol, riding helter-skelter from London, brings him the great news that the old King is as dead as nail in door, and that Harry the Fifth is the man. Sir John, in wild excitement, taking any man's horses, rushes to London; and he carries Shallow with him, for he longs to reward all his friends. We find him standing with his companions just outside Westminster Abbey, in the crowd that is waiting for the King to come out after his coronation. He himself is stained with travel, and has had no time to spend any of the thousand pounds in buying new liveries for his men. But what of that? This poor show only proves his earnestness of affection, his devotion, how he could not deliberate or remember or have patience to shift himself, but rode day and night, thought of nothing else but to see Henry, and put all affairs else in oblivion, as if there were nothing else to be done but to see him. And now he stands sweating with desire to see him, and repeating and repeating this one desire of his heart—'to see him.' The moment comes. There is a shout within the Abbey like the roaring of the sea, and a clangour of trumpets, and the doors open and the procession streams out.

> FAL. God save thy grace, King Hal! my royal Hal!
> PIST. The heavens thee guard and keep, most royal imp of fame!
> FAL. God save thee, my sweet boy!
> KING. My Lord Chief justice, speak to that vain man.
> CH. JUST. Have you your wits? Know you what 'tis you speak?
> FAL. My King! my Jove! I speak to thee, my heart!
> KING. I know thee not, old man: fall to thy prayers;
> How ill white hairs become a fool and jester!
> I have long dream'd of such a kind of man,
> So surfeit-swell'd, so old and so profane;
> But being awaked I do despise my dream.
> Make less thy body hence, and more thy grace;
> Leave gormandizing; know the grave doth gape
> For thee thrice wider than for other men.
> Reply not to me with a fool-born jest
> Presume not that I am the thing I was;
> For God doth know, so shall the world perceive,
> That I have turn'd away my former self;
> So will I those that kept me company.
> When thou dost hear I am as I have been,
> Approach me, and thou shalt be as thou vast,
> The tutor and the feeder of my riots
> Till then, I banish thee, on pain of death,
> As I have done the rest of my misleaders,
> Not to come near our person by ten mile.
> For competence of life I will allow you,
> That lack of means enforce you not to evil:
> And, as we hear you do reform yourselves,
> We will, according to your strengths and qualities,

Give you advancement. Be it your charge, my lord,
To see perform'd the tenour of our word.
Set on.

The procession passes out of sight, but Falstaff and his friends remain. He shows no resentment. He comforts himself, or tries to comfort himself— first, with the thought that he has Shallow's thousand pounds, and then, more seriously, I believe, with another thought. The King, he sees, must look thus to the world; but he will be sent for in private when night comes, and will yet make the fortunes of his friends. But even as he speaks, the Chief Justice, accompanied by Prince John, returns, and gives the order to his officers

Go, carry Sir John Falstaff to the Fleet;
Take all his company along with him.

Falstaff breaks out, 'My lord, my lord,' but he is cut short and hurried away; and after a few words between the Prince and the Chief Justice the scene closes, and with it the drama.

What are our feelings during this scene? They will depend on our feelings about Falstaff. If we have not keenly enjoyed the Falstaff scenes of the two plays, if we regard Sir John chiefly as an old reprobate, not only a sensualist, a liar, and a coward, but a cruel and dangerous ruffian, I suppose we enjoy his discomfiture and consider that the King has behaved magnificently. But if we *have* keenly enjoyed the Falstaff scenes, if we have enjoyed them as Shakespeare surely meant them to be enjoyed, and if, accordingly, Falstaff is not to us solely or even chiefly a reprobate and ruffian, we feel, I think, during the King's speech, a good deal of pain and some resentment; and when, without any further offence on Sir John's part, the Chief Justice returns and sends him to prison, we stare in astonishment. These, I believe, are, in greater or less degree, the feelings of most of those who really enjoy the Falstaff scenes (as many readers do not). Nor are these feelings diminished when we remember the end of the whole story, as we find it in *Henry V.*, where we learn that Falstaff quickly died, and, according to the testimony of persons not very sentimental, died of a broken heart.[2] Suppose this merely to mean that he sank under the shame of his public disgrace, and it is pitiful enough: but the words of Mrs. Quickly, 'The king has killed his heart'; of Nym, 'The king hath run bad humours on the knight; that's the even of it'; of Pistol,

> Nym, thou hast spoke the right,
> His heart is fracted and corroborate,

assuredly point to something more than wounded pride; they point to wounded affection, and remind us of Falstaffs own answer to Prince Hal's question, 'Sirrah, do I owe you a thousand pound?' 'A thousand pound, Hal? a million: thy love is worth a million: thou owest me thy love.'

Now why did Shakespeare end his drama with a scene which, though undoubtedly striking, leaves an impression so unpleasant? I will venture to put aside without discussion the idea that he meant us throughout the two plays to regard Falstaff with disgust or indignation, so that we naturally feel nothing but pleasure at his fall; for this idea implies that kind of inability to understand Shakespeare with which it is idle to argue. And there is another and a much more ingenious suggestion which must equally be rejected as impossible. According to it, Falstaff, having listened to the King's speech, did not seriously hope to be sent for by him in private; he fully realised the situation at once, and was only making game of Shallow; and in his immediate turn upon Shallow when the King goes out, 'Master Shallow, I owe you a thousand pound,' we are meant to see his humorous superiority to any rebuff, so that we end the play with the delightful feeling that, while Henry has done the right thing, Falstaff, in his outward overthrow, has still proved himself inwardly invincible. This suggestion comes from a critic who understands Falstaff, and in the suggestion itself shows that he understands him.[3] But it provides no solution, because it wholly ignores, and could not account for, that which follows the short conversation with Shallow. Falstaff's dismissal to the Fleet, and his subsequent death, prove beyond doubt that his rejection was meant by Shakespeare to be taken as a catastrophe which not even his humour could enable him to surmount.

Moreover, these interpretations, even if otherwise admissible, would still leave our problem only partly solved. For what troubles us is not only the disappointment of Falstaff, it is the conduct of Henry. It was inevitable that on his accession he should separate himself from Sir John, and we wish nothing else. It is satisfactory that Sir John should have a competence, with the hope of promotion in the highly improbable case of his reforming himself. And if Henry could not trust himself within ten miles of so fascinating a companion, by all means let him be banished that distance: we do not complain. These, arrangements would not have prevented a satisfactory ending: the King could have communicated his decision, and Falstaff could have accepted it, in a private interview rich in humour and merely touched with pathos. But Shakespeare has so contrived matters that Henry could not send a private warning to Falstaff even if he wished to, and in their public meeting Falstaff is made to behave in so infatuated and outrageous a manner that great sternness on the King's part was unavoidable. And the curious thing is that Shakespeare did not stop here. If this had been all we should have felt pain for Falstaff, but not, perhaps, resentment against Henry. But two things we do resent. Why, when this painful incident seems to be over, should the Chief justice return and send Falstaff to prison? Can this possibly be meant for an act of private vengeance on the part of the Chief justice, unknown to the King? No; for in that case Shakespeare would have shown at once that the King disapproved and cancelled it. It must have been the King's own act. This is one thing we resent; the other is the King's sermon. He had a right to turn away his former self, and his old companions with it, but he had no right to talk all of a sudden like a clergyman; and surely it was both ungenerous and insincere to speak of them as his 'misleaders,' as though in the days of Eastcheap and Gadshill he had been a weak and silly lad. We have seen his former self, and we know that it was nothing of the kind. He had shown himself, for all his follies, a very strong and independent young man, deliberately amusing himself among men over whom he had just as much ascendency as he chose to exert. Nay, he amused himself not only among them, but at their expense. In his first soliloquy—and first soliloquies are usually significant—he declares that he associates with them in order that, when at some future time he shows his true character, he may be the more wondered at for his previous aberrations. You may think he deceives himself here; you may believe that he frequented Sir John's company out of delight in it and not merely with this cold-blooded design; but at any rate he *thought* the design was his one motive. And, that being so, two results follow. He ought in honour long ago to have given Sir John clearly to understand that they must say good-bye on the day of his accession. And, having neglected to do this, he ought not to have lectured him as his misleader. It was not only ungenerous, it was dishonest. It looks disagreeably like an attempt to buy the praise of the respectable at the cost of honour and truth. And it succeeded. Henry *always* succeeded.

You will see what I am suggesting, for the moment, as a solution of our problem. I am suggesting that our fault lies not in our resentment at Henry's conduct, but in our surprise at it; that if we had read his character truly in the light that Shakespeare gave us, we should have been prepared for a display both of hardness and of policy at this point in his career.And although this suggestion does not suffice to solve the problem before us, I am convinced that in itself it is true. Nor is it rendered at all improbable by the fact that Shakespeare has made Henry, on the whole, a fine and very attractive character, and that here he makes no one express any disapprobation of the treatment of Falstaff. For in similar cases Shakespeare is constantly misunderstood. His readers expect him to mark in some distinct way his approval or disapproval of that which he represents; and hence where *they* disapprove and *he* says nothing, they fancy that he does *not* disapprove, and they blame his indifference, like Dr. Johnson, or at the least are puzzled. But the truth is that he shows the fact and leaves the judgment to them. And again, when he makes us like a character we expect the character to have no faults that are not expressly pointed out, and when other faults appear we either ignore them or try to explain them away. This is one of our methods of conventionalising Shakespeare. We want the world's population to be neatly divided into sheep and goats, and we want an angel by us to say, 'Look, that is a goat and this is a sheep,' and we try to turn Shakespeare into this angel. His impartiality makes us uncomfortable: we cannot bear to see him, like the sun, lighting up everything and judging nothing. And this is perhaps especially the case in his historical plays, where we are always trying to turn him into a partisan. He shows us that Richard II. was unworthy to be king, and we at once conclude that he thought Bolingbroke's usurpation justified; whereas he shows merely, what under the conditions was bound to exist, an inextricable tangle of right and unright. Or, Bolingbroke being evidently wronged, we suppose Bolingbroke's statements to be true, and are quite surprised when, after attaining his end through them, he mentions casually on his death-bed that they were lies. Shakespeare makes us admire Hotspur heartily; and accordingly, when we see Hotspur discussing with others how large his particular slice of his mother-country is to be, we either fail to recognise the monstrosity of the proceeding, or, recognising it, we complain that Shakespeare is inconsistent. Prince John breaks a tottering rebellion by practising a detestable fraud on the rebels. We are against the rebels, and have heard high praise of Prince John, but we cannot help seeing that his fraud is detestable; so we say indignantly to Shakespeare, 'Why, you told us he was a sheep'; whereas, in fact, if we had used our eyes we should have known beforehand that he was the brave, determined, loyal, cold-blooded, pitiless, unscrupulous son of a usurper whose throne was in danger.

To come, then, to Henry. Both as prince and as king he is deservedly a favourite, and particularly so with English readers, being, as he is, perhaps the most distinctively English of all Shakespeare's men. In *Henry V.* he is treated as a national hero. In this play he has lost much of the wit which in him seems to have depended on contact with Falstaff, but he has also laid aside the most serious faults of his youth. He inspires in a high degree fear, enthusiasm, and affection; thanks to his beautiful modesty he has the charm which is lacking to another mighty warrior, Coriolanus; his youthful escapades have given him an understanding of simple folk, and sympathy with them; he is the author of the saying, 'There is some soul of goodness in things evil'; and he is much more obviously religious than most of Shakespeare's heroes. Having these and other fine qualities, and being without certain dangerous tendencies which mark the tragic heroes, he is, perhaps, the most *efficient* character drawn by Shakespeare, unless Ulysses, in *Troilus and Cressida*, is his equal. And so he has been described as Shakespeare's ideal man of action; nay, it has even been declared that here for once Shakespeare plainly disclosed his own ethical creed, and showed us his ideal, not simply of a man of action, but of a man.

But Henry is neither of these. The poet who drew Hamlet and Othello can never have thought that even the ideal man of action would lack that light upon the brow which at once transfigures them and marks their doom. It is as easy to believe that, because the lunatic, the lover, and the poet are not far apart, Shakespeare would have chosen never to have loved and sung. Even poor Timon, the most inefficient of the tragic heroes, has something in him that Henry never shows. Nor is it merely that his nature is limited: if we follow Shakespeare and look closely at Henry, we shall discover with the many fine traits a few less pleasing. Henry IV. describes him as the noble image of his own youth; and, for all his superiority to his father, he is still his father's son, the son of the man whom Hotspur called a 'vile politician.' Henry's religion, for example, is genuine, it is rooted in his modesty; but it is also superstitious—an attempt to buy off supernatural vengeance for Richard's blood; and it is also in part political, like his father's projected crusade. Just as he went to war chiefly because, as his father told him, it was the way to keep factious nobles quiet and unite the nation, so when he adjures the Archbishop to satisfy him as to his right to the French throne, he knows very well that the Archbishop wants the war, because it will defer and perhaps prevent what he considers the spoliation of the Church. This same strain of policy is what Shakespeare marks in the first soliloquy in *Henry IV.*, where the prince describes his riotous life as a mere scheme to win him glory later. It implies that readiness to use other people as means to his own ends which is a conspicuous feature in his father; and it reminds us of his father's plan of keeping himself out of the people's sight while Richard was making himself cheap by his incessant public appearances. And if I am not mistaken there is a further likeness. Henry is kindly and pleasant to every one as Prince, to every one deserving as King; and he is so not merely out of policy: but there is no sign in him of a strong affection for any one, such an affection as we recognise at a glance in Hamlet and Horatio, Brutus and Cassius, and many more. We do not find this in *Henry V.*, not even in the noble address to Lord Scroop, and in *Henry IV.* we find, I think, a liking for Falstaff and

Poins, but no more: there is no more than a liking, for instance, in his soliloquy over the supposed corpse of his fat friend, and he never speaks of Falstaff to Poins with any affection. The truth is, that the members of the family of Henry IV. have love for one another, but they cannot spare love for any one outside their family, which stands firmly united, defending its royal position against attack and instinctively isolating itself from outside influence.

Thus I would suggest that Henry's conduct in his rejection of Falstaff is in perfect keeping with his character on its unpleasant side as well as on its finer; and that, so far as Henry is concerned, we ought not to feel surprise at it. And on this view we may even explain the strange incident of the Chief Justice being sent back to order Falstaff to prison (for there is no sign of any such uncertainty in the text as might suggest an interpolation by the players). Remembering his father's words about Henry, 'Being incensed, he's flint,' and remembering in *Henry V.* his ruthlessness about killing the prisoners when he is incensed, we may imagine that, after he had left Falstaff and was no longer influenced by the face of his old companion, he gave way to anger at the indecent familiarity which had provoked a compromising scene on the most ceremonial of occasions and in the presence alike of court and crowd, and that he sent the Chief Justice back to take vengeance. And this is consistent with the fact that in the next play we find Falstaff shortly afterwards not only freed from prison, but unmolested in his old haunt in Eastcheap, well within ten miles of Henry's person. His anger had soon passed, and he knew that the requisite effect had been produced both on Falstaff and on the world.

But all this, however true, will not solve our problem. It seems, on the contrary, to increase its difficulty. For the natural conclusion is that Shakespeare *intended* us to feel resentment against Henry. And yet that cannot be, for it implies that he meant the play to end disagreeably; and no one who understands Shakespeare at all will consider that supposition for a moment credible. No; he must have meant the play to end pleasantly, although he made Henry's action consistent. And hence it follows that he must have intended our sympathy with Falstaff to be so far weakened when the rejection-scene arrives that his discomfiture should be satisfactory to us; that we should enjoy this sudden reverse of enormous hopes (a thing always ludicrous if sympathy is absent); that we should approve the moral judgment that falls on him; and so should pass lightly over that disclosure of unpleasant traits in the King's character which Shakespeare was too true an artist to suppress. Thus our pain and resentment, if we feel them, are wrong, in the sense that they do not answer to the dramatist's intention. But it does not follow that they are wrong in a further sense. They may be right, because the dramatist has missed what he aimed at. And this, though the dramatist was Shakespeare, is what I would suggest. In the Falstaff scenes he overshot his mark. He created so extraordinary a being, and fixed him so firmly on his intellectual throne, that when he sought to dethrone him he could not. The moment comes when we are to look, at Falstaff in a serious light, and the comic hero is to figure as a baffled schemer; but we cannot make the required change, either in our attitude or in our sympathies. We wish Henry a glorious reign and much joy of his crew of hypocritical politicians, lay and clerical; but our hearts go with Falstaff to the Fleet, or, if necessary, to Arthur's bosom or wheresomever he is.[4]

In the remainder of the lecture I will try to make this view clear. And to that end we must go back to the Falstaff of the body of the two plays, the immortal Falstaff, a character almost purely humorous, and therefore no subject for moral judgments, I can but draw an outline, and in describing one aspect of this character must be content to hold another in reserve.

2.

Up to a certain point Falstaff is ludicrous in the same way as many other figures, his distinction lying, so far, chiefly in the mere abundance of ludicrous traits. *Why* we should laugh at a man with a huge belly and corresponding appetites; at the inconveniences he suffers on a hot day, or in playing the footpad, or when he falls down and there are no levers at hand to lift him up again; at the incongruity of his unwieldy bulk and the nimbleness of his spirit, the infirmities of his age and his youthful lightness of heart; at the enormity of his lies and wiles, and the suddenness of their exposure and frustration; at the contrast between his reputation and his real character, seen most absurdly when, at the mere mention of his name, a redoubted rebel surrenders to him—*why*, I say, we should laugh at these and many such things, this is no place to inquire; but unquestionably we do. Here we have them poured out in endless profusion and with that air of careless ease which is so fascinating in Shakespeare; and with the enjoyment of them I believe many readers stop. But while they are quite essential to the character, there is in it much more. For these things by themselves do not explain why, beside laughing at Falstaff, we are made happy by him and laugh *with* him. He is not, like Parolles, a mere *object* of mirth.

The main reason why he makes us so happy and puts us so entirely at our ease is that he himself is happy and entirely at his ease. 'Happy' is too weak a word; he is in bliss, and we share his glory. Enjoyment—no fitful pleasure crossing a dull life, nor any vacant convulsive mirth—but a rich deep-toned chuckling enjoyment circulates continually through all his being.

If you ask what he enjoys, no doubt the answer is, in the first place, eating and drinking, taking his ease at his inn, and the company of other merry souls. Compared with these things, what we count the graver interests of life are nothing to him. But then, while we are under his spell, it is impossible to consider these graver interests; gravity is to us, as to him, inferior to gravy; and what he does enjoy he enjoys with such a luscious and good-humoured zest that we sympathise and he makes us happy. And if any one objected, we should answer with Sir Toby Belch, 'Dost thou think, because thou art virtuous, there shall be no more cakes and ale?'

But this, again, is far from all. Falstaff's ease and enjoyment are not simply those of the happy man of appetite;[5] they are those of the humorist, and the humorist of genius. Instead of being comic to you and serious to himself, he is more ludicrous to himself than to you; and he makes himself out more ludicrous than he is, in order that he and others may laugh. Prince Hal never made such sport of Falstaff's person as he himself did. It is *he* who says that his skin hangs about him like an old lady's loose gown, and that he walks before his page like a sow that hath o'erwhelmed all her litter but one. And he jests at himself when he is alone just as much as when others are by. It is the same with his appetites. The direct enjoyment they bring him is scarcely so great as the enjoyment of laughing at this enjoyment; and for all his addiction to sack you never see him for an instant with a brain dulled by it, or a temper turned solemn, silly, quarrelsome, or pious. The virtue it instils into him, of filling his brain with nimble, fiery, and delectable shapes— this, and his humorous attitude towards it, free him, in a manner, from slavery to it; and it is this freedom, and no secret longing for better things (those who attribute such a longing to him are far astray), that makes his enjoyment contagious and prevents our sympathy with it from being disturbed.

The bliss of freedom gained in humour is the essence of Falstaff. His humour is not directed only or chiefly against obvious absurdities; he is the enemy of everything that would interfere with his ease, and therefore of anything serious, and especially of everything respectable and moral. For these things impose limits and obligations, and make us the subjects of old father antic the law, and the categorical imperative, and our station and its duties, and conscience, and reputation, and other people's opinions, and all sorts of nuisances. I say he is therefore their enemy; but I do him wrong; to say that he is their enemy implies that he regards them as serious and recognises their power, when in truth he refuses to recognise them at all. They are to him absurd; and to reduce a thing *ad absurdum* is to reduce it to nothing and to walk about free and rejoicing. This is what Falstaff does with all the would-be serious things of life, sometimes only by his words, sometimes by his actions too. He will make truth appear absurd by solemn statements, which he utters with perfect gravity and which he expects nobody to believe; and honour, by demonstrating that it cannot set a leg, and that neither the living nor the dead can possess it; and law, by evading all the attacks of its highest representative and almost forcing him to laugh at his own defeat; and patriotism, by filling his pockets with the bribes offered by competent soldiers who want to escape service, while he takes in their stead the halt and maimed and the gaol-birds; and duty, by showing how he labours in his vocation—of thieving; and courage, alike by mocking at his own capture of Colvile and gravely claiming to have killed Hotspur; and war, by offering the Prince his bottle of sack when he is asked for a sword; and religion, by amusing himself with remorse at odd times when he has nothing else to do; and the fear of death, by maintaining perfectly untouched, in the face of imminent peril and even while he *feels* the fear of death, the very same power of dissolving it in persiflage that he shows when he sits at ease in his inn. These are the wonderful achievements which he performs, not with the sourness of a cynic, but with the gaiety of a boy. And, therefore, we praise him, we laud him, for he offends none but the virtuous, and denies that life is real or life is earnest, and delivers us from the oppression of such nightmares, and lifts us into the atmosphere of perfect freedom.

No one in the play understands Falstaff fully, any more than Hamlet was understood by the persons round him. They are both men of genius. Mrs. Quickly and Bardolph are his slaves, but they know not why. 'Well, fare thee well,' says the hostess whom he has pillaged and forgiven; 'I have known thee these twenty-nine years, come peas-cod time, but an honester and truer-hearted man-well, fare thee well.' Poins and the Prince delight in him; they get him into corners far the pleasure of seeing him escape in ways they cannot imagine; but they often take him much too seriously. Poins, for instance, rarely sees, the Prince does not always see, and moralising critics never see, that when Falstaff speaks ill of a companion behind his back, or writes to the Prince that Poins spreads it abroad that the Prince is to marry his sister, he knows quite well that what he says will be repeated, or rather, perhaps, is absolutely indifferent whether it be repeated or not, being certain that it can only give him an opportunity for humour. It is the same with his lying, and almost the same with his cowardice, the two main vices laid to his charge even by sympathisers. Falstaff is neither a liar nor a coward in the usual sense, like the typical cowardly boaster of comedy. He tells his lies either for their own humour, or on purpose to get himself into a difficulty. He rarely expects to be believed, perhaps never. He abandons a statement or contradicts it the moment it is made. There is scarcely more intent in his lying than in the humorous exaggerations which he pours out in soliloquy just as much as when others are by. Poins and the Prince understand this in part. You see them waiting eagerly to convict him, not that they may really put him to shame, but in order to enjoy the greater lie that will swallow up the less. But their sense of humour lags behind his. Even the Prince seems to accept as half-serious that remorse of his which passes so suddenly into glee at the idea of taking a purse, and his request to his friend to bestride him if he should see him down in the battle. Bestride Falstaff! 'Hence! Wilt thou lift up Olympus?' Again, the attack of the Prince and Poins on Falstaff and the other thieves on Gadshill is contrived, we know, with a view to the incomprehensible lies it will induce him to tell. But when, more than rising to the occasion, he turns two men in buckram into four, and then seven, and then nine, and then eleven, almost in a breath, I believe they partly misunderstand his intention, and too many of his critics misunderstand it altogether. Shakespeare was not writing a mere farce. It is preposterous to suppose that a man of Falstaff's intelligence would utter these gross, palpable, open lies with the serious intention to deceive, or forget that, if it was too dark for him to see his own hand, he could hardly see that the three misbegotten knaves were wearing Kendal green. No doubt, if he *had* been believed, he would have been hugely tickled at it, but he no more expected to be believed than when he claimed to have killed Hotspur. Yet he is supposed to be serious even then. Such interpretations would destroy the poet's whole conception; and of those who adopt them one might ask this out of some twenty similar questions:—When Falstaff, in the men in buckram scene, begins by calling twice at short intervals for sack, and then a little later calls for more and says, 'I am a rogue if I drunk to-day,' and the Prince answers, 'O villain, thy lips are scarce wiped since thou drunk'st last,' do they think that *that* lie was meant to deceive? And if not, why do they take it for granted that the others were? I suppose they consider that Falstaff was in earnest when, wanting to get twenty-two yards of satin on trust from Master Dombledon the silk-mercer, he offered Bardolph as security; or when he said to the Chief Justice about Mrs. Quickly, who accused him of breaking his promise to marry her, 'My lord, this is a poor mad soul, and she says up and down the town that her eldest son is like you'; or when he explained his enormous bulk by exclaiming, 'A plague of sighing and grief! It blows a man up like a bladder'; or when he accounted for his voice being cracked by declaring that he had 'lost it with singing of anthems'; or even when he sold his soul on Good-Friday to the devil for a cup of Madeira and a cold capon's leg. Falstaff's lies about Hotspur and the men in buckram do not essentially differ from these statements. There is nothing serious in any of them except the refusal to take anything seriously.

This is also the explanation of Falstaff's cowardice, a subject on which

I should say nothing if Maurice Morgann's essay,[6] now more than a century old, were better known. That Falstaff sometimes behaves in what we should generally call a cowardly way is certain; but that does not show that he was a coward; and if the word means a person who feels painful fear in the presence of danger, and yields to that fear in spite of his better feelings and convictions, then assuredly Falstaff was no coward. The stock bully and boaster of comedy is one, but not Falstaff. It is perfectly clear in the first place that, though he had unfortunately a reputation for stabbing and caring not what mischief he did if his weapon were out, he had not a reputation for cowardice. Shallow remembered him five-and-fifty years ago breaking Scogan's head at the court-gate when he was a crack not thus high; and Shallow knew him later a good back-swordsman. Then we lose sight of him till about twenty years after, when his association with Bardolph began; and that association implies that by the time he was thirty-five or forty he had sunk into the mode of life we witness in the plays. Yet, even as we see him there, he remains a person of consideration in the army. Twelve captains hurry about London searching for him. He is present at the Council of War in the King's tent at Shrewsbury, where the only other persons are the King, the two princes, a nobleman and Sir Walter Blunt. The messenger who brings the false report of the battle to Northumberland mentions, as one of the important incidents, the death of Sir John Falstaff. Colvile, expressly described as a famous rebel, surrenders to him as soon as he hears his name. And if his own wish that his name were not so terrible to the enemy, and his own boast of his European reputation, are not evidence of the first rank, they must not be entirely ignored in presence of these other facts. What do these facts mean? Does Shakespeare put them all in with no purpose at all, or in defiance of his own intentions? It is not credible.

And when, in the second place, we look at Falstaff's actions, what do we find? He boldly confronted Colvile, he was quite ready to fight with him, however pleased that Colvile, like a kind fellow, gave himself away. When he saw Henry and Hotspur fighting, Falstaff, instead of making off in a panic, stayed to take his chance if Hotspur should be the victor. He *led* his hundred and fifty ragamuffins where they were peppered, he did not *send* them. To draw upon Pistol and force him downstairs and wound him in the shoulder was no great feat, perhaps, but the stock coward would have shrunk from it. When the Sheriff came to the inn to arrest him for an offence whose penalty was death, Falstaff, who was hidden behind the arras, did not stand there quaking for fear, he immediately fell asleep and snored. When he stood in the battle reflecting on what would happen if the weight of his paunch should be increased by that of a bullet, he cannot have been in a tremor of craven fear. He *never* shows such fear; and surely the man who, in danger of his life, and with no one by to hear him, meditates thus: 'I like not such grinning honour as Sir Walter hath. Give me life: which if I can save, so; if not, honour comes unlooked-for, and there's an end,' is not what we commonly call a coward. 'Well,' it will be answered, 'but he ran away on Gadshill; and when Douglas attacked him he fell down and shammed dead.' Yes, I am thankful to say, he did. For of course he did not want to be dead. He wanted to live and be merry. And as he had reduced the idea of honour *ad absurdum*, had scarcely any self-respect, and only a respect for reputation as a means of life, naturally he avoided death when he could do so without a ruinous loss of reputation, and (observe) with the satisfaction of playing a colossal practical joke. For *that* after all was his first object. If his one thought had been to avoid death he would not have faced Douglas at all, but would have run away as fast as his legs could carry him; and unless Douglas had been one of those exceptional Scotchmen who have no sense of humour, he would never have thought of pursuing so ridiculous an object as Falstaff running. So that, as Mr. Swinburne remarks, Poins is right when he thus distinguishes Falstaff from his companions in robbery: 'For two of them, I know them to be as true-bred cowards as ever turned back; and for the third, if he fight longer than he sees reason, I'll forswear arms.' And the event justifies this distinction. For it is exactly thus that, according to the original stage-direction, Falstaff behaves when Henry and Poins attack him and the others. The rest run away at once; Falstaff, here as afterwards with Douglas, fights for a blow or two, but, finding himself deserted and outmatched, runs away also. Of course. He saw no reason to stay. *Any* man who had risen superior to all serious motives would have run away. But it does not follow that he would run from mere fear, or be, in the ordinary sense, a coward.[7]

3.

The main source, then, of our sympathetic delight in Falstaff is his humorous superiority to everything serious, and the freedom of soul enjoyed in it. But, of course, this is not the whole of his character. Shakespeare knew well enough that perfect freedom is not to be gained in this manner; we are ourselves aware of it even while we are sympathising with Falstaff; and as soon as we regard him seriously it becomes obvious. His freedom is limited in two main ways. For one thing he cannot rid himself entirely of respect for all that he professes to ridicule. He shows a certain pride in his rank: unlike the Prince, he is haughty to the drawers, who call him a proud Jack. He is not really quite indifferent to reputation. When the Chief Justice bids him pay his debt to Mrs. Quickly for his reputation's sake, I think he feels a twinge, though to be sure he proceeds to pay her by borrowing from her. He is also stung by any thoroughly serious imputation on his courage, and winces at the recollection of his running away on Gadshill; he knows that his behaviour there certainly looked cowardly, and perhaps he remembers that he would not have behaved so once. It is, further, very significant that, for all his dissolute talk, he has never yet allowed the Prince and Poins to *see* him as they saw him afterwards with Doll Tearsheet; not, of course, that he has any moral shame in the matter, but he knows that in such a situation he, in his old are, must appear contemptible—not a humorist but a mere object of mirth. And, finally, he has affection in him—affection, I think, for Poins and Bardolph, and certainly for the Prince; and that is a thing which he cannot jest out of existence. Hence, as the effect of his rejection shows, he is not really invulnerable. And then, in the second place, since he is in the flesh, his godlike freedom has consequences and conditions; consequences, for there is something painfully wrong with his great toe; conditions, for he cannot eat and drink for ever without money, and his purse suffers from consumption, a disease for which he can find no remedy.[8] As the Chief Justice tells him, his means are very slender and his waste great; and his answer, 'I would it were otherwise; I would my means were greater and my waist slenderer,' though worth much money, brings none in. And so he is driven to evil deeds; not only to cheating his tailor like a gentleman, but to fleecing Justice Shallow, and to highway robbery, and to cruel depredations on the poor woman whose affection he has secured. All this is perfectly consistent with the other side of his character, but by itself it makes an ugly picture.

Yes, it makes an ugly picture when you look at it seriously. But then, surely, so long as the, humorous atmosphere is preserved and the humorous attitude maintained, you do not look at it so. You no more regard Falstaff's misdeeds morally than you do the much more atrocious misdeeds of Punch or Reynard the Fox. You do not exactly ignore them, but you attend only to their comic aspect. This is the very spirit of comedy, and certainly of Shakespeare's comic world, which is one of make-believe, not merely as his tragic world is, but in a further sense—a world in which gross improbabilities are accepted with a smile, and many things are welcomed as merely laughable which, regarded gravely, would excite anger and disgust. The intervention of a serious spirit breaks up such a world, and would destroy our pleasure in Falstaff's company. Accordingly through the greater part of these dramas Shakespeare carefully confines this spirit to the scenes of war and policy, and dismisses it entirely in the humorous parts. Hence, if *Henry IV.* had been a comedy like *Twelfth Night*, I am sure that he would no more have ended it with the painful disgrace of Falstaff than he ended *Twelfth Night* by disgracing Sir Toby Belch.[9]

But *Henry IV.* was to be in the main a historical play, and its chief hero

Prince Henry. In the course of it his greater and finer qualities were to be gradually revealed, and it was to end with beautiful scenes of reconciliation and affection between his father and him, and a final emergence of the wild Prince as a just, wise, stern, and glorious King. Hence, no doubt, it seemed to Shakespeare that Falstaff at last must be disgraced, and must therefore appear no longer as the invincible humorist, but as an object of ridicule and even of aversion. And probably also his poet's insight showed him that Henry, as be conceived him, would behave harshly to Falstaff in order to impress the world, especially when his mind had been wrought to a high pitch by the scene with his dying father and the impression of his own solemn consecration to great duties.

This conception was a natural and a fine one; and if the execution was not an entire success, it is yet full of interest. Shakespeare's purpose being to work a gradual change in our feelings towards Falstaff, and to tinge the humorous atmosphere more and more deeply with seriousness, we see him carrying out this purpose in the Second Part of *Henry IV.* Here he separates the Prince from Falstaff as much as he can, thus withdrawing him from Falstaff's influence, and weakening in our minds the connection between the two. In the First Part we constantly see them together; in the Second (it is a remarkable fact) only once before the rejection. Further, in the scenes where Henry appears apart from Falstaff, we watch him growing more and more grave, and awakening more and more poetic interest; while Falstaff, though his humour scarcely flags to the end, exhibits more and more of his seamy side. This is nowhere turned to the full light in Part I.; but in Part II. we see him as the heartless destroyer of Mrs. Quickly, as a ruffian seriously defying the Chief Justice because his position as an officer on service gives him power to do wrong, as the pike preparing to snap up the poor old dace Shallow, and (this is the one scene where Henry and he meet) as the worn-out lecher, not laughing at his servitude to the flesh but sunk in it. Finally, immediately before the rejection, the world where he is king is exposed in all its sordid criminality when we find Mrs. Quickly and Doll arrested for being concerned in the death of one man, if not more, beaten to death by their bullies; and the dangerousness of Falstaff is emphasised in his last words as he hurries from Shallow's house to London, words at first touched with humour but at bottom only too seriously meant: 'Let us take any man's horses; the laws of England are at my commandment. Happy are they which have been my friends, and woe unto my Lord Chief Justice.' His dismissal to the Fleet by the Chief Justice is the dramatic vengeance for that threat.

Yet all these excellent devices fail. They cause us momentary embarrassment at times when repellent traits in Falstaff's character are disclosed; but they fail to change our attitude of humour into one of seriousness, and our sympathy into repulsion. And they were bound to fail, because Shakespeare shrank from adding to them the one device which would have ensured success. If, as the Second Part of *Henry IV.* advanced, he had clouded over Falstaff's humour so heavily that the man of genius turned into the Falstaff of the *Merry Wives*, we should have witnessed his rejection without a pang. This Shakespeare was too much of an artist to do—though even in this way he did something—and without this device he could not succeed. As I said, in the creation of Falstaff he overreached himself. He was caught up on the wind of his own genius, and carried so far that he could not descend to earth at the selected spot. It is not a misfortune that happens to many authors, nor is it one we can regret, for it costs us but a trifling inconvenience in one scene, while we owe to it perhaps the greatest comic character in literature. For it is in this character, and not in the judgment he brings upon Falstaff's head, that Shakespeare asserts his supremacy. To show that Falstaff's freedom of soul was in part illusory, and that the realities of life refused to be conjured away by his humour—this was what we might expect from Shakespeare's unfailing sanity, but it was surely no achievement beyond the power of lesser men. The achievement was Falstaff himself, and the conception of that freedom of soul, a freedom illusory only in part, and attainable only by a mind which had received from Shakespeare's own the inexplicable touch of infinity which he bestowed on Hamlet and Macbeth and Cleopatra, but denied to Henry the Fifth.

NOTES

1. In this lecture and the three that follow it I have mentioned the authors my obligations to whom I was conscious of in writing or have discovered since; but other debts must doubtless remain, which from forgetfulness I am unable to acknowledge.

2. See on this and other points Swinburne, *A Study of Shakespeare*, p. 106 ff.

3. Rötscher, *Shakespeare in seinen höchsten Charaktergebilden*, 1864.

4. That from the beginning Shakespeare intended Henry's accession to be Falstaff's catastrophe is clear from the fact that, when the two characters first appear, Falstaff is made to betray at once the hopes with which he looks forward to Henry's reign. See the First Part of *Henry IV.*, Act I., Scene ii.

5. Cf. Hazlitt, *Characters of Shakespear's Plays*.

6. See Note at end of lecture.

7. It is to he regretted, however, that in carrying his guts away so nimbly he 'roared for mercy'; for I fear we have no ground for rejecting Henry's statement to that effect, and I do not see my way to adopt the suggestion (I forget whose it is) that Falstaff spoke the truth when he swore that he knew Henry and Poins as well as he that made them.

8. Panurge too was 'naturally subject to a kind of disease which at that time they called lack of money'; it was a 'flux in his purse' (Rabelais, Book II., chapters xvi., xvii.).

9. I seem to remember that, according to Gervinus, Shakespeare did disgrace Sir Toby—by marrying him to Maria!.

NOTE

For the benefit of readers unacquainted with Morgann's Essay I reproduce here, with additions, some remarks omitted from the lecture for want of time. 'Maurice Morgann, Esq. the ingenious writer of this work, descended from an ancient and respectable family in Wales; he filled the office of under Secretary of State to the late Marquis of Lansdown, during his first administration; and was afterwards Secretary to the Embassy for ratifying the peace with America, in 1783. He died at his house in Knightsbridge, in the seventy-seventh year of his age, on the 28th March, 1802' (Preface to the edition of 1825). He was a remarkable and original man, who seems to have written a good deal, but, beyond this essay and some pamphlets on public affairs, all or nearly all anonymous, he published nothing, and at his death he left orders that all his papers should be destroyed. The *Essay on the Dramatic Character of Sir John Falstaff* was first published in 1777. It arose out of a conversation in which Morgann expressed his belief that Shakespeare never meant Falstaff for a coward. He was challenged to explain and support in print what was considered an extraordinary paradox, and his essay bears on its title-page the quotation, 'I am not John of Gaunt, your grandfather: but yet no coward, Hal'—one of Falstaff's few serious sentences. But Morgann did not confine himself to the question of Falstaff's cowardice; he analysed the whole character, and incidentally touched on many points in Shakespearean criticism. 'The reader,' he observes, 'will not need to be told that this inquiry will resolve itself of course into a critique on the genius, the arts, and the conduct, of Shakespeare: for what is Falstaff, what Lear, what Hamlet, or Othello, but different modifications of Shakespeare's thought? It is true that this inquiry is narrowed almost to a single point; but general criticism is as uninstructive as it is easy: Shakespeare deserves to be considered in detail; a task hitherto unattempted.'

The last words are significant. Morgann was conscious that he was striking out a new line. The Eighteenth Century critics had done much for Shakespeare in the way of scholarship; some of them had praised him well and blamed him well; but they had done little to interpret the process of his imagination from within. This was what Morgann attempted. His attitude towards Shakespeare is that of Goethe, Coleridge, Lamb, Hazlitt. The dangers of his method might be illustrated from the Essay, but in his hands it yielded most valuable results. And though he did not attempt the eloquence of some of his successors, but wrote like a cultivated ironical man of the world, he wrote delightfully; so that in all respects his Essay, which has long been out of print, deserves to be republished and better known. [It was republished in Mr. Nichol Smith's excellent *Eighteenth Century Essays an Shakespeare*, 1903; and, in 1912, by itself, with an introduction by W. A. Gill.]

Readers of Boswell (under the year 1783) will remember that Morgann, who once met Johnson, favoured his biographer with two most characteristic anecdotes. Boswell also records Johnson's judgment of Morgann's Essay, which, says Mr. Swinburne, elicited from him 'as good a jest and as bad a criticism as might have been expected.' Johnson, we are told, being asked his opinion of the Essay, answered: 'Why, Sir, we shall have the man come forth again; and as he has proved Falstaff to be no coward, he may prove Iago to be a very good character.' The following passage from Morgann's *Essay* (p. 66 of the 1825 edition, p. 248 of Mr. Nichol Smith's book) gives, I presume, his opinion of Johnson. Having referred to Warburton, he adds: 'Another has since undertaken the custody of our author, whom he seems to consider as a sort of wild Proteus or madman, and accordingly knocks him down with the butt-end of his critical staff, as often as he exceeds that line of sober discretion, which this learned Editor appears to have chalked out for him: yet is this Editor, notwithstanding, "a man, take him for all in all," very highly respectable for his genius and his learning.'

HAROLD C. GODDARD

Henry IV, *Part I*; Henry IV, *Part II*
(The Merry Wives of Windsor)

VI

And now we come to the third candidate for the role of "hero" in these plays.

Who at this late date can hope to say a fresh word about Falstaff? Long since, his admirers and detractors have drained language dry in their efforts to characterize him, to give expression to their fascination or detestation. Glutton, drunkard, coward, liar, lecher, boaster, cheat, thief, rogue, ruffian, villain are a few of the terms that have been used to describe a man whom others find the very incarnation of charm, one of the liberators of the human spirit, the greatest comic figure in the history of literature. "A besotted and disgusting old wretch," Bernard Shaw calls him. And isn't he?—this man who held up unprotected travelers for pastime, betrayed innocence in the person of his page, cheated a trusting and hard-working hostess, borrowed a thousand pounds from an old friend with no intention of repaying it, abused his commission by taking cash in lieu of military service, and insinuated his way into the graces of the heir apparent with an eye to later favor. And yet after three centuries there the old sinner sits, more invulnerable and full of smiles than ever, his sagging paunch shaking like a jelly, dodging or receiving full on, unperturbed, the missiles his enemies hurl at him. Which is he? A colossus of sack, sensuality, and sweat—or a wit and humorist so great that he can be compared only with his creator, a figure, to use one of

From *The Meaning of Shakespeare.* ©1951 by the University of Chicago Press.

Shakespeare's own great phrases, livelier than life? One might think there were two Falstaffs.

The trouble with the "besotted and disgusting old wretch" theory is that Shakespeare has given us that old wretch exactly, and he is another man: the Falstaff of *The Merry Wives of Windsor*. The disparagers of Falstaff generally make him out a mixture, in varying proportions, of this other Falstaff, Sir Toby Belch, and Parolles, each of whom was an incalculably inferior person. But to assert that Falstaff is another man is not saying that he does not have many or even all of the vices of the "old wretch" for whom his defamers mistake him. Salt is not sodium, but that is not saying that sodium is not a component of salt. The truth is that there *are* two Falstaffs, just as there are two Henrys, the Immortal Falstaff and the Immortal Falstaff, and the dissension about the man comes from a failure to recognize that fact. That the two could inhabit one body would not be believed if Shakespeare had not proved that they could. That may be one reason why he made it so huge.

Curiously, there is no more convincing testimony to this double nature of the man than that offered by those who are most persistent in pointing out his depravity. In the very process of committing the old sinner to perdition they reveal that they have been unable to resist his seductiveness. Professor Stoll, for instance, dedicates twenty-six sections of a long and learned essay to the annihilation of the Falstaff that his congenital lovers love. And then he begins his twenty-seventh and last section with the words: "And yet people like Falstaff"! And before his first paragraph is done, all his previous labor is obliterated as we find him asserting that Falstaff is "supremely poetic" (even his most ardent admirers would hardly venture that "supremely") and that "his is in many ways the most marvellous prose ever penned." (It is, but how did the old sot, we wonder; ever acquire it?) Before his next paragraph is over, Stoll has called Falstaff "the very spirit of comradeship," "the king of companions," and "the prince of good fellows." "We, too, after all, like Prince Hal and Mrs. Quickly," he goes on, "take to a man because of his charm, if it be big enough, not because of his virtue; and as for Falstaff, we are bewitched with the rogue's company." (A Falstaff idolater could scarcely ask for more than that.) "Under the spell of his presence and speech," Stoll concludes, we should forget, as she does, the wrong he has done Mrs. Quickly, "did we not stop to think."

"Stop to think"! One may determine the orbit of the moon, or make an atomic bomb, by stopping to think, but when since the beginning of time did one man ever get at the secret of another by means of the intellect? It is all right to stop to think after we have taken a character to our hearts, but to do so before we have is fatal. Dr. Johnson stopped to think about Falstaff and as a result he decided that "he has nothing in him that can be esteemed." A child would be ashamed of such a judgment. But a child would never be guilty of it. "As for *Henry IV,*" wrote one of the most imaginatively gifted young women I have ever known, "I love it. And I must have an utterly vulgar nature, for I simply adore Falstaff. He is perfectly delightful—not a fault in his nature, and the Prince is a DEVIL to reject him." That young woman evidently did not "stop to think." When she does, she will moderate that "not a fault in his nature," for that is the function of thinking—to hold our imagination within bounds and cut down its excrescences. Meanwhile, Falstaff has captured her, and she has captured Falstaff, for, as Blake said, enthusiastic admiration is the first principle of knowledge, and the last. Those who think about Falstaff before they fall in love with him may say some just things about him but they will never enter into his secret. "Would I were with him, wheresome'er he is, either in heaven or in hell!" Those words of poor Bardolph on hearing the account of Falstaff's death remain the highest tribute he ever did or ever could receive. In their stark sincerity they are worthy (irreverent as the suggestion will seem to some) to be put beside Dante's sublime incarnation of the same idea in the Paolo and Francesca incident in *The Inferno*, or even beside the words addressed to the thief who repented on the cross.

The scholars have attempted to explain Falstaff by tracing his origins. He has been found, variously, to have developed from the Devil of the miracle plays, the Vice of the morality plays, the boasting soldier of Plautine comedy, and so on. Now roots, up to a certain point, are interesting, but it takes the sun to make them grow and to illuminate the flower. And I think in this case we can find both roots and sun without going outside Shakespeare. If so, it is one of the most striking confirmations to be found of the embryological nature of his development.

If I were seeking the embryo of Falstaff in Shakespeare's imagination, I should consider the claims of Bottom—of Bottom and another character in *A Midsummer-Night's Dream.* "What!" it will be said, "the dull realistic Bottom and the lively witty Falstaff? They are nearer opposites." But embryos, it must be remembered, seldom resemble what they are destined to develop into. Bottom, like the physical Falstaff at least, is compact of the heaviness, the materiality, the reality of earth; and the ass's head that Puck bestows on him is abundantly deserved, not only in special reference to his brains but in its general implication of animality. But instead of letting himself be humiliated by it, Bottom sings, and Titania, Queen of the Fairies, her eyes anointed by the magic flower, awakening, mistakes him for an angel, and taking him in her arms, lulls him to sleep. The obvious meaning of the incident of course is that love is blind. Look at the asinine thing an infatuated woman will fall in love with! But whoever stops there, though he may have gotten the fun, has missed the beauty. The moment when Bottom emerges from his dream, as we pointed out when discussing *A Midsummer-Night's Dream*, is Shakespeare at one of his pinnacles. By a stroke of genius he turns a purely farcical incident into nothing less than a parable of the Awakening of Imagination within Gross Matter. It is the poet's way of saying that even within the head of this foolish plebeian weaver a divine light can be kindled. Bottom is conscious of transcendent things when he comes to himself. A creation has taken place within him. He struggles, in vain, to express it, and, in his very failure, succeeds:

> God's my life! ... I have had a most rare vision. I have had a dream, past the wit of man to say what dream it was. Man is but an ass, if he go about to expound this dream. Methought I was—there is no man can tell what. Methought I was,—and methought I had,—but man is but a patch'd fool, if he will offer to say what methought I had. The eye of man hath not heard, the ear of man hath not seen, man's hand is not able to taste, his tongue to conceive, nor his heart to report, what my dream was. I will get Peter Quince to write a ballad of this dream. It shall be called "Bottom's Dream," because it hath no bottom.

The dreamer may still be Bottom. But the dream itself is Puck. For one moment the two are one. Ass or angel? Perhaps Titania was not so deluded after all.

Do not misunderstand me. I am not suggesting that Shakespeare ever consciously connected Puck and Bottom with Falstaff in his own mind. But having achieved this inconceivable integration of the two, how easily his genius would be tempted to repeat the miracle on a grander scale: to create a perfect mountain of flesh and show how the same wonder could occur within it, not momentarily, but, humanly speaking, perpetually. That at any rate is what Falstaff is: Imagination conquering matter, spirit subduing flesh. Bottom was a weaver—a weaver of threads. "I would I were a weaver," Falstaff once exclaimed. He was a weaver—a weaver of spells. Here, if ever, is the embryology of the imagination. "Man is but a patch'd fool, if he will offer to say...." Who cannot catch the very accent of Falstaff in that?

> I'll put a girdle round about the earth
> In forty minutes.

It might have been said of Falstaff's wit. His Bottom-like body is continually being dragged down, but his Puck-like spirit can hide in a thimble or pass through a keyhole as nimbly as any fairy's. What wonder that this contradictory being—as deminatured as a satyr or a mermaid—who is forever repeating within himself the original miracle of creation, has taken on the proportions of a mythological figure. He seems at times more like a god than a man. His very solidity is solar, his rotundity cosmic. To estimate the refining power we must know the grossness of what is to be refined. To be astounded by what lifts we must know the weight of what is to be lifted. Falstaff is levitation overcoming gravitation. At his wittiest and most aerial, he is Ariel tossing the terrestrial globe in the air as if it were a ball. And yet— as we must never forget—he is also that fat old sinner fast asleep and snoring behind the arras. The sins, in fact, are the very things that make the miracle astounding, as the chains and ropes do a Houdini's escape.

To grasp Falstaff thus *sub specie aeternitatis* we must see him, as Titania did Bottom, with our imagination, not with our senses. And that is why we shall never see Falstaff on the stage. On the stage there the monster of flesh stands—made, we know, mainly of pillows—with all his sheer material bulk end greasy beefiness, a palpable candidate for perdition. It takes rare acting to rescue him from being physically repulsive. And as for the miracle—it just refuses to happen in a theater. It would take a child to melt this too too solid flesh into spirit. It would take Falstaff himself to act Falstaff. But in a book! On the stage of our imagination! That is another matter. There the miracle can occur—and does for thousands of readers. Falstaff is a touchstone to tell whether the juice of the magic flower has been squeezed into our eyes. If it has not, we will see only his animality. To the vulgar, Falstaff will be forever just vulgar.

The problem of Falstaff himself cannot be separated from the problem of the fascination he exercises over us. Critics have long since put their fingers on the negative side of that secret. Half his charm resides in the fact that he is what we long to be and are not: *free*. Hence our delight in projecting on him our frustrated longing for emancipation. It is right here that those who do not like Falstaff score a cheap victory over those who do. The latter, say the former, are repressed or sedentary souls who go on a vicarious spree in the presence of one who commits all the sins they would like to commit but do not dare to. Like some of Falstaff's own hypotheses, the idea has an air of plausibility. But it involves a pitifully superficial view of Falstaff—as if his essence lay in his love of sack! No! it is for liberation from what all men want to be rid of, not just the bloodless few, that Falstaff stands: liberation from the tyranny of things as they are. Falstaff is immortal because he is a symbol of the supremacy of imagination over fact. He forecasts man's final victory over Fate itself. Facts stand in our way. Facts melt before Falstaff like ice before a summer sun—dissolve in the *aqua regia* of his resourcefulness and wit. He realizes the age-old dream of all men: to awaken in the morning and to know that no master, no employer, no bodily need or sense of duty calls, no fear or obstacle stands in the way—only a fresh beckoning day that is wholly ours.

But we have all awakened that way on rare occasions without becoming Falstaffs. Some men often do. An untrammeled day is not enough; we must have something to fill it with—besides lying in bed. Freedom is only the negative side of Falstaff. Possessing it, he perpetually does something creative with it. It is not enough for him to be the sworn enemy of facts. Any lazy man or fool is that. He is the sworn enemy of the factual spirit itself, of whatever is dull, inert, banal. Facts merely exist—and so do most men. Falstaff lives. And where he is, life becomes bright, active, enthralling.

Who has not been a member of some listless group on whom time has been hanging heavy when in the twinkling of an eye a newcomer has altered the face of everything as utterly as the sun, breaking through clouds, transforms the surface of a gray lake? Boredom is banished. Gaiety is restored. The most apathetic member of the company is laughing and alert and will shortly be contributing his share to the flow of good spirits. What has done it? At bottom, of course, the mysterious fluid of an infectious personality. But so far as it can be analyzed, some tall tale or personal adventure wherein a grain of fact has been worked up with a pound of fiction, some impudent assumption about the host or absurd charge against somebody present rendered plausible by a precarious resemblance to the truth. Always *something made out of nothing*, with power, when added to the facts, to get the better of them. Never an unadulterated lie, but always some monstrous perversion, some scandalous interpretation, of what actually happened. An invention, yes, but an invention attached to reality by a thread of truth—the slenderer the better, so long as it does not break. What is Falstaff but an aggrandized, universalized, individualized version of this familiar phenomenon? He makes life again worth living.

And so, whether we approach Falstaff from the mythological or the psychological angle, we reach the same goal.

But alas! we have been neglecting the other Falstaff, the old sot. Unluckily—or perhaps luckily—there is another side to the story. Having fallen in love with Falstaff, we may now "stop to think" about him without compunction. And on examining more closely this symbol of man's supremacy over nature we perceive that he is not invulnerable. He has his Achilles heel. I do not refer to his love of Hal. That is his Achilles heel in another and lovelier sense. I refer to a tiny fact, two tiny facts, that he forgets and that we would like to: the fact that his imagination is stimulated by immense potations of sack and that his victories are purchased, if necessary, at the price of an utter disregard for the rights of others. We do not remember this until we stop to think. And we do not want to stop to think. We want to identify ourselves with the Immortal Falstaff. Yet there the Immoral Falstaff is all the while. And he must be reckoned with. Shakespeare was too much of a realist to leave him out.

The Greeks incarnated in their god Dionysus the paradox of wine, its combined power to inspire and degrade. *The Bacchae* of Euripides is the profoundest treatment of this theme in Hellenic if not in any literature. "No one can hate drunkenness more than I do," says Samuel Butler, "but I am confident the human intellect owes its superiority over that of the lower animals in great measure to the stimulus which alcohol has given to imagination—imagination being little else than another name for illusion."[1] "The sway of alcohol over mankind," says William James, "is unquestionably due to its power to stimulate the mystical faculties of human nature [the imagination, that is, in its quintessence], usually crushed to earth by the cold facts and dry criticisms of the sober hour. Sobriety diminishes, discriminates, and says no; drunkenness expands, unites, and says yes. It is in fact the great exciter of the *Yes* function in man ... it is part of the deeper mystery and tragedy of life that whiffs and gleams of something that we immediately recognize as excellent should be vouchsafed to so many of us only in the fleeting earlier phases of what in its totality is so degrading a-poisoning."

James's contrast between the earlier and the later phases of alcoholic intoxication inevitably suggests the degeneration that Falstaff undergoes in the second part of *Henry IV.* That degeneration is an actual one, though several recent critics have tended to exaggerate it. Dover Wilson thinks that Shakespeare is deliberately trying to make us fall out of love with Falstaff so that we may accept with good grace his rejection by the new king. If so, for many readers he did not succeed very well. (Of that in its place.)

It is significant that we never see Falstaff drunk. His wit still scintillates practically unabated throughout the second part of the play, though some critics seem set on not admitting it. He is in top form, for instance, in his interview with the Chief Justice, and, to pick a single example from many, the reply he gives to John of Lancaster's reproach,

When everything is ended, then you come,

is one of his pinnacles: "Do you think me a swallow, an arrow, or a bullet?" No, the degeneration of Falstaff is not so much in his wit or even in his imagination as in his moral sensibility. The company he keeps grows more continuously low, and his treatment of Shallow and of his recruits shows an increasing hardness of heart. Shakespeare inserts too many little realistic touches to let us take these scenes as pure farce, and while no one in his senses would want to turn this aspect of the play into a temperance tract it seems at times like an almost scientifically faithful account of the effect of an excess of alcohol on the moral nature. In view of what Shakespeare was at, this time on the verge of saying about drunkenness in *Hamlet* and of what he was to say about it later in *Othello*, *Antony and Cleopatra*, and *The Tempest*, it is certain that he was profoundly interested in the subject; and it is not far-fetched to suppose that he had in the back of his mind in portraying the "degeneration" of Falstaff the nemesis that awaits the artificially stimulated mind. If so, the fat knight is Shakespeare's contribution, in a different key, to the same problem that is treated in *The Bacchae*, and his conclusions are close to those at which Euripides arrives.

VII

And then there is *The Merry Wives of Windsor*. (Here appears to be the right place for a brief interlude on that play.) Criticism has been much concerned over the connection, if any, between the Falstaff of *The Merry Wives* and the Falstaff of *Henry IV*—with something like a consensus that with the exception of a few dying sparks of the original one this is another man. Yet one link between the two Falstaffs cannot be denied: with respect to wit and resourcefulness they are exact opposites. The Falstaff we admire is an incarnation of readiness; this one of helplessness. Nothing is too much for the former. Anything is too much for the latter. They are, respectively, presence and absence of mind. Such an utter antithesis is itself a connection. Shakespeare must have meant something by it.

Nearly everyone is acquainted with the tradition that *The Merry Wives of Windsor* was written in a fortnight at the command of Queen Elizabeth, who wished to see the fat man in love. Shakespeare does appear to have "tossed off" this sparkling farce-comedy, his one play of purely contemporary life and of almost pure prose, and, along with *The Comedy of Errors*, his most inconsequential and merely theatrical one. Several hypotheses, or some combination of them, may account for the Falstaff of this play.

Poets, as distinct from poets laureate, do not like commissions. It would be quite like Shakespeare, ordered by the Queen to write another play about Falstaff, to have his playful revenge by writing one about another man entirely, under the same name. That was precisely the sort of thing that Chaucer did when commanded by another Queen to write a *Legend of Good Women*. It is fun to make a fool of royalty. Then, too, the conditions under which the play was written, if the tradition is true, practically compelled it to keep close to farce. And farce is the very atmosphere in which parody thrives.

This Falstaff is a kind of parody of the other one. But the closer Shakespeare gets to farce, fancy, or nonsense, as he proves over and over, the more certain he is to have some serious underintention. On that principle, what better place than *The Merry Wives of Windsor* in which to insert an oblique comment on the Falstaff of *Henry IV*? Be that as it may, the Falstaff of this play is, as we said, an almost perfect picture, in exaggerated form and in a farcical key, of the Immoral Falstaff of the other plays, the old wretch of Bernard Shaw. Only the light tone of the piece keeps him from being "besotted and disgusting" also. Critics have seriously tried to determine at what spot chronologically this play should be inserted in the Henry series. Such an attempt betrays a curious ignorance of the ways of the imagination. But, after all due discount for the farce and fooling, the Falstaff of *The Merry Wives* looks like pretty good natural history of the latter end of an "old soak." From him it is a relief to get back, after our interlude, to the Immortal Falstaff, who, however entangled with the Immoral Falstaff, as the soul is with the body, breathes another and more transcendental air.

VIII

Is there any activity of man that involves the same factors that we find present in this Falstaff: complete freedom, an all-consuming zest for life, an utter subjugation of facts to imagination, and an entire absence of moral responsibility? Obviously there is. That activity is play.

Except for that little item of moral responsibility, "play" expresses as nearly as one word can the highest conception of life we are capable of forming: life for its own sake, life as it looks in the morning to a boy with

> no more behind
> But such a day to-morrow as to-day,
> And to be boy eternal,

life for the fun of it, as against life for what you can get out of it—or whom you can knock out of it. "Play" says what the word "peace" tries to say and doesn't. "Play" brings down to the level of everyone's understanding what "imagination" conveys to more sophisticated minds. For the element of "imagination" is indispensable to true play. Play is not sport. The confusion of the two is a major tragedy of our time. A crowd of fifteen-year-old schoolboys "playing" football on a back lot are indulging in sport. They are rarely playing. The one who is playing is the child of five, all alone, pretending that dirty rag doll is the rich mother of a dozen infants—invisible to the naked eye. Even boys playing war, if they are harmonious and happy, are conducting an experiment in peace. Play is the erection of an illusion into a reality. It is not an escape from life. It is the realization of life in something like its fulness. What it is an escape from is the boredom and friction of existence. Like poetry, to which it is the prelude, it stands for a converting or winning-over of facts on a basis of friendship, the dissolving of them in a spirit of love, in contrast with science (at least the science of our day), which, somewhat illogically, stands first for a recognition of the absolute autonomy of facts and then for their impressment and subjection to human demands by a kind of military conquest.

Now Falstaff goes through life playing. He coins everything he encounters into play, often even into a play. He would rather have the joke on himself and make the imaginative most of it than to have it on the other fellow and let the fun stop there. Whenever he seems to be taken in because he does not realize the situation, it is safer to assume that he does realize it but keeps quiet because the imaginative possibilities are greater in that case.

Watching him, we who in dead earnest have been attending to business or doing what we are pleased to call our duty suddenly realize what) we have been missing. "The object of a man's life," says Robert Henri, "should be to play as a little child plays." If that is so we have missed the object of life, while Falstaff has attained it, or at least not missed it completely, ash we have. It is his glory that, like Peter Pan, he never grew up, and that glory is the greater because he is an old man. As his immense size and weight were utilized by Shakespeare as a foil for the lightness of his spirit, so his age is used to stress its youthfulness. "You that are old," he says to the Chief Justice, who has been berating him for misleading the Prince, "consider not the capacities of us that are young." The Chief Justice replies that Falstaff is in every part "blasted with antiquity," his belly increasing in size, his voice broken, "and will you yet call yourself young? Fie, fie, fie, Sir John!" Falstaff retorts that as for his belly, he was born with a round one; as for his voice, he has lost it hollaing and singing of anthems; and as for his age, he is old only in judgment and understanding. Though the Lord Chief Justice has all the facts on his side, Falstaff has the victory. There has seldom been a more delicious interview.

As this scene suggests, the right way to take the Falstaff whom we love is to take him as a child. Mrs. Quickly did that in her immortal account of his death: he went away, she said, "an it had been any christom child." To call him a liar and let it go at that is like being the hardheaded father of a poetic little son who punishes him for falsehood when he has only been relating genuine imaginative experiences—as Blake's father thrashed him for saying he had seen angels in a tree. And to call him a coward and let it go at *that* is being no profounder.

But if it is the glory of the Immortal Falstaff that he remained a child, it is the shame of the Immoral Falstaff that he never became a man—for it is a child's duty to become a man no less than it is a man's duty to become a child. Falstaff detoured manhood instead of passing through it into a higher childhood. He is like the character in *The Pilgrim's Progress* who tried to steal into Paradise by climbing over the wall near its entrance instead of passing through the wicket gate and undergoing the trials that it is the lot of man to endure. He wanted the victory without paying the price. He wanted to be an individual regardless of the social consequences, to persist in the prerogatives of youth without undertaking the responsibilities of maturity. But if his virtues are those of a child rather than those of a man, that does not prevent him from being immensely superior to those in these plays who possess the virtues of neither man nor child, or from giving us gleams of a life beyond good and evil.

Dover Wilson[2] would have us take *Henry IV* as a morality play wherein a madcap prince grows up into an ideal king. Falstaff is the devil who temps the Prince to Riot. Hotspur and especially the Lord Chief Justice are the good angels representing Chivalry and justice or the Rule of Law. It is a struggle between Vanity and Government for the possession of the Royal Prodigal.

The scheme is superbly simple and as moral as a Sunday-school lesson. But it calmly leaves the Immortal Falstaff quite out of account! If Falstaff were indeed just the immoral creature that in part he admittedly is, Wilson's parable would be more plausible, though even then the words he picks to characterize Falstaff are singularly unfortunate. "Vanity" by derivation means emptiness or absence of substance, and "riot" quarrelsomeness. Imagine calling even the Immoral Falstaff empty or lacking in substance—or quarrelsome! He had his vices but they were not these. For either vanity or riot there is not a single good word to be said. To equate Falstaff with them is to assert that not a single good word can be said for him—a preposterous proposition. Wit, humor, laughter, good-fellowship, insatiable zest for life: are these vanity or does Falstaff *not* embody them? That is the dilemma in which Mr. Wilson puts himself. And as for the Lord Chief Justice, he is indeed an admirable man; a more incorruptible one in high position is not to be found in Shakespeare. But if the poet had intended to assign him any such crucial role as Mr. Wilson thinks, he certainly would have presented him more fully and would have hesitated to let Falstaff make him look so foolish. For the Chief Justice's sense of justice was better developed than his sense of humor. And even justice is not all.

Henry IV does have a certain resemblance to a morality play. The two, however, between whom the younger Henry stands and who are in a sense contending for the possession of his soul are not Falstaff and the Chief Justice, but Falstaff and the King. It is between Falstaff and the Father—to use that word in its generic sense—that Henry finds himself.

Now in the abstract this is indeed Youth between Revelry and Responsibility. But the abstract has nothing to do with it. Where Henry really stands is between this particular companion, Falstaff, and this particular father and king, Henry IV. Of the two, which was the better man?

Concede the utmost—that is, take Falstaff at his worst. He was a drunkard, a glutton, a profligate, a thief, even a liar if you insist, but withal a fundamentally honest man. He had two sides like a coin, but he was not a counterfeit. And Henry? He was a king, a man of "honour," of brains and ability, of good intentions, but withal a "vile politician" and respectable hypocrite. He was a counterfeit. Which, if it comes to the choice, is the better influence on a young man? Shakespeare, for one, gives no evidence of having an iota of doubt.

But if even Falstaff at his worst comes off better than Henry, how about Falstaff at his best? In that case, what we have is Youth standing between Imagination and Authority, between Freedom and Force, between Play and War. My insistence that Falstaff is a double man, and that the abstract has nothing to do with it, will acquit me of implying that this is the whole of the story. But it is a highly suggestive part of it.

The opposite of war is not "peace" in the debased sense in which we are in the habit of using the latter word. Peace ought to mean far more, but what it has come to mean on our lips is just the absence of war. The opposite of war is creative activity, play in its loftier implications. All through these dramas the finer Falstaff symbolizes the opposite of force. When anything military enters his presence, it instantly looks ridiculous and begins to shrink. Many methods have been proposed for getting rid of war. Falstaff's is one of the simplest: laugh it out of existence. For war is almost as foolish as it is criminal. "Laugh it out of existence"? If only we could! Which is the equivalent of saying: if only more of us were like Falstaff! These plays should be required reading in all military academies. Even the "cannon-fodder" scenes of Falstaff with his recruits have their serious implications and anticipate our present convictions on the uneugenic nature of war.

How far did Shakespeare sympathize with Falstaff's attitude in this matter? No one is entitled to say. But much further, I am inclined to think, than he would have had his audience suspect or than the world since his time has been willing to admit. For consider the conditions under which Falstaff finds himself:

Henry has dethroned and murdered the rightful king of England. The Percys have helped him to obtain the crown, but a mutual sense of guilt engenders distrust between the two parties, and the Percys decide to dethrone the dethroner. Falstaff is summoned to take part in his defense. "Life is given but once." Why should Falstaff risk his one life on earth, which he is enjoying as not one man in a hundred million does, to support or to oppose the cause of either of two equally selfish and equally damnable seekers after power and glory? What good would the sacrifice of his life accomplish comparable to the boon that he confers daily and hourly on the world, to say nothing of himself, by merely being? This is no case of tyranny on one side and democracy on the other, with the liberty or slavery of a world at stake. This is a strictly dynastic quarrel. When two gangs of gunmen begin shooting it out on the streets of a great city, the discreet citizen will step behind a post or into a doorway. The analogy may not be an exact one, but it enables us to understand Falstaff's point of view. And there is plenty of Shakespearean warrant for it.

See the coast clear'd, and then we will depart,

says the Mayor of London when caught, in *1 Henry VI,* between similar brawling factions,

Good God! these nobles should such stomachs bear;
I myself fight not once in forty year.

And Mercutio's "A plague o' both your houses!" comes to mind. Shakespeare meant more by that phrase than the dying man who coined it could have comprehended.

"But how about Falstaff's honor?" it will be asked. "Thou owest God a death," says the Prince to him before the battle of Shrewsbury. "'Tis not due yet," Falstaff answers as Hal goes out,

I would be loath to pay him before his day. What need I be so forward with him that calls not on me? Well, 'tis no matter; honour pricks me on. Yea, but how if honour prick me off when I came on? how then? Can honour set to a leg? No. Or an arm? No. Or take away the grief of a wound? No. Honour hath no skill in surgery, then? No. What is honour? A word. What is in that word honour? What is that honour? Air; a trim reckoning! Who hath it? He that died o' Wednesday. Doth he feel it? No. Doth he hear it? No. 'Tis insensible, then? Yea, to the dead. But will it not live with the living? No. Why? Detraction will not suffer it. Therefore I'll none of it. Honour is a mere scutcheon: and so ends my catechism.

"You must be honorable to talk of honor," says a character in *A Raw Youth*, "or, if not, all you say is a lie." The word "honor," as that sentence of Dostoevsky's shows, is still an honorable word. It can still mean, and could in Shakespeare's day, the integrity of the soul before God. The Chief Justice had honor in that sense. But "honour" in its decayed feudal sense of glory, fame, even reputation, as page after page of these Chronicle Plays records, had outlived its usefulness and the time had come to expose its hollowness. The soul, lifted up, declared Saint Teresa (who died in 1582), sees in the word "honor" "nothing more than an immense lie of which the world remains a victim.... She laughs when she sees grave persons, persons of orison, caring for points of honor for which she now feels profoundest contempt.... With what friendship we would all treat each other if our interest in honor and in money could but disappear from the earth! For my own part, I feel as if it would be a remedy for all our ills."

Saint Teresa and Sir John Falstaff! an odd pair to find in agreement— about honor if not about money. In the saint's case no ambiguity is attached to the doctrine that honor is a lie. In the sinner's, there remains something equivocal and double-edged. Here, if ever, the two Falstaffs meet. The grosser Falstaff is himself a parasite and a dishonorable man, and coming from him the speech is the creed of Commodity and the height of irony. But that does not prevent the man who loved Hal and babbled of green fields at his death from revealing in the same words, as clearly as Saint Teresa, that life was given for something greater than glory or than the gain that can be gotten out of it.

"Give me life," cries Falstaff on the field of Shrewsbury. "Die all, die merrily," cries Hotspur. That is the gist of it. The Prince killed Hotspur in the battle, and Falstaff, with one of his most inspired lies, claimed the deed as his own. But Falstaff's lies, scrutinized, often turn out to be truth in disguise. So here. Falstaff, not Prince Henry, did kill Hotspur. He ended the outworn conception of honor for which Hotspur stood. The Prince killed his body, but Falstaff killed his soul—or rather what passed for his soul.

The dying Hotspur himself sees the truth. The verdict of his final breath is that life is "time's fool" and he himself dust. And the Prince, gazing down at his dead victim, sees it too, if only for a moment.

> Ill-weav'd ambition, how much art thou shrunk!
> When that this body did contain a spirit,
> A kingdom for it was too small a bound,

he exclaims, and, turning, he catches sight of another body from which life has also apparently departed:

What, old acquaintance! could not all this flesh
Keep in a little life? Poor Jack, farewell!
I could have better spar'd a better man.

But nobody was ever more mistaken on this subject of life and flesh than was Henry on this occasion, as the shamming Falstaff proves a moment later, when the Prince goes out, by rising from the dead. "'Sblood," he cries,

> 'twas time to counterfeit, or that hot termagant Scot had paid me scot and lot too. Counterfeit? I lie, I am no counterfeit. To die is to be a counterfeit; for he is but the counterfeit of a man who hath not the life of a man; but to counterfeit dying, when a man thereby liveth, is to be no counterfeit, but the true and perfect image of life indeed. The better part of valour is discretion.

> I fear thou art another counterfeit,

Douglas had cried, coming on Henry IV on the field of Shrewsbury,

> Another king! they grow like Hydra's heads.
> I am the Douglas, fatal to all those
> That wear those colours on them. What art thou,
> That counterfeit'st the person of a king?

The literal reference of course is to the knights, disguised to represent the King, that Henry had sent into the battle to divert the enemy from his own person. "The better part of valour is discretion." This, and that repeated word "counterfeit," is Shakespeare's sign that he intends the contrast, and the deeper unconscious meaning of Douglas'

> What art thou,
> That counterfeit'st the person of a king?

(a king, notice, not the king) is just one more of the poet's judgments upon Henry. For all his "discretion," the Douglas would have killed this counterfeit king who tries to save his skin by the death of others if the Prince had not come to his rescue in the nick of time.

But that was earlier in the battle. At the point we had reached the Prince comes back with his brother John and discovers the "dead" Falstaff staggering along with the dead Hotspur on his back—a symbolic picture if there ever was one.

> Did you not tell me this fat man was dead?

cries Lancaster.

> I did; I saw him dead,
> Breathless and bleeding on the ground,

replies Henry. He has underrated the vitality of the Imagination, and even now thinks he sees a ghost:

> Art thou alive?
> Or is it fantasy that plays upon our eyesight?
> I prithee, speak; we will not trust our eyes
> Without our ears. Thou art not what thou seem'st.

"No: that's certain," retorts Falstaff, "I am not a double man." And to prove it, he throws down the body of Hotspur he is carrying. But beyond this obvious meaning, who can doubt that Falstaff, in the phrase "double man," is also having a thrust at the dual role of the man he is addressing, or that Shakespeare, in letting Falstaff deny his own doubleness, is thereby calling our attention to it? At the very least the expression proves that the world did not have to wait for Dostoevsky before it heard of the double man.

Truth has made it necessary to say some harsh things about Prince Henry; so it is a pleasure to recognize the character of his conduct on the field of Shrewsbury: his valor in his encounter with Hotspur, his courage and loyalty in rescuing his father from Douglas, and his generosity in letting Falstaff take credit for Hotspur's death. Dover Wilson makes much of this last point—too much, I think, for the good of his own case—declaring that it proves the Prince thought nothing of renown, of "the outward show of honour in the eyes of men, so long as he has proved himself worthy of its, inner substance in his own." But if he was as self-effacing as all that, why did he cry at the moment he met Hotspur?—

> all the budding honours on thy crest
> I'll crop, to make a garland for my head.

Those words flatly contradict the "grace" he does Falstaff in surrendering to him so easily the greatest honor of his life. The paradox arises, I think, from the presence of those conflicting personalities, Hal and the Prince. Touched momentarily at the sight of what he believes to be his old companion dead at his feet, the fast-disappearing Hal returns and survives long enough after the surprise and joy of finding him still alive to accept Falstaff's lie for truth. But we wonder how much longer. Wilson's assumption that the Prince would or could have kept up the fiction permanently is refuted by the fact that Morton had observed the death of Hotspur at Henry's hands and reports the event correctly:

> these mine eyes saw him in bloody state,
> Rendering faint quittance, wearied and outbreath'd,
> To Harry Monmouth; whose swift wrath beat down
> The never-daunted Percy to the earth,
> From whence with life he never more sprung up.

Everything, from the famous first soliloquy on, proves that the Prince not only craved renown but craved it in its most theatrical form.

Notes

1. It is usually presumptuous to disagree with Samuel Butler's use of words. But if he had substituted "mind" for "intellect" in the foregoing quotation I think he would have been nearer the mark. And only the unwary reader will think that by "illusion" Butler means the same thing as delusion or lie.

2. Following Professor R. A. Law.

KENNETH TYNAN

The Old Vic 'Henry IV', Parts 1 and 2, at the New Theatre

From a production so unobtrusive that at times it looked positively mousy, three very great pieces of acting emerged. The Old Vic was now at its height: the watershed had been reached, and one of those rare moments in the theatre had arrived when drama paused, took stock of all that it had learnt since Irving, and then produced a monument in celebration. It is surprising, when one considers it, that English acting should have reached up and seized a laurel crown in the middle of a war, and that the plays in which the prize was won should have been plays of battle, tumult, conspiracy and death, as the histories are. There was a bad atmosphere then amongst the acting clubs of London—an atmosphere such as one finds in the senior common-rooms of the women's colleges at Oxford: an air of pugnacious assurance and self-sufficiency mixed with acrid misogyny. There were roughly two groups of actors: the elder, who seemed to be suffering from thyroid deficiency, a condition which induces a blunt and passive sedentariness in the sufferer: and the very young ones, afflicted by the opposite sickness, thyroid excess, whose symptoms are emaciation and nervous constriction. The good, mature players were silent: the state of society had tied their hands, and they tied their own tongues. It was left to Richardson and Olivier to sum up English acting in themselves; and this was what, in *Henry IV*, they achieved.

Richardson's Falstaff was not a comic performance: it was too rich and

From *He That Plays the King: A View of the Theatre*. © 1950 by Longmans, Green and Co.

many-sided to be crammed into a single word. The humour of it, as in Max Beerbohm's prose, was in the texture: there were no deliberate farcical effects. This was the down-at-heel dignity of W. C. Fields translated into a nobler language: here was a Falstaff whose principle attribute was not his fatness but his knighthood. He was Sir John first, and Falstaff second, and let every cock-a-hoop young dog beware. The spirit behind all the rotund nobility was spry and elastic: that, almost, of what Skelton in a fine phrase called 'friskajolly younkerkins'; there was also, working with great slyness but great energy, a sharp business sense: and, when the situation called for it, great wisdom and melancholy ('Peace, good Doll! do not speak like a death's-head: do not bid me remember my end' was done with most moving authority). Each word emerged with immensely careful articulation, the lips forming it lovingly and then spitting it forth: in moments of passion, the wild white halo of hair stood angrily up and the eyes rolled majestically: and in rage one noticed a slow meditative relish taking command: 'Marry, there is another indictment upon thee, for suffering flesh to be eaten in thy house, contrary to the law; for the which I think—thou—wilt—howl': the last four words with separate thrice-chewed pungency. Richardson never rollicked or slobbered or staggered: it was not a sweaty fat man, but a dry and dignified one. As the great belly moved, step following step with great finesse lest it overtopple, the arms flapped fussily at the sides as if to paddle the body's bulk along. It was deliciously and subtly funny, not riotously so: from his height of pomp Falstaff was chuckling at himself: it was not we alone, laughing at him. He had good manners and also that respect for human dignity which prevented him from openly showing his boredom at the inanities of Shallow and Silence: he had only recently sunk from the company of kings to the company of heirs-apparent. None of the usual epithets for Falstaff applied to Richardson: he was not often jovial, laughed seldom, belched never. In disgrace, he affected the mask of a sulky schoolboy, in the manner of Charles Laughton: in command, he would punch his wit at the luckless heads of his comrades, and their admiration would forbid response. The rejection scene at the end of Part 2 came off heartrendingly well: with his back to the audience Richardson thumped forward to welcome the new king, his whilom jackanapes: and after the key-cold rebuke which is his answer, the old man turned, his face red and working in furious *tics* to hide his tears. The immense pathos of his reassuring words to Shallow even now wets my eyes: 'I shall be sent for soon at night.' He hurried, whispered through the line very energetically, as if the whole matter were of no consequence: the emptiness of complete collapse stood awfully behind it. It was pride, not feasting and foining, that laid this Falstaff low: the youthful, hubristic heart inside the corporeal barrel had flown too high, and must be crushed. Cyril Connolly might have been speaking of this performance when he said: 'Imprisoned in every fat man a thin one is wildly signalling to be let out' let out, and slaughtered. Beside this Falstaff, Nicholas Breton's picture of a drunkard seems almost blasphemous: 'a tub of swill, a spirit of sleep, a picture of a beast and a monster of a man'.

Enough has already been written of Olivier's Hotspur, that ferocious darling of war. With the roughness and heedlessness of the warrior chieftain, he mixed the heavyhanded tenderness of the very virile husband: and knotted the performance into a unity by a trick, the stammer which prefaced every word beginning with the letter 'w'. This clever device fitted perfectly with the over-anxiousness, the bound-burstingness, the impotent eagerness of the character. The long speech of explanation to the king about the unransomed prisoners, beginning 'My liege, I did deny no prisoners', is essentially an apology: for this Hotspur it was an aggressive explosion of outraged innocence:

> ... for it made me *mad* [almost a shriek]
> To see him shine so brisk and smell so sweet
> And talk so like a waiting-gentlewoman
> Of guns and drums and w— w—

(Here the face almost burst for frenzy: the actor stamped the ground to loosen the word from his mouth. Finally, in a convulsion of contempt, it sprang out)

> w-*wounds*—God save the mark!

This impediment dovetailed so well with Hotspur's death that one could not escape concluding that Olivier had begun his interpretation of the part at the end and worked backwards: the dying speech ends thus:

> ... no, Percy, thou art dust,
> And food for—
> HENRY: For worms, brave Percy.

I need not add that Olivier died in the throes of uttering that maddening, elusive consonant.

The most treasurable scenes in these two productions were those in Shallow's orchard: if I had only half an hour more to spend in theatres, and could choose at large, no hesitation but I would have these. Richardson's performance, coupled with that of Miles Malleson as Silence; beak-nosed, pop-eyed, many-chinned and mumbling, and Olivier as Shallow, threw across the stage a golden autumnal veil, and made the idle sporadic chatter of the lines glow with the same kind of delight as Gray's *Elegy*. There was a sharp scent of plucked crab-apples, and of pork in the larder: one got the sense of life-going-on-in-the-background, of rustling twigs underfoot and the large accusing eyes of cows, staring through the twilight. Shakespeare never surpassed these scenes in the vein of pure naturalism: the subtly criss-crossed counterpoint of the opening dialogue between the two didderers, which skips between the price of livestock at market and the philosophic fact of death ('Death, saith the Psalmist, is certain; all must die'), is worked out with fugal delicacy: the talk ends with Shallow's unanswered rhetorical question: 'And is old Double dead?' No reply is necessary: the stage is well and truly set, and any syllable more would be superfluous. The flavour of sharp masculine kindness Olivier is adept in: for me the best moment in his 'Hamlet' film was the pat on the head for the players' performing dog which accompanied the line: 'I am glad to see thee well.' And it was in the very earth of this Gloucestershire orchard. Olivier was the Old Satyr in this Muses' Elizium; 'Through his lean chops a chattering he doth make, which stirs his staring, beastly-drivell'd beard.' This Shallow (pricked with yet another nose, a loony apotheosis of the hook-snout he wore as Richard) is a crapulous, paltering scarecrow of a man, withered up like the slough of a snake; but he has quick, commiserating eyes and the kind of delight in dispensing food and drink that one associates with a favourite aunt. He pecks at the lines, nibbles at them like a parrot biting on a nut; for all his age, he darts here and there nimbly enough, even skittishly; forgetting nothing, not even the pleasure of Falstaff's page, that 'little tiny thief'. The keynote of the performance is old-maidishness, agitated and pathetically anxious to make things go with a swing: a crone-like pantomime dame, you might have thought, were it not for the beady delectation that steals into his eyes at the mention of sex. (Shallow was, as Falstaff later points out, 'as lecherous as a monkey'.) His fatuous repetitions are those of importunate female decrepitude: he nags rather than bores. Sometimes, of course, he loses the use of one or more of his senses: protesting, over the table, that Falstaff must not leave, he insists, emphasizing the words by walking his fingers over the board: 'I will not excuse you, sir; you shall not be excused; excuses shall not be admitted; there is no excuse shall serve; you shall not be excused'—and after his breathless panic of hospitality, he looks hopefully up: but Falstaff has long since gone. Shallow had merely forgotten to observe his departure: and the consequent confusion of the man, as he searches with his eyes for his vanished guest, is equalled only by his giggling embarrassment at finding him standing behind him.

Of all the wonderful work Olivier did in this and the previous Old Vic season, I liked nothing more than this. A part of this actor's uniqueness lies in the restricted demands he makes on his, audience's rational and sensual capacities. Most actors invite the spectator either to pass a *moral* judgment on the characters they are representing; or to pass a *physical* judgment on their own appearance. A normal actor playing a moderately sympathetic part will go all out to convince the audience that he is a thoroughly good man, morally impeccable; playing a villain, he will force them to see the enormity of the man's sins. He will translate the character into the terms of a bad nineteenth-century novel. An attractive actor playing the part of a *jeune premier* will try primarily to arouse the admiration of the women and the envy of the men; a player of farce will rely chiefly on grotesque make-up to establish the character for him. But most actors do insist on a judgment of one kind or another: and they are better or worse actors according to the degree to which it is obvious that they are *insisting*. Olivier makes no such attempts to insist, and invites no moral response: simply the thing he is shall make him live. It is a rare discretion, an ascetic tact which none but he dares risk.

LEO SALINGAR

Falstaff and the Life of Shadows

THESEUS. *The best in this kind are but shadows; and the worst are no worse,*
  if imagination amend them.
HIPPOLYTA. *It must be your imagination then, and not theirs.*
                                      A Midsummer Night's Dream, 5.1.211–14

What is it that makes us laugh about Falstaff? This is perhaps a naive,
unanswerable question. In his magisterial lecture on "The Rejection of
Falstaff," Bradley set even a part of it, the query why we laugh at the fat
knight, judiciously aside. Nevertheless, it is still tempting to assail the
indefinable and, throwing caution to the winds, to try to sprinkle salt on the
tail of that particularly large but paradoxically lively bird, even at the risk of
losing, along with the caution, the salt. It is particularly tempting if we want
to examine the general nature of comedy and—a related but distinct set of
questions—the place Falstaff occupies in the two parts of *Henry IV*.

Some of the unavoidable niggles that beset this sort of inquiry are that
we do not all, as readers, laugh at the same things or even twice at the same
place; that we are much more prone to laugh in company than alone; and
that, even in the theater, our laughter depends to some extent on accidents
of the occasion. Further, the impulse to laugh, when studying Shakespeare,
is to some extent lumbered with the ponderous gear of annotations. And,

From *Shakespearean Comedy* 5–6 (1980). ©1980 by New York Literary Forum.

more generally, a perfect, utopian theory of laughter would take care of the difference between the occasions when we laugh outright and the occasions when we merely feel an inclination to laugh. But the present essay—caution having been disregarded—cannot pause over such niceties (just as it will only be concerned with the canonical or *echt* Falstaff, as the two historical plays body him forth).

Perhaps the best starting-place is Bergson's theory of laughter, insufficient though it is. According to Bergson, then, we laugh when we perceive "something mechanical encrusted on something living," the physical encroaching upon the sphere of mental freedom, a human being behaving like a physical object; at bottom, our laughter is prompted by *raideur* rather than *laideur*, by "the unsprightly" rather than "the unsightly."[1] In comedy, it is directed against the personage who has sunk his individuality in the routines of a social or professional or temperamental type, who has forfeited his waking spontaneity to some automatism of behavior resembling absentmindedness. And, since mechanical thought or behavior, though necessary within limits, is ultimately hostile to social evolution, or the *élan vital*, the underlying function of comedy is to marshal our collective and corrective laughter against such obstacles to freedom. This theory applies well to a great deal in Molière, and to Labiche, Bergson's second choice for purposes of illustration; equally, it could apply almost intact to the superbly intricate contraptions for laughter devised by Bergson's contemporary, Georges Feydeau.

However, Bergson's purview is limited by assumptions traditional with criticism, especially in France, such as the assumption that comedy and laughter are very nearly the same thing. Even within those limits, he pays no attention to those characters who make us laugh *with* them and not at them. And, as Albert Thibaudet noted in his study of Bergson, the philosopher's analysis of stage comedy, even in Molière, omits the indispensable factor of mobility: "a comedy is a movement, I don't mean necessarily an action."[2] For Thibaudet, this is a correlative to the subliminal movement we experience inwardly when responding to any work of art. However, by the same token, it is also an expression of Bergsonian *élan*. And perhaps one can carry this observation a step further and save the appearances for Bergson's theory of the comic by supposing that those stage characters who make us laugh intentionally, and not inadvertently, have become, at least for the time being, delegates for the author by anticipating some threatened incursion of the mechanical upon the vital and triumphantly reversing the flow. If so, they represent the upsurge of spontaneity over automatism, a process more fundamental to comedy than any enforcement of social correction. This line of reasoning may account also for those stimuli to laughter that other theorists have emphasized, though they are only marginal from Bergson's point of view, such as the laughter due to surprise or incongruity or to release from the breaking of a taboo. Although in cases like those our laughter may not have been prompted by "something mechanical encrusted on something living," it could still be argued that the cause of it was the mental jolt of expecting to see a logical or a moral rule at work but finding instead that the mechanism of the rule had been overcome. This still has less to do with social solidarity than with the subconscious pleasure of release. But in the theater there is surely also a further level of interplay on some such lines between the mechanical and the vital. Once the train of laughter has been set going, we seem to store up a reserve for extra additional laughter precisely in our altered uncertainty as to when next and which way the cat is going to jump.

Falstaff is surely the grand example of such multiplicity, or deep duplicity, in the causes of laughter. "The brain of this foolish compounded clay, man," he can fairly claim, "is not able to invent anything that intends to laughter more than I invent or is invented on me. I am not only witty in myself, but the cause that wit is in other men" (*Henry IV, Part 2*, 1.2.7–10). When Bradley and like-minded critics gloss over the causes why others laugh *at* Falstaff, it must be because they seem so obvious—"gross as a mountain"—and not because they are unfathomable. First, of course, his fatness, a classic instance of what Aristotle would call the ludicrous arising from a defect that is not destructive or what Bergson would call the physical encroaching upon the mental (since it is represented as a consequence of his chosen way of life). Then his drinking, his cowardice (or, if you prefer, his "instinct" not to be heroic), his apparently compulsive lying. Poins and the Prince foresee very well what mechanisms they will spring in him when they plan their "jest" at Gad's Hill. And Shakespeare has made him a perpetual comic butt, because, as Harry Levin has pointed out, he has staged him as a walking paradox, a Renaissance knight without a horse; "uncolted" (*Henry IV, Part 1*, 2.2.39) by the Prince, and commissioned with nothing better for the war than "a charge of foot" (2.4.550).[3]

On the other hand, when Poins anticipates "the incomprehensible" (the illimitable) "lies that this same fat rogue will tell" (*Henry IV, Part 1*, 1.2.183–4), he hints at just the opposite side of Falstaff, his inventiveness, his inexhaustible resilience, his predictable unpredictability. These have to do with the reasons why we laugh *with* him. He is always quick at changing an awkward subject. And his lies are foxy evasions, not empty fantasies like the boasts of Baron Munchausen or the daydreams of Walter Mitty. They match the positive resourcefulness of his wit, his ability to play with words and, beyond that, to disconnect and recombine the accepted rules of moral judgment. In thought as in act, he is the arch-opponent of regularity: "Give you a reason on compulsion? If reasons were as plentiful as blackberries, I would give no man a reason upon compulsion, I" (*Henry IV, Part 1*, 2.3.239–42). We laugh, one may suggest, at sallies like this both because he is cornered and knows he is cornered and because he can nevertheless trump up something almost indistinguishable from a valid reply, unexpected and, in the fullest sense, diverting. We laugh because he is caught out, because just the same he has been too quick for us, and further (I believe) because we are not sure which of these thoughts is uppermost. This kind of uncertainty is fundamental in comic tradition.

FALSTAFF'S LANGUAGE

Falstaff's puns form one of his ways of circumventing mechanisms of thought, by taking advantage of what are possibly no more than accidental associations of ideas in language. He can treat "reasons" like "blackberries," for instance because the word was pronounced *raisins*; thereby evading an awkward truth. Or he can pun spontaneously, from high spirits, as when, later in the same tavern scene, he enjoins his companions to "clap to the doors. Watch tonight, pray tomorrow" (*Henry IV, Part 1*, 2.4.279–80)—out of sheer relief on learning that the stolen money he thought he had been filched of could be used for his benefit after all. His biblical "Watch and pray" not merely pretends to sanctify their proposed drinking-bout (or *watch*), but also recalls his fellow-thieves to their predatory highway code, thus covertly reinstating his own manliness at the same time.[4]

He is similarly inventive in the vocabulary of aggression, protestation, belittlement, and abuse. If the others will not credit his valor on Gad's Hill, he is "a shotten herring" (*Henry IV, Part 1*, 2.4.131) or "a bunch of radish." Hal, disbelieving him, becomes "you starveling, ... you dried neat's-tongue, you bull's pizzle, you stockfish" (2.4.246–7). All this Carnival, or Billingsgate, raillery is, of course, part of the game that he shares with the Prince. In their first scene together, when Hal has disobligingly knocked down his attempts to find expressions for his alleged "melancholy," Falstaff retorts, "Thou hast the most unsavory similes, and art indeed the most comparative, rascalliest, sweet young prince (*Henry IV, Part 1*, 1.2.80–82). Set point to the "fat-witted" knight; but it seems clear enough why the Prince should enjoy his company.

The game they play calls for stylistic agility (for the copiousness in words the Elizabethans admired and for skill in calculated breaches of literary decorum) besides licensing a free-for-all of mock-aggression. It was fashionable in the 1590s and was related to the new literary conception of wit that was then emerging. Nashe, for example, relishes what he calls the "sport" of railing; after a two-page effusion over a literary enemy, he characteristically adds,

> *Redeo ad vos, mei auditores* [back to you, listeners]: have I not an indifferent pretty vein in spur-galling an ass? If you knew how extemporal it were at this instant, and with what haste it is writ, you would say so. But I would not have you think that all this that is set down here is in good earnest, for then you go by St. Giles the wrong way to Westminster; but only to show how for a need I could rail if I were thoroughly fired.[5]

Shakespeare's courtly wits, as in *Love's Labor's Lost*, indulge themselves in a similar vein. But it is specially appropriate to a Bohemian or adventurer of the pen like Nashe; indeed, it becomes Nashe's principal stock in trade, as he bawls his academically certified wares in the marketplace. And it is peculiarly appropriate to Falstaff's position as a gentle-bred adventurer who compensates through language for deficiencies in the more solid advantages due to his rank. In language, Falstaff is a lord. He commands a ruffianly composure of speech, a leisured pace permitting lightning thrusts, and a compendious range of tone including masterful coarseness. It is the coarseness that Hotspur wants to hear from Lady Percy when she swears (*Henry IV, Part 1*, 3.1.245–54). It distinguishes Falstaff completely from a mere "swaggerer" of the day and ranter of playhouse tags like Pistol; style is his real, and his only real, ground of equality with the Prince. Yet his speech is repeatedly ambiguous in tone, corresponding to the indeterminateness of his social position. As William Empson has put it, "Falstaff is the first major joke by the English against their class system; he is a picture of how badly you can behave, and still get away with it, if you are a gentleman—a mere common rogue would not have been nearly so funny."[6]

Whether his tone for the moment is aggressive or not, Falstaff habitually asserts himself by defeating expectation. His very first appearance must have come as a surprise to the Elizabethans; they could have anticipated a wild gallant or a rumbustious clown to accompany Hal onto the stage, but not a corpulent, benevolent, apparently deliberative grayhead. On his opening words, noncommittal in tone ("Now, Hal, what time of day is it, lad?" [*Henry IV, Part 1*, 1.2.1]), the Prince pounces with the imputation that his proper qualities are gluttony and sloth, which are much what stage tradition, if not historical legend, would attach to such a personage:

> Thou art so fat-witted with drinking of old sack, and unbuttoning
> thee after supper, and sleeping upon benches after noon, that

thou hast forgotten to demand that truly which thou wouldest
truly know. What a devil hast thou to do with the time of the day?
[1.2.2–6]

But Falstaff at once shows that he has, on the contrary, a concern of sorts
with the passage of time, by asking a series of questions about the future, in
the course of which, far from admitting to sloth or gluttony, he fleetingly
adopts the voices of manly "resolution," "melancholy" solicitation, and even
sorrowful "amendment of life" (1.2.103). He may resemble Gluttony or
Sloth—or alternatively, Riot—but in himself, his manner implies, he is not
to be identified with any of them (any more than Jaques's melancholy is the
scholar's or the musician's or the courtier's, "but it is a melancholy of mine
own, compounded of many simples, extracted from many objects" [*As You
Like It*, 4.1.15–17]).

And Falstaff's personality seems always in movement, going against the
stream of opinion. He repeatedly advances the idea of his own worth, not simply
by bragging when occasion favors, but by jocular assertion and, especially in his
early scenes, by insinuating that the standards he could be criticized by, the
yardsticks that society commonly applies to worthiness, are habitually
misconceived or misplaced. He does not expect his assertions to be taken "in
good earnest" any more (or any less) than Nashe; and, at least before the battle
scenes, he does not single out any one of society's values for direct criticism
(which might seem to fix him in the vulnerable position of a malcontent or
satirist). Instead, he works through parody and calculated irrelevance, or the
dissociation of received ideas. His counterattack on public values is mobile and
indirect, as, in the opening dialogue, when he responds to the, Prince's sarcasm
by dignifying (or affecting to dignity?) his occupation as a thief:

Indeed you come near me now, Hal; for we that take purses go by
the moon and the seven stars, and not by Phoebus, he, that
wand'ring knight so fair [which disposes of Hal's question about
"the time of the day."]

And I prithee, sweet wag, when thou art king ... let not us that are
squires of the night's body be called thieves of the day's beauty.
Let us be Diana's foresters, gentlemen of the shade, minions of
the moon; and let men say we be men of good government, being
governed, as the sea is, by our noble and chaste mistress the
moon, under whose countenance we steal.

(*Henry IV, Part 1*, 1.2.14–17; 24–30)

Hearing this, an Elizabethan audience must have been so sidetracked, or delighted, by the pell-mell parodies of euphuism, balladry, popular romance, and even of the worship of Cynthia, mistress of the sea, herself, that they could not muster any of their proper indignation at the naked proposal Falstaff is putting forward or at his hint that it is only fancy names, arbitrary titles, that distinguish the honest citizen from the thief (as Gadshill supportively observes a few scenes later, "'homo' is a common name to all men" [2.1.97–8]).

Whatever else Falstaff may be set to do in *Henry IV*, he has begun with the ancient comic operation of turning the world upside-down. And soon he returns to this even more insidiously. After the Prince has rebuffed him with reminders about the gallows and has teased him with the promise of a hangman's job, instead of the momentarily hoped-for office of a judge, Falstaff shifts his key to the Biblical:

> But, Hal, I prithee trouble me no more with vanity. I would to God thou and I knew where a commodity of good names were to be bought.

and, as if mounting the pulpit:

> An old lord of the council rated me the other day in the street about you, sir, but I marked him not; and yet he talked very wisely, but I regarded him not; and yet he talked wisely, and in the street too.
>
> (Henry IV, Part 1, 1.2.82–7)

Part of Falstaff's ploy here is to pretend, in all generosity, that he has been receiving blame because of Hal and not the other way about. And in the midst of his sermonizing he can suddenly swerve into a good, downright tavernly oath: "I'll be damned for never a king's son in Christendom" (1.2.7–8). But as soon as Hal, taking his cue from this, quips him with a reminder about taking purses, Falstaff reverts to his Biblical strain: "Why, Hal, 'tis my vocation, Hal. 'Tis no sin for a man to labor in his vocation" (1.2.105–6). Critics, noting Falstaff's very frequent allusions to the Bible (particularly the book of Proverbs and the parable of the Prodigal Son), are fond of explaining that he is ridiculing the language of Puritanism; but it was equally the language of the Book of Homilies and the established Church.[7] As far as parody goes, his subversiveness is comprehensive.

FALSTAFF'S ROLES

Yet he is not simply a stage jester any more than he is simply a rogue. None of the roles that critics or other characters on the stage attribute to him define him adequately as a character or as a figure in the play. He is not, for instance, a Morality-play Vice, however he may be compared to such. Apart from anything else, it makes nonsense of his relations with Hal to think of him as a personification of the Prince's human proneness to sin or to speak as if he ever tempts the Prince successfully in the course of the play or gains any ascendancy over his will. He is not a traditional braggart soldier, if only because he is far too intelligent. He is not exactly a Lord of Misrule; if he can be said to preside over revels in Eastcheap, it is more in our imagination than in the view of his company as a whole. Nor is he exactly a trickster, or ironic buffoon, in the line of classical comedy, in spite of his aptitude for turning the world upside-down. He neither pursues any ingenious intrigue in the manner of New Comedy (though he swindles Mrs. Quickly and Shallow) nor consistently entertains any world-changing fantasy like a hero from Aristophanes. He is too deeply enmeshed in common reality to imagine that he can change the world, and he takes his adventures as they come. He is constantly improvising, assuming a role. In the extemporized play scene that marks the highest point of his concord with Hal, he revels in parodying an actor; but through all his assumed voices we can hear a voice of his own, coming out most clearly perhaps in soliloquies—of which he has more than any other speaker in the play. It seems no accident that he became, in his own name, a legendary figure, as quickly and as lastingly as Hamlet. We seem to be in the presence of a richly complex personality, with a reserve of self-awareness underneath all his clowning.

In Maurice Morgann's apologia for Falstaff, there is a striking footnote where Morgann outlines the principles that, in his view, require a critic of Shakespeare to explain the characters of Shakespeare's people "from those parts of the composition which are *inferred* only, and not distinctly shewn," and "to account for their conduct from the *whole* of character, from general principles, from latent motives, and from policies not avowed."[8] The "historic" or biographical method of interpretation that Morgann erected upon this insight has been thoroughly, perhaps too thoroughly, exploded. And in Falstaff's case, such apparently solid biographical facts as we are given—that as a boy he had been "page to Thomas Mowbray, Duke of Norfolk" and had known John of Gaunt—are not disclosed until the second half of the second play (*Henry IV, Part 2*, 3.2.26–73, 328). Nevertheless, one can hardly deny that Morgann brought out something vital about the *impression* (to use his own term) that Shakespeare gives us about Falstaff and gives us from the outset. Only, Shakespeare's methods were not biographical in anything like the way that (for example) Ibsen's methods could be so described. One of the means that Shakespeare uses is to suggest through the dialogue that a particular role will fit Falstaff or that he will display a particular disposition of mind, and then almost at once to make the character belie it. As Falstaff speaks, we perceive that the characteristics we have been led to expect of him are incorrect or incomplete or shadowy approximations at best. It quickly turns out that Hal's first description of him as Sloth and Gluttony is no more than a caricature. When he has behaved like a braggart soldier, he can switch to the ironic buffoon. When he is patently and professedly acting ("as like one of these harlotry players as ever I see!" says the Hostess [*Henry IV, Part 1*, 2.4.400–1]), it turns out that he is pleading his own cause. He is reputed to be misleading the Prince, but Falstaff himself says just the opposite, and in any case we never see him do it.

Watching or reading the play, of course, we do not sift such conflicting bits of evidence and work out a decisive verdict that would satisfy a jury in a court of law. There is nothing like the question whether Hal is really the irresponsible his father and the others suppose him to be, a question Shakespeare takes care to set at rest very soon. But with Falstaff, allegations and half-truths are allowed to remain at the back of our minds, without being clearly dispelled. We neither confirm nor reject them completely but are allowed and even prompted to imagine that they may be true, but only to limited facets of his character, or true to something in his unseen conduct off-stage. These half-defined approximations are like shadows in a picture that throw the figure into relief. To defeat our expectations, then, is part of Falstaff's comic tactics, and to keep us uncertain about the essential Falstaff is part of Shakespeare's strategy as a comic playwright. But further, Shakespeare has given Falstaff hints of an inner consciousness, at variance with his outward roles, that go some way towards justifying Morgann's search for "latent motives" and "policies not avowed."

Critics have been reluctant to consider that Falstaff has anything like a conscience or any doubts about himself. Hazlitt praises his "absolute self-possession" and "self-complacency,"[9] and Bradley insists that we laugh *with* Falstaff precisely because he is so "happy and entirely at his ease" in "his humorous superiority to everything serious, and the freedom of soul enjoyed in it."[10] And in W. H. Auden's view, "time does not exist" for Falstaff (but then Auden holds that the essential man belongs to *opera buffa*, and is out of place in *Henry IV*).[11] However, Falstaff (a "proud Jack" [*Henry IV, Part 1*, 2.4.11] to the tavern-drawers, according to Hal) is not remarkable for *bonhomie*; and he never expresses himself as cheerful or satisfied for long. On the contrary, his favorite terms of reference for his favorite subject, himself, imply, if they are taken in earnest, a sense of injury and regret for neglected valor, lost innocence, and either material or spiritual insecurity. His first speeches are questions about the future, which we are given no reason to think are totally flippant. If he can loudly contradict his years in the heat of the robbery scene ("What, ye knaves, young men must live" [2.2.92–31]), his next scene shows him affectedly brooding over them: "There lives not three good men unhanged in England; and one of them is fat, and grows old" (2.4.131–3). This cadence swerves, of course, into ludicrous self-mockery— "I would I were a weaver; I could sing psalms or anything" (2.4.133–5)—and this whole speech (125–35) is a typical mock-diatribe or mock-complaint, in which Falstaff's claims of "manhood" and self-righteousness are incongruous with one another and doubly incongruous in the light of his behavior.

Still, these are his two most frequent themes, with particular emphasis on the theme of religion. "Before I knew thee, Hal," he has affirmed, "I knew nothing; and now am I, if a man should speak truly, little better than one of the wicked" (*Henry IV, Part 1*, 1.2.93–6). And later, with no one more appreciative than Bardolph to hear him:

> Well, I'll repent, and that suddenly, while I am in some liking ...
> And I have not forgotten what the inside of a church is made of,
> I am a peppercorn, a brewer's horse. The inside of a church!
> Company, villainous company, hath been the spoil of me.[12]
>
>   (3.3.4–11)

Naturally, each of these outbursts of elderly grumbling, sorrowful grievance, or rueful contrition on the part of "Monsieur Remorse," as Poins calls him, strikes us as yet another of Falstaff's jokes. And whenever he alludes to repentance, he quickly veers away from it. Nevertheless, persistent jokes on the same topic tell us something about what weighs on a man's mind; it seems as if Falstaff were one of those fat men in whom a thin man is struggling to get out. Without probing into "latent motives," Shakespeare has portrayed in him, not "absolute self-possession," but the condition of mind of a man of intellectual power, wounded in his self-esteem and conscience, who cannot bring himself to do anything about it, but finds an escape from his self-image in joking. Far from expressing "self-complacency" or complete "freedom of soul," his "humorous superiority to everything serious," if it exists, seems to be gained at the cost of self-mockery—which mocks the world as well, in order to redress the balance. But without the potential, camouflaged seriousness in his jokes (together with the background of seriousness in the political action in the play), many of them would lose their force and point.

To return to his first scene for an example:

> But, Hal, I prithee trouble me no more with vanity. I would to
> God thou and I knew where a commodity of good names were to
> be bought....
>
> (*Henry IV, Part 1*, 1.2.82–4)

The word *vanity*, which initiates Falstaff's diversion to Biblical parody, is not
simply a pretended rebuke to Hal's "unsavory similes" (1.2.80) but also an
oblique acknowledgment of the seriousness running through their previous
talk, particularly by way of Hal's references to hanging. And the irony about
"good names" (loaded with the word *commodity*, which usually has a smack of
skulduggery about it in Shakespeare)[13] would lose half its dramatic point if it
were no more than a capricious quip or satiric side-thrust against the
established order. There is the second irony that Falstaff is pretending to be
in earnest, while hinting to the Prince, without openly admitting, that on
another level he is seriously engaged as well. That the two ironies should
work against one another both contributes to the continuity of Falstaff's part
in the play and adds to the store of laughter from uncertainty in the minds
of the audience.

By way of contrast, consider the tone Shakespeare was to give to an
ironist of a different stamp, Iago:

> Good name in man and woman, dear my lord,
> Is the immediate jewel of their souls.
> Who steals my purse steals trash; 'tis something, nothing....
>
> (*Othello*, 3.3.157–9)

These are the sententious accents of hypocrisy. Iago is quite indifferent to
the maxim he is manipulating, and must be felt to be indifferent so that we
can concentrate on the effect of his words upon Othello, whereas Falstaff
knows very well that he is not really pulling the wool over the eyes of the
Prince, but he is personally, if covertly, involved in what he says.

Once or twice in *Part 1* this concern shows more directly. When
Falstaff has to hide from the sheriff, Hal tells the others, "Now, my masters,
for a true face and good conscience" (2.4.506–7) while Falstaff exists with an
aside—"Both of which I have had; but their date is out, and therefore I'll hide
me" (2.4.508–9). And as he approaches the battlefield, he is given his second
soliloquy. Since he comes on here in the contemporary guise of a fraudulent
recruiting officer and since this is the first time he has gained any profit in
the course of the play, we should expect to find him in a mood of malicious
glee if he were simply a conventional stage rogue or Morality Vice. But
instead, he is unexpectedly "ashamed":

> If I be not ashamed of my soldiers, I am a soused gurnet. I have
> misused the king's press damnably ... No eye hath seen such
> scarecrows. I'll not march through Coventry with them, that's
> flat....
>
> (*Henry IV, Part 1*, 4.2.11–13; 38–40)

He shrugs off this mood almost at once:

> There's not a shirt and a half in all my company ... But that's all
> one; they'll find linen enough on every hedge.
>
> (42–3.47–8)

We are very nearly back to the atmosphere of Eastcheap and Gad's Hill. All
the same, the tone of genuine surprise, a novel tone in Falstaff's voice, shows
that there has been a progression in his part. The war becomes a testing
experience for Falstaff as, on a very different scale, it becomes a testing
experience for Hal. It imparts a continuous movement to Falstaff's share in
the play, from his early, half-comic protest to Hal—"I must give over this life,
and I will give it over!" (1.2.46–7)—to the slyly conditional resolution or
prediction in his last soliloquy, which is also his closing speech:

> If I do grow great, I'll grow less; for I'll purge [*repent*], and leave
> sack, and live cleanly, as a nobleman should do.
>
> (5.4.161–4)

From beginning to end in *Part 1*, Falstaff is engaged with the passage of time,
with concern about the future.

FALSTAFF AND THE THEME OF TIME

The theme of time is crucial to Shakespeare's presentation of what
Edward Hall had described as "The Unquiet Time of King Henry IV." The
guiding thought in the overplot of *Part 1* is the thought of "redeeming time,"
with implications at once religious,[14] financial, chivalric, and political. In
financial terms, it branches out by way of talk about ransom and theft,
auditing, debt, and repayment, to return, as it were, to the main line of the
action by way of Hal's determination to "pay the debt I never promised.
Redeeming time when men think least I will" (1.2.206; 214). In the opening
scene, though he does not use the word, Henry IV dwells on the thought of
the Redeemer (1.1.18–27). Shakespeare has antedated his project to lead a
crusade, treating it as Henry's intended means of absolving England from

civil war and, by inference, absolving himself from his guilt as an usurper.[15] Hotspur, eager to "redeem" "drowned honor," (1.3.205), tells his father and uncle that "yet time serves wherein you may redeem / Your banished honors" (1.3.178–9)—by changing allegiance for a second time in rebellion.[16] On his side, Hal promises to "redeem" his reputation "on Percy's head" and his father confirms that he has "redeemed ... lost opinion" in the battle (3.2.132; 5.4.46). For the leading political actors, "time serves," not to achieve honor, like knights-errant, but to redeem the honor they have already lost, or appear to have lost.

FALSTAFF AND THE POLITICAL WORLD

With his ignoble ambition to find out "where a commodity of good names were to be bought" (*Henry IV, Part 1*, 1.2.83–4), Falstaff is a parody of this political world. In Hal's company he is like a grotesque father-substitute, and he echoes the king in his grumbles over time misspent. His lawlessness and braggartism throw light on Hotspur. Above all, Falstaff is a man in a false position, just as the king, Hotspur, and Hal are all, in their different ways, men in false positions. But Falstaff, of course, has the saving grace of humor. He has an inclusive, if usually ironic, self-awareness that men like Henry IV and Hotspur cannot afford, though some of it seems to have rubbed off onto Hal. This is the obverse of his comic "remorse": not a "superiority to everything serious" or simply an addiction to the pleasures of the flesh, but a warm belief in the immediacy and, in the end, authenticity, of his personal existence. "Banish plump Jack, and banish all the world!" (2.4.484–5) he exclaims to Hal, as their improvised play-acting breaks down in a moment of truth; and then, as he prepares to hide from the sheriff, "Dost thou hear, Hal? Never call a true piece of gold a counterfeit" (2.4.496–7). This cryptic admonition takes on fuller significance later, in the battle scenes. Falstaff's development there, in close proximity to the political actors, is far from one-sided. His cynical betrayal of his troop of "rag-of-muffins" (5.3.36) matches Worcester's double dealing. His low-minded "discretion" is pitched against Hotspur's high-minded but futile "valor" (117–8). The conclusion to his famous "catechism," that "Honor is a mere scutcheon" (*Henry IV, Part 1*, 5.1.140) cannot efface the resplendent heroism that Shakespeare gives the Prince, though it still leaves the purely chivalric motives in war and politics open to question.

But at the same time, as at the beginning of the play, the dramatist sets Falstaff in relation to the king, by his arrangement of the kaleidoscopic battle episodes. Taking a hint from Holinshed's statement that at Shrewsbury there were several knights "apparelled in the king's suit and clothing" (but reducing the chronicler's emphasis on the king's "high manhood"),[17] Shakespeare shows two episodes in which Douglas is engaged with the "likeness" or the "shadows" or the "counterfeit" of the king. In the first (*Henry IV, Part 1*, 5.3.1–29) Douglas kills Sir Walter Blunt, as he says he has already killed Lord Stafford, believing him to be the king himself, until Hotspur undeceives him ("The king hath many marching in his coats"). In the second (5.4.23–36), meeting the king in person, he can hardly believe that Henry is not "another counterfeit." Hal drives Douglas off. Then, while Hal encounters Hotspur in resonantly epic style, in the action to which the whole course of the play has pointed, Douglas reenters briefly and, in dumb show, apparently kills Falstaff.

But as soon as Falstaff has been left alone on the stage, he jumps up again, undercutting the lofty tones of the champions' verse in his savory prose:

> 'Sblood, 'twas time to counterfeit, or that hot termagant Scot had paid me scot and lot too. Counterfeit? I lie; I am no counterfeit. To die is to be a counterfeit, for he is but the counterfeit of a man who hath not the life of a man; but to counterfeit dying when a man thereby liveth, is to be no counterfeit, but the true and perfect image of life indeed....
>
> (*Henry IV, Part 1*, 5.4.111–17)

In this folk-play-style sham resurrection, and in his farcical sham killing of Hotspur immediately afterwards, Falstaff counteracts the high talk of politics and war. Courage in battle has been shown as a reality in the play, and the need for royal authority has been vindicated. But the political scenes have revealed expediency, double dealing, and even a kind of inward privation, not because Henry IV has been shown as a downright Machiavellian like Richard III, but because his rule has been established on false foundations and because the forward drives of conflicting political interests have generated their own ruthless momentum. Falstaff's counterfeiting here revives basic human impulses which the affairs of state would have thwarted or excluded.

THE FUNCTION OF SHADOWS IN THE *HENRY IV* PLAYS

At Shrewsbury, Henry has safeguarded his life by the employment of "shadows." In another sense also, Shakespeare has extensively used "shadows" in both parts of the play to give life and imagined reality to the world in which Henry and Falstaff belong. History could be said to require that the action should shift across the country between north and south and that the main actors should refer to characters and events that are not shown on the stage. But in *Henry IV* Shakespeare has taken particular pains, more I think than in any other of his plays, to go beyond the strict requirements of dramatizing history and conjure up the thought of England as a country and, even more strikingly, to conjure up images of individuals offstage, known to the speakers in the play though unrecorded by the chroniclers.

What is at stake in the Percies' rebellion is the territory of England— "this soil," as Henry calls it in his opening lines (*Henry IV, Part 1*, 1.1.5). Shakespeare imagines this, in its continuity and specific variety, as no other poet before him had done. In the first scene of *Part 1*, for instance, we hear of "stronds" and "fields" and "acres," of Herefordshire and Windsor, and all "the variation of each soil / Betwixt that Holmedon and this seat of ours" (64–5). Later, in the scene between Hotspur, Mortimer, and Glendower, a map is an essential property. And when Hotspur falls, Hal reflects that

> When that this body did contain a spirit
> A kingdom for it was too small a bound;
> But now two paces of the vilest earth
> Is room enough. The earth that bears thee dead
> Bears not alive so stout a gentlemen.
>
> (5.4.87–91)

Meanwhile, we have heard, for instance, of "Severn's sedgy bank" and of Berkeley Castle (the name Hotspur cannot remember [1.3.97; 240–6]) of Moorditch and the Wild of Kent and Falstaff's route through Coventry. And in *Part 2*, to say nothing of Falstaff's boasted acquaintance with "all Europe" (2.2.133), we hear of Northumberland's "worm-eaten hole of ragged stone" at Warkworth (Induction 135), of Oxford and Stamford fair, and particularly of localities in or near London—Eastcheap, the St. Alban's road, Clement's Inn, Mile-End Green, Turnbull Street, Windsor, the Jerusalem chamber, the Fleet. Both parts are busy with the images of messengers, especially horsemen, hurrying with instructions or news or rushing to or from a battlefield. And each virtually begins with a striking image of this sort, of Sir Walter Blunt "new lighted" (*Henry IV, Part 1*, 1.1.63) after his long ride from Holmedon or of the unnamed gentleman met by Northumberland's servant, Travers, "spurring hard" and "almost forspent with speed" on his "bloodied horse," who had paused only to ask the road to Chester and then "seemed in running to devour the way" (*Henry IV, Part 2*, 1.1.36; 37; 38; 47) in his headlong flight from Shrewsbury. Amid all this evocation of England's place-names and roads and "uneven ground" (*Henry IV, Part 1*, 2.2.25) the earthy and earthbound figure of Falstaff seems solidly congenial; he "lards the lean earth as he walks along" (2.2.111–12).

Even closer to the sense of animated reality in both parts of the play are the allusive sketches of nonhistorical characters whom we hear of though never see. In *Part 1*, they range from the "old lord of the council" who (allegedly) had "rated" Falstaff about Hal "the other day in the street" (1.2.85–6) by way of Hotspur's acid sketch of the "popin-gay" who had "so pest'red" (1.3.49) him after the fighting at Holmedon (the "certain lord" whose "chin new reaped / Showed like a stubble land at harvest home" [1.32–4]—men and country are thought of together), on to the "mad fellow" by the wayside who had taunted Falstaff about his troop of "tattered prodigals," and to the prodigals' victim, "the rednose innkeeper at Daventry" (4.2.36; 34–5; 47). These marginal, off-stage figures, shadowlike but with separate lives of their own, intensify our sense of varied life in the stage characters themselves. They supply precisely what Morgann would call "those parts of the composition which are *inferred* only, and not distinctly shewn."

They are even more numerous in *Part 2*, especially in direct or indirect contact with Falstaff. Falstaff's first dialogue opens with a sarcasm reported from his doctor and with the knight's abuse of that "yea forsooth knave" (1.2.36), his obdurate mercer, Master Dummelton. (It is striking how, in *Part 2*, off-stage characters, as well as minor actors on the stage, are now given expressive, caricatural names.[18]) Through Mrs. Quickly's chatter, we hear of her "gossip," "goodwife Keech, the butcher's wife" (2.1.92–3) and of "Master Tisick, the deputy," who had admonished her while "Master Dumbe, our minister" (2.4.86; 89) was standing by. And in Shallow's scenes, at least (on my count) sixteen off-stage characters are identified, mostly by the aging justice himself—from the three invisible Silences he asks after, and the four "swinge-bucklers" and old Double (the bowman beloved of John of Gaunt), recalled from his "Inns o' Court" days (3.2.23) back to the "arrant knave" (5.1.42) William Visor of Woncot, whom nevertheless his servant Davy trusts he will "countenance" (5.1.39) in a lawsuit. With the help of names like Keech (butcher's fat), Simon Stockfish, Jane Nightwork, and Silence's champion fat man, "goodman Puff of Barson" (5.3.93–4) as well as with drinking episodes and snatches of song, these Boar's Head and Cotswold scenes project a continuing, subdued impression as of a sort of scrimmage between representatives of Carnival and of Lent. From another point of view, it is a confused medley between everyday rascality and everyday law, complicating and enriching the historical theme of high justice, now central to the main plot. And with grimly sympathetic touches, sharp as engravings by Callot, these profusely inventive comic scenes bring home the rhythm of insignificant lives and insignificant deaths that shadow the high historical drama of war and statecraft. Moreover, they contribute something vital to the state of mind or quality of experience projected by *Part 2* as a whole, especially by way of Justice Shallow, that marvellous latecomer to *Henry IV*, with his trivial comforts and his senile reminiscences.

The predominant experience conveyed by *Part 2*, it seems to me, is the experience of uncertainty. It is the uncertainty, suspense, indecision that Northumberland expresses when he says:

> 'Tis with my mind
> As with the tide swelled up unto his height,
> That makes a still-stand, running neither way.
>   (2.3.62–4)

Shakespeare makes the historical action unexciting, by contrast with *Part 1*, showing the rebellion suppressed, well before the end, by cold-blooded stratagem, not by fighting. He reduces even the death of Northumberland in battle to an incidental anticlimax, stripping it of the animation of circumstantial report (*Henry IV, Part 2*, 4.4.97–101). He treats the passage of history he is dealing with as an interim period, a period of waiting rather than doing, thus throwing new emphasis on the way the actors perceive themselves as "time's subject" (1.3.110), peering into the future, reconsidering the past. One of his innovations in both parts of *Henry IV*, concurrent with the use of so many off-stage personalities, is the way Shakespeare now makes his characters recall past events at length, and this is particularly noticeable and effective in *Part 2*. The historical speakers think back to the battle of Shrewsbury and its antecedents—even, while Henry is dying, to the time before Richard II, as the anxious princes recall omens and popular beliefs preceding the death of Edward III:

> The river hath thrice flowed, no ebb between,
> And the old folk, time's doting chronicles,
> Say it did so a little time before
> That our great-grandsire, Edward, sicked and died.
>   (4.4.125–8)

This speech echoes both Northumberland's image about the tide and the theme introduced in the prologue by Rumour, the theme of "surmises" and "conjectures," of "Conjecture, expectation, and surmise" (Induction 16; 1.3.23).

Throughout the play, remembrance of the past is set in tension against "likelihoods and forms of hope" (*Henry IV, Part 2*, 1.3.35) about the future or else "forms imaginary" (4.4.59) of apprehension, which run from the uncertainties agitating the rebel camp in the early scenes to the anxieties, even in victory, surrounding the deathbed of Henry IV. It is this form of mental tension, this general human experience, that Shakespeare is dramatizing here (though it must have struck a specially contemporary chord at the moment when the play first appeared). About midway (in Act 3, scene 1), there is a turning point in the speeches rehearsing past events, when Henry has been questioning his whole troubled career and Warwick tries to explain that "There is a history in all men's lives" (3.1.80) linking past and future in intelligible sequence. Whereupon the king exclaims, "Are these things then necessities? / Then let us meet them like necessities" (3.1.92–3). But even here, what emerges is the expression of a frame of mind, not any decision affecting the plot. It is the characters' attitude towards current realities that Shakespeare is concerned with. As in *Part 1*, they are conscious of the pressures of "time." But in *Part 2*, it is more especially "the condition of these *times*" that preoccupies them—"The times are wild" ... "these coster-mongers' times" ... "the revolution of the times"—together with the signs they seem to hold about the "times that you shall look upon" (4.1.99; 1.1.93; 1.2.70–1; 3.1.46; 4.4.60).

"Old folk" dominate the stage in *Part 2*, whereas youth is either dead and gone with Hotspur or subject to fears about the future with Hal (whose glory gained at Shrewsbury is kept, for good dramatic reasons, out of sight).[19] As L. C. Knights has pointed out, *Part 2* dwells on "age, disappointment and decay."[20] But this elegiac mood is countered in the comic scenes by the enjoyment of immediate, if trivial, pleasures, such as Mrs. Quickly's appreciation of goodwife Keech's "good dish of prawns" (2.1.95) or Shallow's enjoyment of "any pretty little tiny kickshaws" to be produced by "William cook" (5.1.28) and his anticipation of eating "a last year's pippin of [his] own graffing, with a dish of caraways, and so forth" (5.3.2–3). On the other side, Hal is obliged to regret that his princely appetite can still "remember the poor creature, small beer. But indeed," he adds, "these humble considerations make me out of love with my greatness" (2.2.10–12). Such "humble considerations" are made to seem relatively timeless; particularly where, towards the climax for Falstaff, Shakespeare cuts from the scene of preparations for dinner at Shallow's house (Act 5, scene 1) to the scene at London announcing Henry IV's death and showing Henry V's reconciliation with the Chief Justice, and then back to Shallow's house for the fruit (Act 5, scene 3)—as if, for the moment, the national crisis belonged not only to a different world but to a different order of time. Yet the distinction between the low world and the high is finely shaded. There is no more than a shaky grasp of reality in Mrs. Quickly's muddled, rambling, suggestive mind, and in Shallow's gullible self-importance and his vanity about the past. Doll Tearsheet and Silence are complementary, if opposite, types. Altogether, since he is kept at a distance from the Prince, Falstaff's chosen company in *Part 2* is more easygoing, less sharp-witted, than his company in *Part 1*.

There are corresponding changes in Falstaff himself. In spite of the credit he has gained, with the help of Rumour, from Shrewsbury, he still depends ultimately on patronage from Hal. But he is thrown more upon his own resources, so that his capture of a prisoner of war seems like an accident; and the main line of his action, until the last moments of the play, is a spiraling progress from debt to debt. We see more of his social versatility than before, but we also hear more of his private reflection, as he sizes up himself and his world. He can inspire affection, at least the maudlin affection of Doll and Mrs. Quickly. He is given less to outbursts of "remorse" than before and more to exploiting the world as he finds it: "A good wit will make use of anything. I will turn diseases to commodity" (something he can sell, this time, not something he wants to buy [*Henry IV, Part 2*, 1.2.250–1]). He will fleece Justice Shallow if he can, on the strength of their old acquaintance, in sardonic complicity with "the law of nature" (3.2.336). He is as evasive and resourceful as before, but less impulsive, more detached and calculating. We hear more of the mellow, observant, leisured cadences in his prose. He is more of a philosopher and more of a rogue.

A recurrent subject of wryly amused reflection with Falstaff, in connection with the Page and then Prince John and finally Shallow, is the inequality between the Fat and the Lean. What occupies his mind is not so much thoughts of his own age and sickness, which he will evade if he can, as the contrast between his sense of implantation in life and the unsteadiness of his fortunes. His antipathy to Prince John inspires his most elaborate set speech (*Henry IV, Part 2*, 4.3.86–125), his soliloquy of mock-humanistic encomium in praise of drink and of wine-inspired wit, "apprehensive, quick, forgetive, full of nimble, fiery and delectable shapes" (4.3.99–101). This is his most defiant plea for laughter and his own style of life. But his meeting with Shallow has begun to elicit another style from Falstaff, more objectively humorous but also more contemplative, as he measures the squire's history against his own. "Lord, Lord, how subject we old men are to this vice of lying!" (3.2.307–8) is a spontaneous (if ironic) reflection, not a set speech. And his first, richly grotesque, soliloquy about Shallow and how "This same starved justice hath done nothing but prate to me of the wildness of his youth" (3.2.308–10) is also Falstaff's first excursion of any length into his own past (3.2.305–37); but "now has he land and beeves" (3.2.332). His second soliloquy on the same topic (5.1.64–88) is more detached, with exactly balanced clauses of amused observation:

> If I were sawed into quantities, I should make four dozen of such
> bearded hermits' staves as Master Shallow. It is a wonderful thing
> to see the semblable coherence of his men's spirits and his. They,
> by observing him, do bear themselves like foolish justices. He, by
> conversing with them, is turned into a justice-like serving-man....
> It is certain that either wise bearing or ignorant carriage is
> caught, as men take diseases, one of another. Therefore let men
> take heed of their company....
>
> (*Henry IV, Part 2*, 5.1.64–71; 77–80)

This has the ring of shrewd, almost homely, unforced practical wisdom, so much that the dramatic irony in the last sentence is almost submerged. This speech marks the high point of Falstaff's role as an unruffled humorous critic of mechanical behavior in other men. He goes on to anticipate how he will make "Prince Harry" laugh over Shallow, though with a rueful glance at the gap between jester and patron—"a fellow that never had the ache in his shoulders!" (*Henry IV, Part 2*, 5.1.80–2; 85–6). In his next scene (Act 5, scene 3), the news that Pistol (of all select companions) brings from court releases a mechanism in Falstaff himself, in the wild dream that "the laws of England are at my commandment" (5.3.140–1).

It seems almost impossible for critics to agree about the rejection of Falstaff. Perhaps this shows a flaw in the writing of the play as a whole. Admittedly, there is a jarring note in Henry's rejection speech, though on the other hand the whole action ends on an unheroic note of subdued expectation, on the *diminuendo* of a half-line of verse. But perhaps also those who, like Bradley, deplore the dismissal of a comic spirit of freedom and those who, like Dover Wilson, justify the regal severity of Henry V, both minimize the comic side of Falstaff's downfall and his own share in bringing it about. A Falstaff temperate enough to approach the new king for favors privately or submissive enough to wait until sent for would be less funny than the Falstaff we see. A more amiable separation from Hal would be less in keeping with the character of Falstaff and less true to the logic of comedy, which does not require benevolence, still less indulgence, so much as what Shaw called disillusionment or, rather, a developed engagement between our sense of reality and fixed habits of human behavior or else between realism and voluntary fantasy. But a realistic appraisal of the sustained business of government cannot be the province of comedy, as distinct from satire, at all.

The two Parts of *Henry IV* form an unprecedented study of statecraft and of the relations of statecraft to other sides of life. More than any other English plays, I think, they suggest the continuousness of the life of a whole people, through space and time and the mixture of typical human qualities. As such they must include more than comedy. On the other hand, the inclusive vision they contain of the ways men and women of different sorts confront social reality gives perspective and more salience than entirely comic surroundings could provide to the uniquely comic figure of Falstaff.

NOTES

1. Henri Bergson, *Laughter* (1900), Eng. trans. in Wylie Sypher, ed., *Comedy* (Garden City, N.Y.: Doubleday, 1956), pp. 79, 97.

2. Albert Thibaudet, *Le Bergsonisme* (Paris, 1923), II, 93; cf. pp. 59–60.

3. See Harry Levin, "Falstaff Uncolted" (1946), in *Shakespeare and the Revolution of the Times* (New York: Oxford Univ. Press, 1976).

4. See A. R. Humphreys, ed., *1 Henry IV*, New Arden ed. (London: Methuen, 1960), p. 71n.

5. Thomas Nashe, *Pierce Penniless* (1592), in *Selected Works*, ed. Stanley Wells (Stratford-upon-Avon Library, London: Arnold, 1964), p. 55. Cf. parallels with Nashe in *1 Henry IV*, ed. John Dover Wilson, New Cambridge ed. (Cambridge: Cambridge Univ. Press, 1946), pp. 191–6.

6. William Empson, "Falstaff and Mr. Dover Wilson" (1953), in *Shakespeare, Henry IV, Parts I and II; a Casebook*, ed. G. K. Hunter (London: Macmillan, 1970 [referred to below as *Casebook*]), p. 145.

7. See Richmond Noble, *Shakespeare's Biblical Knowledge* (London: Society for Promoting Christian Knowledge, 1935), pp. 169–81.

8. Maurice Morgann, "As Essay on the Dramatic Character of Sir John Falstaff" (1777), in *Eighteenth Century Essays on Shakespeare*, ed. D. Nichol Smith, 2d ed. (Oxford: Oxford Univ. Press, 1963), p. 230n.

9. William Hazlitt, *Characters of Shakespear's Plays*, in *Liber Amoris and Dramatic Criticism*, ed. Charles Morgan (London: Peter Nevill, 1948), p. 309.

10. A. C. Bradley, "The Rejection of Falstaff" (1902), in *Oxford Lectures on Poetry*, 2d ed. (London: Macmillan, 1909), pp. 261, 269.

11. W. H. Auden, "The Prince's Dog" (1959), in *Casebook*, p. 188.

12. Cf. *Henry IV, Part 1*, 1.2.83–4; 2.2.10–20; 3.4.334–6; 3.3.172–6; and so on.

13. Cf. *King John*, 2.1.561–98; *Measure for Measure*, 4.3.5. (Perhaps Falstaff is thinking of *Proverbs*, xxii.1 at this point; cf. Noble, p. 169.)

14. See Paul A. Jorgensen, "'Redeeming Time' in Shakespeare's *Henry IV*" (1960), in *Casebook*, pp. 231–42.

15. See Holinshed, in *Narrative and Dramatic Sources of Shakespeare*, ed. Geoffrey Bullough, IV (London: Routledge, 1962), p. 276.

16. *Henry IV, Part 1*, 1.3.84–7; 178–80; 183–4; 203–5.

17. Holinshed, in Bullough, IV, 191.

18. See A. R. Humphreys, ed., *2 Henry IV*, New Arden ed. (London: Methuen, 1966), p. 20n; Levin, "Shakespeare's Nomenclature" (1963), in *Shakespeare and the Revolution of the Times*, pp. 70, 75.

19. See Humphreys, ed., *2 Henry IV*, Intro., p. xxvi.

20. L. C. Knights, "Time's Subjects: The Sonnets and *2 Henry IV*," in *Some Shakespearean Themes* (London: Chatto and Windus, 1959) (*Casebook*, p. 174).

BIBLIOGRAPHICAL NOTE

This essay has been based in part on Bergson's *Laughter*, in Wylie Sypher's collection, *Comedy*, with some help from W.D. Howarth's Introduction to *Comic Drama, the European Heritage*, ed. Howarth (Methuen: London, 1978) and in part on Morgann's essay on Falstaff and modern studies represented in the *Casebook*, ed. G. K. Hunter. A. R. Humphreys' Introductions to his New Arden editions of *Henry IV, Parts 1* and *2* have been particularly useful.

E. TALBOT DONALDSON

Love and Laughter:
Troilus and Criseyde, Romeo and Juliet,
the Wife of Bath, and Falstaff

W hen I first became interested in the relation of Chaucer to Shakespeare, it was the possible connection between *Troilus and Criseyde* and *Romeo and Juliet* on the one hand and between the Wife of Bath and Falstaff on the other that most engaged me. That was a number of years ago, and the sad fact is that the two connections remain to this day elusive, in many ways beyond my grasp. In my first chapter I pointed out how the authors of *Troilus* and *Romeo* handled melodramatic situations in somewhat the same manner, but a more tangible evidence of an influence that I am persuaded exists eludes me with the two love stories as with the two comic characters. Perhaps in both cases I should settle for analogy, or simple similarity, rather than influence. In that case I can take comfort in what Ann Thompson has written in her consideration of Shakespeare's possible use of Troilus in writing *Romeo and Juliet*: the question of whether or not this can be proved, she says, "need not take absolute precedence over the matter of whether it is valid and interesting to read these great works alongside each other. It is possible that to travel along this road is more important than to arrive."[1] I believe it is proper to extend her remark to include the very crooked road on which Falstaff and the Wife of Bath also traveled. In this chapter I hope that assuming an influence that cannot be proved may enable us at least to see in a new light certain aspects of the poem, the play, and the two characters.

Ann Thompson has written as well as anyone ever has on the subject of

From *The Swan at the Well: Shakespeare Reading Chaucer.* © 1985 by Yale University.

Troilus and Criseyde and *Romeo and Juliet*, and I start with her point that Shakespeare's play succeeded Chaucer's poem as "the single most important and influential love-tragedy in English poetry, the archetype to which situations in both life and literature [are] referred."[2] I should prefer to describe the poems as the two greatest love *poems* in English, rather than love-tragedies, even while emphasizing that they are both tragedies. But it is hard to think of a love-comedy that is comparable to either of these works, as the term love-tragedy suggests that there ought to be; the great love stories must, I guess, be sad. And thereby hangs a moral.

It is, however, a moral so obvious and so discouraging that I should like to defer discussion of it until later. For the moment I should like to make the point that neither the play nor the poem contains an even flatter and staler moral, which is that people should not fall so violently and passionately in love that they are willing to contravene the wishes of their parents (*Romeo and Juliet*) or go to bed with each other without getting married first (*Troilus and Criseyde*). That is, I do not think that the moral of either of these love stories is that one should not fall in love as intensely as at least three of the lovers in these works do. And in this negative point is one of the close similarities of the poem and the play, and their preeminent greatness as love stories.

The chief immediate source for Shakespeare's play, Arthur Brooke's *The Tragical Historye of Romeus and Juliet* is, according to its author, a negative moral exemplum. In a preface to the reader Brooke warns that he has written his "tragicall matter" because "the evill mans mischefe, warneth men not to be evyll."[3] Hence he will describe to us what happens to a

> coople of unfortunate lovers, thralling themselves to unhonest desire, neglecting the authoritie and advise of parents and frendes, conferring their principal) counsels with dronken gossyppes, and superstitious friers (the naturally fitte instrumentes of unchastitie) attemptyng all adventures of peryll, for thattaynyng of their wished lust, usyng auriculer confession (the kay of whoredome, and treason) for furtherance of theyr purpose, abusyng the honorable name of lawefull mariage, [to] cloke the shame of stolne contractes, finallye, by all means of unhonest lyfe, hastyng to most unhappye deathe.

Romeus and Juliet is not a good poem (though not really as bad as many commentators say it is), but it is, despite this horrendously disapproving prospectus, a very humane one. Indeed, the tone of Brooke's prefatory note and the tone of the poem itself are in total opposition. The poem shows almost nothing but sympathy for the lovers, and that "naturally fit instrument of unchastity," the friar, is a very nice man who, like his successor in Shakespeare, does his best to help the lovers stay honest, as well as alive and happy. There are simply no evil people in the poem by whose wickedness the reader is to be warned. Brooke does his Protestant duty by blaming it all on popery, but he actually serves up not the nasty cake he promises but a rather agreeable one.

Shakespeare, imitating what Brooke did and not what he said he was doing, emphasizes the sadness of the story, but nowhere suggests that it is a moral exemplum. The famous Prologue to the play proposes to show "the misadventurous piteous overthrows" of a "pair of star-cross'd lovers" and the "fearful passage of their death-mark'd love." It does not in any way condemn the lovers, but mentions how their sad fate finally brought an end to their families' feud. In the last two lines of the play the Prince offers his own simple summary,

> For never was a story of more woe
> Than this of Juliet and her Romeo.   [V.iii.309–10]

The spokesman for conventional morality within the play is Friar Lawrence, but like everyone else he is so overwhelmed by the rapidity with which events follow one another that he has very little leisure for moralistic preachment. He stops both lovers in turn from suicide, but not with doctrinaire argument but with the reasoning that they must continue to live in order not to deprive the other of his beloved. Lust, part of Brooke's prospectus, is of so little importance in the play that it is not mentioned. The lovers are in full agreement that they must marry before they consummate their love. The moral weight of the play, such as it is, is concentrated in the scene just before the Friar weds the couple. His oft quoted speech—oft quoted because it has no rival in the play for moralization—is an answer to Romeo's challenge to "love-devouring death" to do what it dares so long as Romeo can call Juliet his own for just a moment. In an image that some scholars believe to have been borrowed from Chaucer's Criseyde's meditation, "Ful sharp beginning breaketh oft at ende" (II 791),[4] the Friar observes,

> These violent delights have violent ends,
> And in their triumph die, like fire and powder,
> Which as they kiss consume.   [II.vi.9–11]

But after this generalization with its splendidly prophetic overtones, the Friar subsides into conventional moralization of the drabbest sort, advising Romeo to love moderately, lest he grow tired of Juliet:

> The sweetest honey
> Is loathsome in his own deliciousness,
> And in the taste confounds the appetite.
> Therefore love moderately: long love doth so;
> Too swift arrives as tardy as too slow.

This is simply the advice expected of a late medieval priest before he performs a marriage—indeed, one can't help recalling Chaucer's Parson's sober (and sobering) advice to husbands to love their wives with discretion, patiently, and attemperly (I 860). This piece of singularly ill-directed counsel is interrupted by the sudden appearance of Juliet, who enchants the Friar out of his parsonical persona just as he is sententiously observing that "Too swift arrives as tardy as too slow." Her swift arrival gives him the lie, and his moralization dissolves in appreciation:

> Here comes the lady. O, so light a foot
> Will ne'er wear out the everlasting flint.

From this mixture of unwitting prophecy and admiration of Juliet's grace he makes, or tries to make, a professional recovery:

> A lover may bestride the gossamers
> That idles in the wanton summer air,
> And yet not fall; so light is vanity.

Having marvelously suggested the buoyancy of young love—its ability to defy gravity—he twists the image of weightlessness into moral weightlessness, which is nothing, or vanity. But just as Friar Lawrence's moralization loses its way because of Juliet's charming appearance on the scene, so any attempt to read *Romeo and Juliet* as anything but a celebration of love must fail because of the great charm and intensity of the love affair and of the lovers: their weightlessness is not vanity. This is the last, weak effort Shakespeare allows Friar Lawrence to serve the play as Brooke's preface was supposed to serve the poem.

Brooke was familiar with Chaucer's *Troilus and Criseyde*, and it may be that his preface, so out of keeping with the tone of his poem, is a clumsy attempt to imitate the dichotomy that occasionally divides the narrator of Chaucer's poem from what the poem is saying, and does so especially in its ending. Like Shakespeare, Chaucer begins his work by stressing, indeed overstressing, its sadness, and making no mention of any moral content. The narrator proposes to tell of the "double sorrow" of Troilus in love, how his adventures "fell from woe to weal and after out of joy." He begins with verses so woeful that they weep as he writes them. He calls on the fury Tisiphone to serve as his muse, and she responds at once by helping him overwrite the second stanza of his poem so that its seven lines contain the nouns *torment* and *pain*, the verb *complain*, and the adjectives *cruel, woeful, dreary, sorry, sorrowing,* and *sorrowful* (twice)—an exercise in verbal agony that threatens to drown in its own tears.

But once he has established himself in the first fifty-six lines as the translator of a very sad story and has warned the reader in so many words that Criseyde forsook Troilus before she died, he goes on merrily cheering the principal characters into their love affair and occasionally giving very dubious advice, such as that the ladies in his audience should yield to their lovers as Criseyde finally did to Troilus. There is neither sadness nor morality. For three-fifths of the way through, the story is told as one of romantic sexual love that's going to end splendidly, and the full force of the sadness does not assert itself until the final book. It is only after the narrator has shown us Criseyde accepting Diomede in Troilus' place and Troilus' finally being persuaded of her betrayal that the narrator begins to worry about the morality of his story. This he does after Troilus is killed by Achilles and ascends to the eighth sphere (the seventh, according to the black-letter editions). From there Troilus looks down upon this little spot of earth, laughs at those who weep for his death, and damns all our work that so follows "this blinde lust." And the narrator goes on to exhort "yonge fresshe folkes, he or she" in whom love grows up with their years to love Christ, who will not betray them, and to seek no "feigned" loves (V 1842–48).

This is, of course, a moral with a vengeance, one that converts an 8,200-line poem in praise of love into a negative moral exemplum fifty lines from its end—a tiny tail of extraordinary moral weightiness wagging a huge shaggy dog. In Chaucer criticism, this tiny tail is commonly given the name "Chaucer" to distinguish it from the huge dog "Narrator," to which it is attached. To excuse the imbalance between the two entities, which in its own statistical way is as gross as Brooke's preface is to his poem, it is possible to conjure up at least the wraith of a moral appearing earlier in the poem: Chaucer's narrator does describe his poem as a tragedy, and it is well known that a medieval tragedy always has a moral (and always the same moral), and that the moral of medieval tragedy is at least conformable with Chaucer's advice to young people to restrain themselves from loving one another.

There is some force in this proposition, though I do not think it quite justifies reading the poem as a negative moral exemplum, written to discourage romantic love. Everyone in Chaucer's medieval audience knew what to expect of a tragedy, and though Chaucer does not actually tell us that he is writing a tragedy until about eighty lines from its end (V 1786)—after he has written it, really—the very first stanza of the poem, summarizing Troilus' falling from woe to weal in his love affair, and afterward out of joy, suggests by its terminology that the poem is to be a medieval tragedy, though the fall from woe to weal is against normal tragic gravity. Our most reliable expert on medieval tragedy is, of course, Chaucer's Monk, who defines it as a story such as we find in old books of those who stood in great prosperity and fell out of it, ending wretchedly (B² 3165–67). The Monk's negative exempla teach us, again and again, that this world is governed by the fickle Lady Fortune, who allows some people to ride high on her Ferris wheel for a time but then inevitably hurls them down into the slough, where they end wretchedly. The moral, and a mighty paltry moral it is, is "Fortune will get you in the end." Notice that the moral character of the protagonist (or victim) is not at issue: Nero makes as good a tragic hero as someone far more worthy. To qualify for a tragedy, all one has to do is rise high and fall, and the tragic quotient is determined by the altitude from which one falls.

As defined and practiced by the Monk—and by a number of writers in the Middle Ages, including Boccaccio—tragedy is without doubt the most flaccid literary form that ever gave a writer an excuse to tell a sad story. The morals appended to the *Gesta Romanorum* have at least variety in their idiocy, even if they share the vacuity of the endlessly repeated tragic morals. But there is, of course, a more grown-up form of medieval tragedy than the Monk's. Instead of simply reviling Fortune, its moral warns: "Do not *commit* yourself to Fortune." What this amounts to is a recommendation of a certain wary stoicism—be prepared for the worst and try not to put your whole being into something that may not last; meanwhile, derive what comfort you can from bad experience, and enjoy the good. In Dante and above all in Boethius, Fortune assumes a philosophical dimension of some stature, with at least an educational message for those whom Fortune has spurned.

But is Chaucer's poem a representative of either one of these variations of medieval tragedy, the Monk's or Boethius'? Well, it fits the Monk's, but gains little by doing so. Troilus is a person of high degree who for a time enjoys felicity with Criseyde, then loses her by an act of Fortune, and ends wretchedly. And one might say that the Monk and the narrator of Troilus are alike in that both spend more time recounting the good things the protagonists enjoyed while they were high on the wheel than they do on their wretched endings. But unlike *The Monk's Tale*, where the good things are merely material, the love of Troilus and Criseyde has enormous spiritual urgency; we recognize in it a potentiality of life at its very best. And Chaucer varies from his Monk in that he gives Fortune's wheel a symbolic last turn when, after his death, Troilus is sent up to what seems to me unquestionably a better place (though it is open to question)[5] than this world, there to reside, presumably, permanently. This is a violation of the Monk's tragic rules, which allow no dealings with the afterlife. Chaucer's poem is only most superficially a tragedy in the Monk's sense.

I must digress here for a moment to deal with a matter related to the subject of tragedy that keeps coming up in criticism even though it has no right to. That is, the possibility that the narrator's injunction to "yonge, fresshe folkes, he or she" to place their hearts in Christ rather than in "feigned" loves somehow has application to the lovers Troilus and Criseyde. The medieval proclivity for anachronism is, I admit, outrageous, often worse than Shakespeare's. Criseyde swears by God more often than any other woman in Chaucer, and it is clearly the Christian God by whom the narrator thinks she is swearing. But this is merrily to bring a highborn Trojan lady up-to-date for fourteenth-century Londoners, and not to make her a proleptic Christian. It is not at all the same thing as equipping ancient Troy with the full doctrine of the medieval Church, complete with patristic exegetes. Despite his frequent use of Christian ideas in the story he is telling, the narrator is perfectly aware that the Trojan gods were Jove, Apollo, Mars, and such rascaille, and he curses them roundly at the end for not taking better care of Troilus. Troilus simply did not have a god worthy of being given his heart. In the same realm of improbability is the argument that Troilus and Criseyde were guilty of mortal sin because they committed fornication—some critics accuse them of adultery, apparently feeling that adultery has more hamartialogical dignity than fornication.[6] Troilus and Criseyde knew nothing of Christianity or of medieval restrictions on sex, and are not liable to Christian judgment.

But to return to the moral of medieval tragedy in its relation to the poem. The Boethian lesson of not committing oneself does apply to Troilus, but only obliquely and awkwardly. For it is not Fortune that Troilus commits himself to so much as it is Criseyde. In his naughtier moments Chaucer does play with the idea. that Criseyde is Dame Fortune: at the beginning of Book IV, in outlining the remainder of the plot, his narrator trembles at the thought of relating how Fortune turned her bright face away from Troilus and took no heed of him,

> But caste him clene out of his ladies grace,
> And on her whele she set vp Diomede.   [IV 10–11]

Here the woman Fortune's casting Troilus out of the woman Criseyde's grace and setting up Diomede on her wheel is a maneuver that the mind is much tempted to simplify by having Criseyde do her own casting out and setting

up. And Criseyde's final words in the poem, her farewell to the absent
Troilus, "But all shall passe, and thus take I my leave" (V 1085), are a kind of
identification of herself with Fortune. Yet to press the matter too hard, as
Chaucer knew, would be to reduce the poem to an antifeminist allegory
drained of its lifeblood: an allegory of a paradise in which for Troilus, as for
Adam, every prospect pleases and only Eve is vile. Chaucer is always aware
that the plot of his story is one of the great showpieces of antifeminism, and
he is careful not to let the issue come to the surface—despite moments when
it comes very close to the surface. Still, the poem's moral is not, Don't trust
a woman, which is the moral that comes into being if one allows the full
identification of Criseyde with Fortune.

But even if one rejects—as I do—all these candidates, the poem does
have a moral. This moral, I reiterate, can have no ex post facto application to
Troilus and Criseyde, and it is simply that the best thing we know, love, is
unreliable, like all things human. If you wish to ensure constancy in love, you
had better love God, who will betray none who loves him. And this is true
enough. I have argued elsewhere that the tiny tail we call Chaucer in the
ending of the poem is not really a separate entity from the big dog we call
narrator, but is the narrator's own proper tail.[7] Heartbroken over the way his
poem has come out (as if he had forgotten the end of the story despite his
having warned us of it in the overly emotional beginning), the narrator again
reacts violently and overemotionally. He jumps to the conclusion that no
love affair will work out, hence get thee to a nunnery or a monastery, go. I
think many of us, myself included, have been too anxious to separate the
narrator from the poet Chaucer. Actually, the huge dog is a hybrid,
consisting of a poet who sees the beauty in romantic love and a poet who sees
its instability, and they've been working together all the way through. The
one we call narrator takes the more extreme position in favor of love, and
now that it's let him down, he takes the more extreme position in its
dispraise. Although the universalizing effect of great art suggests that
because this love affair did not work out, no love affair so intense, so
consuming, so lovely will work out, I still very much doubt that the
alternative that is suggested to falling in love, a life of celibacy and human
lovelessness, is one that Chaucer expected many of his young, fresh readers
to choose. They would surely ask themselves in what sense Troilus would
have been better off *not* to fall in love with Criseyde. World-hating is a
medieval occupation, but richness of experience is a timeless need.

And this brings us back to Shakespeare. For the moral—which is not
quite the right word—of *Romeo and Juliet* is the same as that of *Troilus and
Criseyde*: love at its most passionate and its most fulfilling does not last in the
real world. Romeo and Juliet never had a chance of making a go of it over a

longer period of time than the play's brief duration, not even a chance to equal the longer but still brief happiness allotted to Troilus and Criseyde. In neither case is the sad denouement the result of moral principles asserting themselves in opposition to the loves of the characters. Shakespeare's tragedy is more tragic—and more satisfactory—because it is the lovers that the world destroys, not their love. In Chaucer's poem the love is flawed in the person of Criseyde—a much more interesting person than Juliet, but not the stuff of which tragic heroines are made. She cannot sustain the dizzying and unreal rapture of such lovers as Troilus and Juliet and Romeo. Shakespeare, replacing what was the greatest love poem in English with what is the greatest love poem in English, eliminated the traces of medieval antifeminism and made the tragic symmetry perfect. But both poets wrote magnificent celebrations of love, and I can hardly think of anything better to celebrate.

From the sublime to the ridiculous—the sublimely ridiculous. We can never ascertain whether Shakespeare had the Wife of Bath in mind—at least in his unconscious mind—when he created Falstaff.[8] It may be merely a coincidence that Falstaff in one of his early appearances is seen on the pilgrim route to Canterbury; and it may have been merely Shakespeare's instinct that told him that a gross solipsist of enormous vitality would be the proper comic figure to provide an anti-heroic foil for a fledgling monarch and an ironic commentary on the values of English power politics, and that he never thought of that earlier large solipsist of enormous vitality who provides a foil for all the virtuous wives in fact and fiction and an ironic commentary on the Middle Ages' received ideas about marriage and the nature of women. The ironic commentaries that Falstaff and the Wife of Bath make are, because of the assurance and authority of their personalities, as persuasive as is the reality of the milieus in which they live and to which they respond. Both are supremely self-confident in their idiosyncrasy. As is often pointed out, they both use—or rather misuse—in their own defense the verse of St, Paul in the first Epistle to the Corinthians, in which he enjoins Christ's followers to remain in that vocation to which they have been called. Speaking of her total dedication to the vocation of matrimony, the Wife announces

> In such a state as god hath cleped vs
> I wol perseuer: I nam not precious. [D 147–48]

And when the Prince comments on Falstaff's role as a taker of purses, Falstaff replies, "Why, Hal, 'tis my vocation, Hal, 'tis no sin for a man to labor in his vocation" (I.ii.104–05). I am not suggesting that Shakespeare needed the Wife of Bath to put St. Paul's text into Falstaff's mind, for the verse from the Epistle is one of several Pauline texts that were probably often perverted in a way that would have horrified the Apostle. In the C-text of *Piers Plowman*, for example, Long Will beats off an attack by Conscience and Reason on his begging his bread for a living by citing the verse as an excuse for not performing manual labor.[9] All three characters are suggesting, with varying degrees of seriousness, that, although others may find what they do reprehensible, they find their occupations fully justified because they are *their* occupations, and they find them congenial. Their ideas of the world may be at variance with other people's ideas, but they are at home with them, and do not intend to alter their styles for anyone. And, if I may pervert Scripture myself, they speak not as the Scribes and Pharisees, but as those having authority.

Judith Kollmann has recently pointed out a number of similarities between *The Canterbury Tales* and *The Merry Wives of Windsor*,[10] and I myself wonder if that play does not make a backhanded acknowledgment of Shakespeare's awareness of *The Wife of Bath*. The merry wives are in many ways, not including wifely virtue, like the Wife of Bath—independent, resourceful, sturdy women of the same middle-class background as she. This is, indeed, as Professor Kollmann shows, a background one associates with Chaucer's *Canterbury Tales* and hardly at all with Shakespeare's plays, which are mostly aristocratic or upper class, with bits of low life thrown in for spice. But the community of Windsor is made up of the same sort of people as the community of the Canterbury pilgrims, and is complete with the Host of the Garter Inn, whose involvement with what is going on around him is like that of the Host of the Tabard Inn, who leads the Canterbury pilgrims. The two wives of the play administer sorely needed lessons about women to two men, a jealous husband and an unlikely courtly lover, and this is an enterprise that the Wife of Bath would have cheered them on in, especially when they punished that most porcine of male chauvinist pigs, Sir John Falstaff, who had the gall to rival her in comic grandeur. And indeed, the punishment of Falstaff is effected by facsimiles of those very fairies whom the Wife of Bath tells us the Friar has blessed out of existence—one of whom teaches a lesson about women to the young rapist in *The Wife of Bath's Tale*.

Of the many traits the Wife of Bath and Falstaff share, one of the most striking is their wit. Of Falstaff, who boasts that the brain of man "is not able to invent anything that intends to laughter more than I invent or is invented upon me," and that he is "not only witty in [him]self, but the cause that wit is in other men" (*Henry IV Part 2*, I.ii.7–10), no more need be said—though it's tempting to say it anyhow. But the Wife's wit is sometimes underestimated. She is, for instance, a past-mistress of the progressively engulfing squelch, the insult that hurts the victim more the more he thinks about it. At the end of a tirade directed at one of her doddering husbands she asks him, out of the blue, "What aileth soche an old man for to chide?" (D 281). Perhaps one has to be a man of advanced—or advancing—years really to feel how this question goes on subtly cutting deeper after the first superficial wound has been felt: apparently old age cancels a man's right to complain about anything, especially a vigorous wife, for an old man ought, she implies, to feel nothing but gratitude for being allowed to clutter up the house with his useless carcass. One does not have to be a friar to savor the wit of her devastating repayment of the Friar on the pilgrimage for his patronizing comments on her learning and the length of her prologue. She explains that the friars, having blessed fairies out of existence, have taken their place: the result is that women may walk the countryside safely, for where there used to be an incubus there is now only a friar, and he'll do nothing to women—except dishonor them (857–81).

As the quotation from St. Paul suggests, both the Wife of Bath and Falstaff are adept at converting received *dicta*, whether biblical or proverbial, into slightly askew statements critical of other people's values or expressive of their own. I say "converting," for the process is not really one of twisting such texts as it is reinterpreting them by a surprising use of logic. That human flesh is frail is an observation so trite that it has lost its force as a moral warning and has become an extenuating statement. Or so Falstaff suggests when he restates it in the comparative degree: "Thou seest I have more flesh than another man, and therefore more frailty" (*Henry IV Part 1,* III.iii.166–68). "The lion will not touch the true prince" is a statement which, under Falstaff's analysis, serves to excuse Falstaff's unlion-like failure to oppose Hal and Poins when they rob him of the booty of the Gadshill theft, and also to validate both Hal's claim to be a true prince and Falstaff's to be a lion, whose instinct caused him to run away from his sovereign (II.iv.270–75). The Wife of Bath, though her *forte* is the Bible—to which I shall return—matches this refurbishment of an adage by her reinterpretation of the innocent little saying that it is too miserly for a man to refuse to let another man light a candle at his lantern, since he'll have none the less light as a result (D 333–34). When the Wife identifies the man as a husband and the lantern as his wife, the proverb takes on shocking implications, managing to justify a wife's extramarital sexual activity while dutifully preserving the medieval tenet that the wife is the husband's chattel, like any other of his tangible goods.

The Wife of Bath and Falstaff create their individual versions of reality by the protraction of their speech: they erect large verbal structures which fill the listener's mind and exclude from it all other matter. The prologue to the Wife's tale is approximately as long as the Prologue to *The Canterbury Tales*, a proportionment in which she would have found nothing to criticize. In all three of the plays in which Falstaff appears one finds long, long prose passages spoken by Falstaff, sometimes to someone else, but more often to himself, and us. He is a soliloquist more copious than Hamlet. Yet despite the fact that these solipsistic monologists are constantly explaining themselves to us, we are often not sure where to have them. Both make ironic commentaries on their milieus, but both also *are* ironic commentaries on their milieus, and as such they share, along with irony, the effect of making the reader uncertain of the exact locus from which their speeches proceed—their *locus loquendi*, if I may invent a critical term. Sturdy no-nonsense commonsense is the basis for one of their guises, though this can at any time modulate into almost frightening sophistication. And both guises can suddenly give way to childlike naiveté—the kind of thing that enables the child in the old story to see that the emperor has no clothes on. And occasionally both seem genuinely naive, becoming parodies of adult behavior in the same way that small children are. One might say that the Wife of Bath and Falstaff share a Wordsworthian child's vision, uncluttered by conventions, with intimations of immorality. And each has a fourth guise as well, though one they do not share: the Wife's is the ferocious aggressive intensity of the shrew, while Falstaff's, rather surprisingly, is that of injured innocence.

Chaucer is careful to confirm our impression of the Wife of Bath's instability of guise when, after the Pardoner's interruption, she consents to his request that she teach him about marriage with an apology, which under the color of clarification produces obfuscation:

> ... I pray to al this company
> If that I speke after my fantasy
> As taketh not agrefe of that I say,
> For mine entent is not but to playe. [D 189–92]

We know precisely what the meanings of the word *fantasy* are, but unfortunately we do not know which of the two dominant meanings is the right one. Serious scholars—over-serious, in my opinion—have suggested that she means by *fantasy* imagination, not delight and, hence, that the whole story of her marriages is a fabrication, just as she tells us that her version of what her old husbands used to say to her when they came home drunk is a fabrication. But to deny that the Wife's account of her marriages is true is to raise the insuperable problem of evaluating the truth of a fiction in relation to the truth of a fiction within a fiction. Are the separate stories in Don

Quixote more or less true than the story of Don Quixote? And, in order to complicate matters, the Wife does not quite say that she is speaking after her fantasy, but asks her hearers not to be offended *if* she speaks after her fantasy: we do not know when, if ever, the protasis of the conditional sentence begins to govern the discourse. Chaucer has been careful to give the Wife of Bath's ironies an elusiveness that makes them seem to be in perpetual motion.

The Wife tells us that her intent is only to play, and that is perhaps true most of the time of Falstaff. But as with the Wife, we are often unsure where his play begins or leaves off. The most obvious example is at the tavern after the Gadshill robbery. When Falstaff boasts of his heroic behavior, and in doing so multiplies two rogues in buckram suits into eleven and then adds three misbegotten knaves in Kendall green (II.iv.191–224), does he really expect the Prince and Poins to believe him? Actually, the question is easily answered, but answered, unhappily, as easily in the negative as in the affirmative. For Falstaff's expectations are as obscure as those of Chaucer's Pardoner, when, after fully exposing his fraudulence, he tries at the end of his tale to get the Host to buy some of his pardon (C 919–59). Critical argument is unending about whether the Pardoner really thought he could make a sale. The Host's furious response reflects his ill ease, because the Pardoner is a user and exemplifier of irony whose center the Host cannot locate. The reader is apt to be similarly ill at ease with Falstaff, and critics occasionally imitate the Host's treatment of the Pardoner by trying to reduce Falstaff's various guises to mere matter, and to gross matter at that. In a way, that is what Hal is forced to do when he finally rejects Falstaff. He did not overhear Falstaff's catechism on honor at Shrewsbury (V.i.129–41), but as King he would recognize that such playful subversions are more dangerous to his rule than any robberies at Gadshill, despite, or perhaps because of, the catechism's taking the elementary form of a schoolboy's lesson. Such an ambiguously motivated question of Falstaff's when he learns that the party they are about to rob at Gadshill consists of eight or ten men, as "'Zounds, will they not rob us?" (II.ii.65) may appear on the printed page as pure play. But spoken, it develops ambiguity. Should one say, "Will they not *rob* us?" like an honest man fearing to fall among thieves, or "Will *they* not rob *us*?" like a thief recognizing that there may be other thieves with superior numbers?

And what is one to make—and what did Hal make?—of Falstaff's soliloquy just before the robbery, which is overheard by the Prince?

Well, I doubt not but to die a fair death for all this, if I scape hanging for killing that rogue [Prince Hal]. I have forsworn his company hourly any time this two and twenty years, and yet I am

bewitch'd with the rogue's company. If the rascal have not given
me medicines to make me love him, I'll be hanged. It could not
be else, I have drunk medicines.   [II.ii.13–20]

In order to put a consistently cynical and knowing base under Falstaff so he can
be pinned down, critics have suggested that he knows Prince Hal is listening,
and that he is saying what will ingratiate himself with him. But this is to explain
a mystery by denying it existence: It is really another irony that the love of
Falstaff for the Prince is real, though it is expressed here at once with a
childlike naiveté and in the ironical language Falstaff often uses in public, with
the reason for his love being assigned to, even blamed on, the Prince, a rogue
who he feels has corrupted him. Is there some chance that the "reverent vice,"
as the Prince calls him, really has a heart that is suitable for a "goodly portly
man, i' faith, and a corpulent, of a cheerful look, a pleasing eye, and a most
noble carriage" (II.iv.421–23) as Falstaff describes himself? Perhaps.

The Wife of Bath's bases are equally troublesome. Her approach to the
Bible and its commentators is a combination of naive literalism, a somewhat
questioning sense of reverence, and plain commonsense grounded in
experience. She has trouble, as moralistic critics are always pointing out,
understanding that it is not the letter but the spirit that one must heed. The
relevant significance of Christ's remark to the Samaritan women at the well,
"Thou hast had five husbands and that man that now hath thee is not thy
husband" (D 14–25), eludes her. And well it might. The proposition, of
which she has been told, that the text somehow limits the number of
husbands a woman can have to five (six being over the legal limit) stems from
St. Jerome, who heaped his Pelion of antifeminism upon the antifeminist
Ossa of St. Paul. St. Jerome's proposition was based on his misreading of the
biblical story, a confusion worse confounded by the Wife when she fails to
understand that Christ was referring not to a fifth husband, but to a sixth
man to whom the Samaritan woman had said she was not married—a
disclaimer suppressed by St. Jerome in his eagerness to see that his reading
of the spirit should not be belied by the letter.[11] The tenuousness of such
blatantly prejudiced spiritual readings of the Bible is equally reflected in the
Wife of Bath's natural perplexity and the saint's willful inaccuracy. The
absurdity is enhanced by the Wife's attempt to fit the proposition to herself
by misreading St. Jerome's misreading, so that the number of husbands
comes out to four plus one questionable one, instead of five plus one man
unwedded. Five is her current total if, as she carefully says, the fifth was
canonically legal. But she herself can think of no explanation for Christ's
choice of the number four, and seems ultimately to decide that the number
of consecutive husbands she may have is unlimited.

In dealing with St. Paul, the Wife uses a literalist approach worthy of a puritan reformer. She reminds him of his admission that on the subject of matrimony he had no higher authority (79–82). And she uses those texts that please her and lets the others go without notice. She knows that her husband should leave father and mother and take only unto her (30–31), and that she has power over her husband's body and not he (158–59), but she fails to mention any reciprocal obligation. Yet in so doing she is providing a naturally ironic commentary on generations of celibate experts on marriage, who endlessly repeat the woman's obligation and rarely mention the husband's. She is understandably uncertain why, if the patriarchs had a number of wives, multiplicity of spouses is now deemed reprehensible (55–58). She envies Solomon his many spouses, and suppresses—if she is aware of it—the fact that Solomon's uxoriousness in building temples to his wives' strange gods brought the Lord's wrath down on him (35–43).

She even performs a bit of sophisticated biblical interpretation of her own: first she wishes that she had Solomon's gift from God of being "refreshed" by spouses as often as he was (37–38); later she remarks that she is willing to let virgins be bread of pure wheat seed and wives barley bread; but finally she notes that with barley bread Christ "refreshed" many a man (143–46)—a mixture of letter and spirit that would do credit to a patristic, intellectually speaking, if not morally. Her culminating combining of simplicity and sophistication occurs in her lament, "Alas, alas, that euer loue was sin!" (614). Moralists sometimes seize on this as proof that the Wife was aware of her sinfulness and regretted it. But her apparent repentance is actually parody, a parody of the repentance one is led to expect. It is not Christian remorse that provokes her exclamation, but regret that because sexual love is sin its availability to her has been reduced. An old age of repentance is no more the Wife of Bath's prospectus than it ever was Falstaff's.

Both the Wife of Bath and Falstaff are, though utterly charming, perfectly horrible people. It is true that the Wife's victims are mostly husbands who deserved the abuse and exploitation she practiced on them. But she is a habitual fornicator and adulterer, and her ability to be disagreeable when her authority is challenged is not limited to the domestic scene, as any parish wife who gets to the Offering before her learns. Falstaff is not only a drunken old man, but a thief, a deadbeat, an exploiter of poor women and shallow justices from whom he borrows money that he fails to repay, an abuser of the King's press, a lecher, a liar, and heaven knows what else. And as two very dubious citizens, they should *not* be sentimentalized. I say this very sternly, for I am aware that I can never discuss them at length without sentimentalizing them. I blame this on their creators, who seem to have loved them dearly while endowing them with enough vices to supply an army of the wicked-enough vices and enough vitality. I have always supposed that *Henry IV Part 2* exists largely because Falstaff's vitality was too bountiful to be confined in *Part 1*; and surely *The Merry Wives of Windsor* exists because of him. Shakespeare originally promised that Falstaff would show up in *Henry V* (Epilogue to *Henry IV Part 2*), but prudently changed his mind and killed him off before he could stop Hal from ever getting to Agincourt. The Wife of Bath managed to get herself into *The Merchant's Tale* (E 1685–87) and into Chaucer's "Envoy to Bukton"—also an unruly fiction who would not remain on the page where she belonged. Both characters took on life independent of their creators.

And both are associated with passages of unrivaled emotional effectiveness, passages that are as splendid tributes to human vitality as any I know. The Wife of Bath speaks hers, and Falstaff's is spoken about him. The Wife of Bath's is a digression from her account of her fourth husband:

> My fourth husbonde was a reuelour—
> This is to saie, he had a paramour.
> And I was yong, and full of ragerie,
> Stubburne and strong, and ioly as a Pie.
> Well coud I daunce to an Harpe smale,
> And sing, iwis, as a Nitingale,
> Whan I had dronken a draught of swete wine.
> Metellus, the foule churle, the swine,
> That with a staffe biraft his wife her life
> For she dronk wine, though I had be his wife,
> He should not haue daunted me fro drinke.
> And after wine of Venus must I thinke,
> For also seker as cold engendreth haile,
> A likorus mouth must haue a lecherous taile.
> In women vinolent is no defence:
> This knowe lecherous by experience.
>
> But lord Christ, when it remembreth me
> Vpon my youth and my iolite,
> It tickleth me about the hart roote—
> Vnto this daie is doeth my hart boote—
> That I haue had my worlde as in my time.
> But age, alas, that all woll enuenime
> Hath me biraft my beaute and my pith.
> Let go, fare well, the deuile go therwith!

> The Houre is gon, ther nis no more to tell;
> The bran, as I best can, now mote I sell.
> But yet to be right merie woll I fonde.
> Now forth to tell of my fourth husbonde.   [D 453–80]

I doubt that many who have spent their lives far better than the Wife are able to look back with such a sense of benediction as that with which the Wife of Bath looks back on her misspent past. She has enjoyed life, and will go on enjoying it. And although she is a very immoral woman, she has, in her enjoyment, perfect integrity.

Perhaps Falstaff was incapable of so philosophical a looking back—that was not one of his guises. But Shakespeare gives him the same kind of emotional justification in the erstwhile Mistress Quickly's account of his death in *Henry V*, a kind of apology by the dramatist for Hal's shabby treatment of him and the merry wives' triumph over him. In the scene, Bardolph has just reacted violently to Falstaff's death, wishing he were "with him, wheresome'er he is, either in heaven or hell." The Hostess replies:

> Nay sure, he's not in hell; he's in Arthur's bosom, if ever man went to Arthur's bosom. 'A made a finer end, and went away and it had been any christom child. 'A parted ev'n just between twelve and one, ev'n at the turning o' th' tide; for after I saw him fumble with the sheets, and play with flowers, and smile upon his finger's end, I knew there was but one way; for his nose was as sharp as a pen, and 'a [talk'd] of green fields. "How now, Sir John?" quoth I, "what, man? be a' good cheer." So 'a cried out, "God, God, God!" three or four times. Now I, to comfort him, bid him 'a should not think of God; I hop'd there was no need to trouble himself with any such thoughts yet. So 'a bade me lay more clothes on his feet. I put my hand into the bed and felt them, and they were as cold as any stone; then I felt to his knees, [and they were as cold as any stone;] and so up'ard and up'ard, and all was as cold as any stone.[12]

Both passages occur in marvelously comic contexts, and both are perfectly controlled in their tone, with the pathos not spoiling the humor, or vice versa. I don't think we should worry about the Hostess' misplacement of Falstaff in Arthur's bosom, any more than we should worry about the final destination of the wife of Bath's soul—*she* never did. Both characters are in any case still very much alive, very much their creators' celebrations of life, and I can hardly think of anything better to celebrate.

Notes

1. Thompson, *Shakespeare's Chaucer*, p. 109.

2. Ibid., p. 95.

3. Brooke's text is taken from Bullough, *Narrative and Dramatic Sources*, I, 284–88. The bracketed word "to" appears as "the" in the original.

4. P. 98. Quotations from Chaucer are from the edition of 1561; the Shakespeare is from *The Riverside*.

5. As Bonnie Wheeler points out, "Dante, Chaucer, and the Ending of *Troilus and Criseyde*," *PQ*, 61 (1982), p. 110, Troilus' eventual destination, to which Mercury leads him from the seventh/eighth sphere, "is hidden from our knowledge." For further discussion of Troilus' ultimate domicile, see Elizabeth Kirk, "'Paradis Stood Formed in Hire Yen': Courtly Love and Chaucer's Re-Vision of Dante," *Acts of Interpretation: The Text in Its Contexts 700–1600*, ed. Mary J. Carruthers and Elizabeth D. Kirk (Norman: Pilgrim Books, 1982), pp. 257–77. I should perhaps say here that my understanding of Chaucer's poem and that of D. W. Robertson, Jr. (see especially "Chaucerian Tragedy," *ELH*, 19 (1952): 1–37) are so far removed from one another that we seem to lack any common ground on which we might profitably argue.

6. See, e.g., John Gardner, *The Life and Times of Chaucer* (New York: Knopf, 1977), p. 215. Responsibility for the mistake is probably in part C. S. Lewis', who, in *The Allegory of Love*, so stresses the importance of adultery to courtly love and of courtly love ideas to *Troilus and Criseyde*, that one is almost forced to find adultery in it.

7. See Donaldson, "The Ending of Troilus," *Speaking of Chaucer*, pp. 84–101.

8. A number of similarities between the two characters have of course been noted in the criticism, but no actual influence of Chaucer on Shakespeare's concept of Falstaff has been shown. Ann Thompson (*Shakespeare's Chaucer*, p. 83) speaks rather scornfully of "the attempts of some critics to draw comparisons between such figures as Falstaff and the Wife of Bath as 'rich comic characters',," on the uncertain grounds that Shakespeare "seems to have thought of Chaucer *primarily* as a writer of romantic and courtly poetry rather than as a comic naturalist" (p. 82). But this is to allow a preconception to override any evidence the text may provide to the contrary. In "The Non-Comic, Non-Tragic Wife: Chaucer's Alys as Sociopath," *ChauR*, 12 (1978), 171, Donald Sands disallows all comparison between Falstaff and the Wife of Bath by announcing, "There is no abysm of evil in him, and such an abysm may exist in Alys." Against moralization so self-assured and so prejudiced neither the Wife of Bath nor literature itself has any defense. Perhaps the best reply to Sands is to quote an equally surprising statement by Nevill Coghill—here pulled rudely out of context but not falsifying his opinion: "Chaucer had no vision of evil": see *Elizabethan and Jacobean Studies Presented to F. P. Wilson*, p. 99.

9. See *Piers Plowman by William Langland: An Edition of the C-Text*, ed. Derek Pearsall (Berkeley and Los Angeles: University of California Press, 1978), Passus V, lines 32–57.

10. Judith J. Kollmann, "Ther is noon oother incubus but he: *The Canterbury Tales*, *Merry Wives of Windsor* and Falstaff," in *Chaucerian Shakespeare: Adaptation and Transformation*, ed. E. T. Donaldson and J. J. Kollmann ([Detroit:] Michigan Consortium for Medieval and Early Modern Studies, 1983), pp. 43–68.

11. See my "Designing a Camel; or, Generalizing the Middle Ages," *TSL*, 22 (1977), 1–16, for a fuller discussion of Jerome's misinterpretation.

12. *King Henry V*, II.iii.9–26. Despite its brilliance, I find Theobald's famous emendation of F1 "Table" to "babbl'd" too emotive, and prefer the conjectural emendation "talk'd." The bracketed words near the end of the passage are in Q1–3, and seem to me to have been left out of F1 through scribal error.

NORTHROP FRYE

The Bolingbroke Plays
(Richard II, Henry IV)

I've mentioned the sequence of plays, four in all, that Shakespeare produced early in his career, on the period of the War of the Roses between Lancaster and York (so called because the emblem of Lancaster was a red rose and that of York a white one). With *Richard II* we begin another sequence of four plays, continuing through the two parts of *Henry IV* and ending with *Henry V*. The two central characters of the whole sequence are Bolingbroke, later Henry IV, who appears in the first three, and his son, later Henry V, who appears in the second, third and fourth. Although there are ominous forebodings of later events in *Richard II*, the audience would pick up the allusions, and we don't need to assume that Shakespeare began *Richard II* with the ambition of producing another "tetralogy" or group of four plays. The second part of *Henry IV* looks as though it were written mainly to meet a demand for more Falstaff. Still, each play does look back to its predecessors, so there is a unity to the sequence, whether planned in advance or not. And, as the Epilogue to *Henry V* tells us, the story ends at the point where the earlier sequence began.

I've provided a table of the intermarriages of English royalty between the reigns of Edward III and Henry VII, the period that covers the eight history plays. If you add Henry VIII, Henry VII's son, all the histories are covered that Shakespeare wrote except *King John*. In order to show the

From *Northrop Frye on Shakespeare*, edited by Robert Sandler. ©1986 by Northrop Frye.

important marriages, I haven't always listed sons and daughters in order of age, from the left. We can see that there were not many Romeo and Juliet situations: in the aristocracy at that time you simply married the man or woman who would do most for the fortunes of your family.

We start with Edward III's five sons. Shakespeare speaks of seven sons: the other two, both called William, died early on. Edward's eldest son and heir, Edward the "Black Prince," who would normally have succeeded his father, died the year before his father did, and the rules of succession brought his son, Richard, to the throne when he was still a boy. As some of his contemporaries remarked, "Woe to the land that's governed by a child!", and yet Richard lasted for twenty-two years, as long as Henry IV and Henry V together, Shakespeare's play covering only the last year or so of his reign.

The daughter of the second son, Lionel, married into the family of Mortimers; her daughter in turn married Hotspur of the Percy family. When Richard II's life ended in 1399, his heir, by the rules of succession, should have been the third Edmund Mortimer, Earl of March, who was also nominated, according to the conspirators in *Henry IV*, by Richard II as his successor. That was the issue that the revolt against Henry IV, which involved Hotspur so deeply, depended on. Bolingbroke was the son of John of Gaunt, Edward III's third son, and so not the next in line to the crown. However, he succeeded in establishing the Lancastrian house as the royal family, and was followed by his son and grandson. Apart from what the conspirators say, the fact that Bolingbroke seized the crown from Edmund as well as Richard is played down in this sequence, but there is a grimly eloquent speech from this Edmund, dying in prison, in *1 Henry VI* (although Shakespeare, if he wrote the scene, has confused him with someone else).

The Yorkist line came from the fourth son, Edmund, Duke of York, whose dramatic switch of loyalties from Richard to Bolingbroke, and the resulting conflict with his son Edward, called Aumerle, is the real narrative turning point of *Richard II*. The Yorkist line was not consolidated until the marriage of Aumerle's brother, Richard, to a descendant of Lionel produced Richard, Duke of York, who began the War of the Roses. The Yorkists got the upper hand in the war, and the Yorkist heir succeeded as Edward IV. Edward's two young sons, Edward (called Edward V because he had a theoretical reign of two months, although never crowned) and Richard, were supposed to have been murdered in the Tower by their wicked uncle, who became Richard III. Whether Richard III did this, or whether the story came from the Tudor propaganda machine, is still disputed: in any case Shakespeare bought it. Richard III, after a reign of about two years, was defeated and killed in battle by the Duke of Richmond, a descendant of John of Gaunt through a later wife. (She was not his wife when their son was born, and the line had to be legitimized by a special act of Richard II.) The Duke of Richmond then ascended the throne as Henry VII and founded what is called the House of Tudor, from the name of his father. Because of his descent from John of Gaunt, his victory technically restored the House of Lancaster, but one of the first things he did was to marry the Yorkist heiress Elizabeth, and the marriage put a symbolic end to the war by uniting the red and white roses. References to this could easily be turned into a compliment to Queen Elizabeth's complexion: a sonnet by the poet Fulke Greville begins:

> Upon a throne I saw a virgin sit,
> The red and white rose quartered in her face.

The fifth son, Thomas of Woodstock, Duke of Gloucester, had been murdered just before the action of *Richard II* begins, and the duel that Bolingbroke and Mowbray are about to fight in the opening scene of the play results from Mowbray's being implicated in the murder. There was another well-known contemporary play on this subject, *Thomas of Woodstock* (anonymous). This play is probably a source for Shakespeare, as it seems to be earlier, although it loads the case against Richard more heavily than Shakespeare does. According to this play Woodstock lost his life because he was too persistent in giving Richard II advice, and Richard was as much involved with his death as Mowbray.

Shakespeare's play seems to have made a deep impression on his public, and there were six Quartos of it, five of them within his lifetime. The first three omitted the deposing scene at the end of Act IV; the fourth, the first one that had it, appeared five years after Queen Elizabeth's death. The cutting out of the deposing scene could have happened anyway, because of the official nervousness about showing or printing such things, but there is evidence that the play was revived during the conspiracy of Essex against Elizabeth, perhaps for the very purpose the censors worried about, that of accustoming the public to the thought of deposing a monarch. The queen herself made the connection, and is reported, to have said: "I am Richard II, know ye not that? This tragedy was played forty times in open streets and houses." We may perhaps take "forty" to be (literally) Elizabethan rhetoric for at least once," but even the commission of inquiry must have realized that there was no relation between the reckless and extravagant Richard and the cautious and stingy Elizabeth. It is perhaps a measure of her sense of insecurity, even at this period of her reign, that she thought there was.

As for Shakespeare's own dramatic vision, we have that curious garden scene (III.iv), for which scholars have never located a source, and which is two things that Shakespeare's writing practically never is, allegorical and sentimental. Considering the early date of the play (mid-1590s, probably), it is most unlikely that there was any contemporary allusion, but if the Essex group did revive the play for propaganda, this scene would have backfired on them, as it says that a capable ruler ought to cut ambitious nobles down to size before they get dangerous.

In *Richard II* Shakespeare had to make a marriage of convenience between the facts of medieval society, so far as they filtered down to him from his sources, and the Tudor mystique of royalty. That mystique regarded government by a central sovereign to be the form of government most in accord with both human nature and the will of God. It is true that no English sovereign except Henry VIII ever had the unlimited power that was very common on the Continent then and for many centuries thereafter. But still the reigning king or queen was the "Lord's anointed," his or her person was sacred, and rebellion against the sovereign was blasphemy and sacrilege as well as treason. The phrase "Lord's anointed" comes ultimately from the Bible. The Hebrew word Messiah, meaning "the anointed one," is applied in the Old Testament to a lawfully consecrated king, including even the rejected King Saul. The Greek equivalent of Messiah is Christ, and Jesus Christ was regarded as the king of the spiritual world, lawful kings in the physical world being his regents. If a lawful king happened to be a vicious tyrant, that was ultimately the fault of his subjects rather than of him, and they were being punished through him for their sins.

So when Richard II, during the abdication scene particularly, draws so many parallels between his trial and the trial of Christ, he is not comparing himself directly to Christ, but saying that the same situation, of the world rejecting the Lord's anointed, is being enacted once again. Of these echoes from the Passion in the Gospels, perhaps the most striking is that of Pilate's washing of his hands in a futile effort to make himself innocent of the death of Christ. Bolingbroke uses this image when he is making his first act as the next king, in ordering the execution of Bushy and Green; it is repeated in a contrasting context by Richard:

> Not all the water in the rough rude sea
> Can wash the balm off from an anointed king
>
> (III.ii. 54–55)

and explicitly linked with Pilate by Richard in the abdication scene. The closing lines of the play are spoken by Bolingbroke, and express his purpose of going on a crusade "To wash this blood off from my guilty hand."

One awkward question might be raised in connection with this doctrine of the sacredness of the royal person. Suppose you're second in line from the throne, and murder the one who's first in line, do you thereby acquire all the sanctity of the next Lord's anointed? Well, in some circumstances you do. Shakespeare's King John becomes king when his nephew, Prince Arthur, is really in line for the succession, and although the prince technically commits suicide by jumping out of a window, John is certainly not innocent of his murder. John thereby becomes by default the lawful king, and when he dies his son Prince Henry becomes his legitimate heir. The strongest man in the country at the time is Falconbridge, bastard son of Richard I, who would have been king if he were legitimate, and could probably seize power quite easily in any case. But he holds back in favour of Prince Henry, and the play comes to a resounding patriotic conclusion to the effect that nothing can happen "If England to itself do rest but true," which in the context means partly keeping the line of succession intact. You may not find this particular issue personally very involving, but the general principle is that all ideologies sooner or later get to be circumvented by cynicism and defended by hysteria, and that principle will meet you everywhere you turn in a world driven crazy by ideologies, like ours.

A lawful king, as Shakespeare presents the situation, can be ruthless and unscrupulous and still remain a king, but if he's weak or incompetent he creates a power vacuum in society, because the order of nature and the will of God both demand a strong central ruler. So a terrible dilemma arises between a weak king de jure and a de facto power that's certain to grow up somewhere else. This is the central theme of *Richard II*. Richard was known to his contemporaries as "Richard the Redeless," i.e., a king who wouldn't take good advice, and Shakespeare shows him ignoring the advice of John of Gaunt and York. His twenty-year reign had a large backlog of mistakes and oppressions that Shakespeare doesn't need to exhibit in detail. In the scene where his uncle John of Gaunt is dying, John concentrates mainly on the worst of Richard's administrative sins: he has sold, for ready cash, the right of collecting taxes to individuals who are not restrained in their rapacity by the central authority. This forms part of what begins as a superbly patriotic speech: Shakespeare's reason for making the old ruffian John of Gaunt a wise and saintly prophet was doubtless that he was the ancestor of the House of Tudor. We also learn that Richard had a very undesirable lot of court favourites, spent far too much money on his own pleasures, and at the time of the play was involved in a war in Ireland that had brought his finances into a crisis. As we'll see later, getting into a foreign war is normally by far the best way of distracting a disaffected people, but Ireland roused no one's enthusiasm.

In the Middle Ages the effective power was held by the great baronial houses, which drew their income from their own land and tenants, many of them serfs; they could raise private armies, and in a crisis could barricade themselves into some very strong castles. In such a situation a medieval king had a theoretical supremacy, but not always an actual one, and, as his power base was often narrower than that of a landed noble, he was perpetually hard up for money. So if he were stuck with a sudden crisis, as Richard II is with the Irish war, he would often have to behave like a brigand in his own country and find pretexts for seizing and confiscating estates. What kind of law does a lawful king represent who resorts to illegal means of getting money? Or, who resorts to means that are technically legal, but violate a moral right?

Depends on what the moral right is. If it's abstract justice, protection of the poor, the representation of taxpayers in government, the right of the individual to a fair trial or the like, forget it. Shakespeare's *King John* never mentions Magna Carta, and *Richard II* never mentions the most important event of the reign, the Peasants' Revolt (twenty years earlier, but the social issues were still there). But if you take private property away from a noble house that's powerful enough to fight back, you're in deep trouble. The Duke of York tries to explain to Richard that his own position as king depends on hereditary succession, and that the same principle applies to a nobleman's right to inherit the property of his father. When Richard seizes John of Gaunt's property, he's doing something that will make every noble family in England say "Who next?" So John's son Henry Bolingbroke gets a good deal of support when he defies Richard's edict of banishment and returns to claim his own. We don't know much about what is going on in Bolingbroke's mind at any one time, and that's largely because he doesn't let himself become aware of the full implications of what he's doing. When he says at first that he merely wants his rights, it's possible that he means that. But this is the point at which Richard's spectacular incompetence as an administrator begins to operate. In the demoralized state of the nation a de facto power begins to gather around Bolingbroke, and he simply follows where it leads, neither a puppet of circumstances nor a deliberately unscrupulous usurper.

The rest of the play is the working out of this de jure and de facto dilemma. Some, like the Duke of York, come over to Henry's side and transfer the loyalty owed the Lord's anointed to him. So, when York's son Aumerle conspires in favour of Richard, York accuses his son of the same treason and sacrilege he'd previously accused Bolingbroke of before he changed sides. In the scene, where York insists on the king's prosecuting his son for treason and his duchess pleads for pardon, Bolingbroke is at his best, because he realizes the significance of what's happening. He's made the transition from being the de facto king to being the de jure king as well, and after that all he needs to do is get rid of Richard.

There are others, like the Bishop of Carlisle, who take the orthodox Tudor line, and denounce Bolingbroke for what he is doing to the Lord's anointed. As Shakespeare presents the issue, both sides are right. Henry becomes king, and makes a better king, as such things go, than Richard. When his nobles start quarrelling among themselves in a scene that reads almost like a reprise of his own challenge to Mowbray, he puts all the challenges "under gage," postpones all action, and squashes instantly what could become a dangerous brawl. But the way he came to the throne leaves a curse over the House of Lancaster that starts working out after Henry V's death twenty years or so later. Perhaps the only thing that would really resolve the situation is for Henry IV to go on the crusade he keeps talking about, because killing Moslems is so meritorious an act that it wipes out all previous sins, however grievous. John of Gaunt introduces the theme of crusade, as one of the things England was devoted to in its prime: he was doubtless thinking of the contrast between Richard and his namesake, Richard I, who spent so much of his ten-year reign fighting in the Third Crusade. But Henry's plans to go on a crusade are interrupted by revolts against him, and that again is inevitable: one revolt begets another. He carries on as best he can, and the comforting prophecy that he will die in Jerusalem turns out to apply to the name of a room in the palace of Westminster. It is a particularly savage irony, from Bolingbroke's point of view, that his enemy Mowbray, who, unlike him, was banished for life, should have died fighting in a crusade.

It should be clear by now that Shakespeare is not interested in what we would normally think of as history. What is really happening in history is extremely difficult to dramatize. Shakespeare is interested in chronicle, the personal actions and interactions of the people at the top of the social order. And the centre of his interest is in the kind of dramatic performance involved in being a leader in society, more particularly a king. All social relationships are in a sense theatrical ones: as soon as someone we know appears, we throw ourselves into the dramatic situation that our knowledge of him makes appropriate, and act it out accordingly. If we're alone, like Hamlet or like Richard in prison, we soliloquize; that is, we dramatize ourselves to ourselves. And what we all do, the prince makes history, or chronicle, by doing. In his vision of leadership, Shakespeare often comes curiously close to Machiavelli's *The Prince*. Curiously, because it is practically impossible that Shakespeare could have known Machiavelli's writings, and because Shakespeare's social vision is a deeply conservative one, whereas Machiavelli's was realistic enough to make the horrified idealists of his time give him a reputation in England and elsewhere as the voice of the devil himself. He comes in, for example, to emit cynical sentiments as the prologue speaker of Marlowe's *Jew of Malta*. But the theorist and the dramatist converge on two points: the dramatic nature of leadership and the fact that the qualities of the born leader are not moral qualities.

In ancient times stage actors usually wore masks, and the metaphor of the masked actor has given two words to the language. One is "hypocrite," which is Greek in origin and refers to the actor looking through the mask; the other is "person," which is Latin and refers to his speaking through it. Today we also use the word "persona" to mean the social aspect of an individual, the way he encounters other people. To some extent it's a misleading term, because it implies a real somebody underneath the masks, and, as the soliloquy reminds us, there's never anything under a persona except another persona. What there is is a consistency that limits the variety of social relations to a certain repertoire: that is, Hamlet always sounds like Hamlet, and Falstaff like Falstaff, whatever their roles at the moment. But for Shakespeare, as we'll see further later on, the question of identity is connected with social function and behaviour; in other words with the dramatic self, not with some hidden inner essence.

Well, "hypocrite" is a moral term and "person" is not: we accept that everyone has a personality, but it's supposed to be wrong for people to be hypocrites. Hypocrisy has been called the tribute that vice pays to virtue, but to know that you're saying one thing and thinking another requires a self-discipline that's practically a virtue in itself. Certainly it's often an essential virtue for a public figure. Situations change, and the good leader does what the new situation calls for, not what is consistent with what he did before. When Bolingbroke orders the execution of the king's favourites, one of his gravest charges against them is the way that they have separated the king from the queen, but an act or so later he himself is ordering a much more drastic separation of them. A successful leader doesn't get hung up on moral principles: the place for moral principles is in what we'd call now the PR job. The reputation of being virtuous or liberal or gracious is more important for the prince than the reality of these things, or rather, as in staging a play, the illusion is the reality.

Bolingbroke begins and ends the play, and the beginning and ending are in a most symmetrical relationship. At the beginning there is to be a public duel, or trial by battle, between Bolingbroke and Mowbray, over the murder of Thomas of Woodstock. Although Mowbray belongs to the house of Norfolk, not York, here is in embryo the theme of the eight historical plays: two noblemen quarrelling among themselves, with the king driven to stratagems to maintain his ascendancy. Perhaps a shrewder monarch would have left them to fight it out, on the ground that a duel to the death would get rid of at least one dangerous nobleman, but Richard stops the duel and banishes both, Mowbray for life, Bolingbroke for ten years, later reduced to six. The duellists talk so much that we suspect they're both lying, but it's Bolingbroke who drops the key image of civil war, Cain's murder of his brother Abel:

> That he did plot the Duke of Gloucester's death...
> Which blood, like sacrificing Abel's, cries
> Even from the tongueless caverns of the earth.
>
> (I.i. 100–105)

At the end of the play, no Bolingbroke, now Henry IV, hints that the death of the imprisoned Richard would be most convenient to him, and his follower Exton carries out the murder, and returns expecting a reward for faithful service. He forgot that leaders have to dissociate themselves immediately from such acts, whether they ordered them or not, and the play closes with Exton banished and Henry saying, "With Cain go wander thorough shades of night," echoing Mowbray's line about his banishment: "To dwell in solemn shades of endless night."

The play is thus enclosed by the image of the first human crime, Cain's murder of his brother, the archetype of all civil wars that follow. In the middle comes the scene of the queen and the gardener. The gardener is addressed as "old Adam's likeness," which, means that this is not a garden like Eden, where nothing was "unruly" and there were no weeds, but a garden made from the soil that Adam was forced to cultivate after his fall. Another phrase, of the queen's, "To make a second fall of cursed man," is repeated in a very curious context in *Henry V*. Every fall of every consecrated) ruler repeats the original fall of man. Since then, history has proceeded in a series of cycles: Shakespeare's audience was thoroughly familiar with the image he uses constantly in his plays, the wheel of fortune, and would see the entire action of this play, from the murder of Woodstock to the murder of Richard, as a single turn of that wheel. Richard's image for this is that of two buckets, one going up and the other down, "The emptier ever dancing in the air," a most sardonic comment on the sort of person who succeeds in the way that Bolingbroke has succeeded. One corollary from this conception of a wheel of fortune is that in history it is only the past that can be idealized or thought of as, heroic or peaceful. The *Henry VI* plays look back to the great and victorious Henry V; the play of *Henry V* looks back to the time of Richard as a time when there was no curse of usurpation on the royal house; and in this play we have John of Gaunt idealizing an earlier time, apparently the reign of Edward III, the reign that saw the Black Death and the beginning of the Hundred Years' War with France.

What keeps the wheel turning is the fact that people are conditioned to a certain reflex about it: whenever there's a change in personnel in the state, the assumption is normally that somehow or other an old age is going to be renewed. As the Duchess of York says to Aumerle after the king has pardoned him, "Come, my old son: I pray God make thee new." The joyful expectation on the part of the people that a new king will give a new life to the nation is put by York into its proper context:

> As in a theatre the eyes of men,
> After a well-graced actor leaves the stage,
> Are idly bent on him that enters next.   (V.ii. 23–25)

The illusion of movement in history corresponds to the processional aspect of a drama, the series of events that holds the interest. We have to listen on a deeper level, picking up such things as the Cain imagery, to realize that the beginning and the end are much the same point.

We feel this circularity of movement from the very beginning, the ordeal by battle that opens the play. Such ordeals, in medieval times, were surrounded by the most detailed ritual and punctilio. The combatants appeared before the king and formally stated their cases; the king would try to reconcile them; he would fail; he would then allow a trial by battle at a time and place duly stated. As the play goes on, the duel modulates to one between Bolingbroke and King Richard, but the same ritual formality continues, except that there is no longer any question of a fair fight. That is one reason why *Richard II* is written, contrary to Shakespeare's usual practice, entirely in verse: no contrasting force from outside the duelling ritual breaks in to interrupt the action.

Bolingbroke realizes that one of the qualities of the leader is inscrutability, giving the impression that there are great reserves of power of decision not being expressed. Of course many people look inscrutable who are merely stupid: Bolingbroke is not stupid, but he understands that the leaders who attract the greatest loyalty and confidence are those who can suggest in their manner that they have no need of it. Later, in *1 Henry IV*, Bolingbroke is telling his son Prince Hal that, in the dramatic show a leader puts on, the one essential is aloofness. He says that he appeared publicly very seldom, and always with calculation:

> By being seldom seen, I could not stir
> But like a comet I was wond'red at
>   (*1 Henry IV*, III.ii. 46–47)

and contrasts his own skilful performance with Prince Hal's wasting time with low company in Eastcheap, which he says is repeating the mistake of "the skipping king" Richard, who lost his crown mainly because he was seen too often and not with the right people. What Henry says may be true as a general political principle, though whether it was true of his own behaviour at the time or not is another question: certainly the communique from Richard's headquarters about Bolingbroke is very different from what Bolingbroke remembers of it:

> Off goes his bonnet to an oyster-wench;
> A brace of draymen bid God speed him well
> And had the tribute of his supple knee
>
> *(Richard II*, I.iv. 31–33)

One aspect of this question of leadership has been studied in a fine piece of scholarship, a book called *The King's Two Bodies*, by E.H. Kantorowicz. Oversimplifying a bit, the king's two bodies, as distinguished in medieval and Renaissance theory, are his individual body as a man and his symbolic aspect as the body of his nation in an individual form. To extend this in the direction of *Richard II*, if the individual man is A, and the symbol of the nation as a single body is B, then the real king is B, the consecrated and sacrosanct figure, the king de jure. But the stronger the king is as an individual, and the more de facto ability he has, the more nearly A will equal B, and the better off both the king and his society will be. In any case, whether A equals B or not, it is clear that A minus B equals nothing, and that equation is echoed in the words "all" and "nothing" that run through the abdication scene, and in fact are continuing as late as *King Lear*.

Richard has been brought up to believe in the sanctity of his office, and unfortunately that has not made him more responsible but less so. Hence he turns to magic and fantasy as soon as he is even momentarily frustrated. When he goes to see the dying John of Gaunt, thinking of how soon he can get his money, he soliloquizes:

> Now put it, God, into the physician's mind
> To help him to his grave immediately!   (I.iv. 59–60)

This is not the voice of a strong-willed and powerful king, but of a spoiled child, and those who talk in such accents can never get away with what they do for long. John of Gaunt tells him his flatterers have got inside his individual castle, and have cut him off from that identification with his

society that every genuine king must have. Nobody could express the
doctrine of the two bodies more clearly than John of Gaunt does:

> A thousand flatterers sit within thy crown,
> Whose compass is no bigger than thy head;
> And yet, incaged in so small a verge,
> The waste is no whit lesser than thy land.
>
> (II.i. 100–103)

After his return from Ireland, Richard refuses for a time to believe that
anything can affect an anointed king adversely. But after the roll call of
disasters has been recited to him he suddenly reverses his perspective,
fascinated by the paradox that an individual, as vulnerable and subject to
accident as anyone else, could also be the body of his whole kingdom. In
short, he turns introvert, and that is a dangerous thing for a ruler to be who
expects to go on being a ruler.

It is obvious, long before his final murder, that Richard is no coward,
but his growing introversion gives him some of the weaknesses that make
other men cowards. One of them is an overreacting imagination that
sketches the whole course of a future development before anyone else has
had time to figure out the present one. Sometimes these flashes of the future
are unconscious: at the beginning he tells Mowbray that he is not favouring
Bolingbroke and would not "Were he my brother, nay, my kingdom's heir."
That could pass as the straight thematic anticipation that we've met before
in Shakespeare. So, more doubtfully, could his complaint about John of
Gaunt's "frozen admonition":

> chasing the royal blood
> With fury from his native residence.   (II.i. 118–19)

But when disaster becomes objective he instantly begins to see himself as the
central figure of a secular Passion. When Northumberland reports
Bolingbroke's wish for Richard to come down and parley with him in the
"base court" (the *basse cour* or lower courtyard of Flint Castle), the symbolism
of the whole operation flashes at once through his mind:

> Down, down I come, like glist'ring Phaeton ...
> In the base court? Base court, where kings grow base ...
> In the base court? Come down? Down, court! Down, king!
>
> (III.iii. 178–82)

So active an imagination makes Richard a remarkable poet, but cripples him as a practical man, because his mental schedule is so different from those of people who advance one step at a time, like Bolingbroke. We are reminded here, as so often in Shakespeare, that successful action and successful timing are much the same thing. His being a day late in returning from Ireland has resulted in twelve thousand Welshmen, on a rumour that he was dead, deserting to Bolingbroke. Very little is said about fortune or fate or the stars here, because Richard has made so many mistakes in timing that something like this was bound to hit him sooner or later.

Eventually Richard comes to understand, if not consciously at first, that he is programming himself as a loser, and has thrown himself into the elegiac role of one who has lost his throne before he has actually lost it. This in its turn is a kind of self-indulgent retreat from the confronting situation: "that sweet way I was in to despair," as he calls it. In the abdication scene he makes what could look like a last throw of the dice:

> And if my word be sterling yet in England,
> Let it command a mirror hither straight
>
> (IV.i. 264–65)

It is Bolingbroke who gives the order to bring a looking glass: there is nothing sterling about Richard's word anymore. As far as history is concerned, Richard has had it: nothing remains but to find some device for murdering him. But as far as drama is concerned, Richard is and remains the unforgettable central figure, and Bolingbroke is a supporting actor. How does this come about? How does Richard manage to steal the show from Bolingbroke at the very moment when Bolingbroke is stealing his crown?

The reason goes back to the distinction we made earlier between the two forms of mask: the hypocrite and the person. We all have to be persons, and that involves our being hypocrites at times too: there's no way out of that. But Richard is surrounded with nobles solidly encased in hypocrisy of various kinds: many of them, as we'll discover more fully in the next play, are just gangsters glorified by titles and blank verse, and all of them, including Bolingbroke, are engaged in pretending that a bad king is being deposed for a good one. Some truth in it, of course; there's always a lot of truth in hypocrisy.

When Richard says he sees traitors before him, that is only what a loser would be expected to say. But when he goes on:

> Nay, if I turn mine eyes upon myself,
> I find myself a traitor with the rest.   (IV.i. 247–48)

he may sound as though he were saying what Northumberland is trying to bully him into saying, or signing: that he is justly deposed as a criminal. But in fact something else is happening: in that solid mass of rebels ritually carrying out a power takeover, Richard is emerging as a stark-naked personality, and the others can do nothing but stare at it.

There follows the inspired mirror scene, in which he dramatizes his phrase "turn mine eyes upon myself." He's still putting on an act, certainly; but it's a totally different act from what he was expected to put on. In one of his two aspects, the king is a human being: by forcing everyone to concentrate on him as a human being, while he stares in the mirror, a kind of royalty becomes visible from that humanity that Bolingbroke will never in this world find the secret of. We see a principle that we see later on in *King Lear*: that in some circumstances the real royalty is in the individual person, not in the symbolic one. Bolingbroke lives in a world of substance and shadow: power is substantial to him, and Richard with his mirror has retreated to a world of shadows. But a nagging doubt remains, of a kind related to the close of *A Midsummer Night's Dream*: which has the more effective power, the Duke of Athens or the king of shadows in the wood? In the context of a history the issue is clearer cut than in a fantastic comedy, of course, except for the audience's response. The audience takes Richard out of the theatre, and groups everyone else around him.

The contrast between what Bolingbroke has become and what Richard has been all along comes out in the two final episodes of the play. The first episode is the one we've glanced at already: Bolingbroke's pardoning of Aumerle, who conspired against him, in response to the impassioned pleas of the Duchess of York. In this episode there are two themes or verbal phrases to be noticed: the theme of the beggar and the king, and the theme of setting the word against the word. Bolingbroke is now king, and everyone else becomes in a sense a beggar: if a subject does anything that puts his life in danger, he must sue to the king for his life as a beggar would do. The "word" being discussed is the word of royal command, specifically the word "pardon." The Duke of York, as hot for prosecuting his son as ever, urges Bolingbroke to say pardon in French, where *pardonnez-moi* would have the general sense of "sorry, nothing doing." But Bolingbroke knows that he is now in a position where he is the source of the word of command, and must make all such words as unambiguous as possible, even when he does what he is soon to do to Exton.

This scene is immediately followed by Richard's great prison speech, which in many respects sums up the play, and repeats these two themes of the beggar and the king and of setting the word against the word. The prison is the final actualizing of the individual world dramatized by the mirror earlier, and Richard is fascinated by the number of personae he can invoke. His soul and brain become an Adam and an Eve, and they germinate between them a whole new world of thoughts. Some of the thoughts are ambitious, wanting only to get out; some are resigned (perhaps Boethius, writing *The Consolation of Philosophy* while awaiting execution in prison, is in the background here), but all of them are discontented. Not because of the prison: they'd be discontented anywhere. Here, setting "the word against the word" refers to the words of Scripture, the commands that come from the spiritual world and so often seem ambiguous; and the king and beggar are the same identity, different only in mask and context. He concludes:

> Nor I, nor any man that but man is,
> With nothing shall be pleased till be he eased
> With being nothing.   (V.v. 39–41)

Ever since the beginning of language, probably, "nothing" has meant two things: "not anything" and "something called nothing." Richard is saying here (not very grammatically) that every human being, including himself, is discontented, not pleased with anything, until he becomes that something we call nothing, i.e., in this context, dead. This double meaning becomes very central in *King Lear* later.

In *A Midsummer Night's Dream* the two worlds of the play, Theseus's court and Oberon's wood, represent two aspects of the mind, the conscious, rational, daylight aspect and the dreaming and fantasizing aspect. One dwells in a world of things and the other in a world of shadows; the shadow mind may live partly in the imaginary, in what is simply not there, but it may live partly also in the genuinely creative, bringing into existence a "transfigured" entity, to use Hippolyta's word, which is neither substantial nor shadowy, neither illusory nor real, but both at once. In *Romeo and Juliet* we got one tantalizing glimpse of this world in Mercutio's Queen Mab speech, but what we see of it mostly is the world created out of the love of the two young people, a world inevitably destroyed as the daylight world rolls over it, but possessing a reality that its destruction does not disprove.

Richard II is in a more complex social position, and has been caught in the paradox of the king, who, we remember, possesses both an individual and a sacramental body. The latter includes all the subjects in his kingdom; the former, only himself. In the prison, however, an entire world leaps into life within his own mind: the other world he was looking for in the mirror. He has as many thoughts as he has subjects, and, like his subjects, his thoughts are discontented, rebellious and conflicting. But the king's two bodies are also God's two realities, linked by the anointing of they king.

The imagery changes as music sounds in the background: Richard comments on the need for keeping time in music, and applies the word to his own life: "I wasted time, and time doth now waste me." From there two conceptions of time unfold: time as rhythm and proportion, the inner grace of life itself that we hear in music, and time as the mechanical progress of the clock, the time that Bolingbroke has kept so accurately until the clock brought him to power. Near the beginning of the play, John of Gaunt refuses to take active vengeance for Woodstock's death on the Lord's anointed. He leaves vengeance to heaven, which will release its vengeance "when they see the hours ripe on earth." The word "they" has no antecedent: John must mean something like "the gods," but the image of ripening, and of acting when the time is "ripe," brings in a third dimension of time, one that we don't see in this play, or perhaps fully anywhere else, although there are unconscious commitments to it like Edgar's "ripeness is all." There is a power in time, with its own rhythm and form: if we can't see it in action, perhaps it sees us, and touches the most sensitive people, such as Hamlet, with the feeling that it shapes our ends. If we did see it, perhaps the world of history would burst like an eggshell and a new kind of life would come forth.

Richard II was, we said, written entirely in verse, the reason being that the action is centred on what is practically a ritual, or inverted ritual: the deposing of a lawful king and the crowning of the successor who has forced him out. At the beginning of *Henry IV*, the hangover has set in. Bolingbroke, realizing that there is nothing worse for a country than a civil war, has determined at the outset to get started on a crusade. The idea, we said, was partly that God would forgive anyone anything, even deposing an anointed king, if he went on a crusade. But even more, an external enemy unites a country instead of dividing it. Shortly before his death, Henry IV tells Prince Henry that when he becomes king he should make every effort to get a foreign war started, so that the nobles will be interested in killing foreigners instead of intriguing against each other and the king—advice Prince Henry is not slow to act on. But at this point the new king's authority is not well enough established for a foreign war, much less a crusade. Henry finds that there are revolts against him in Scotland and Wales, and that many of the lords who backed him against Richard II are conspiring against him now. So *Henry IV* contains a great deal of prose, because this play is taking a much broader survey of English society, and showing the general slump in morale of a country whose chain of command has so many weak links. Falstaff speaks very early of "old father antic the law," and both the Eastcheap group and the carriers and ostlers in the curious scene at the beginning of the second act illustrate that conspiracy, at all levels, is now in fashion.

In the opening scenes two issues make their way into the foreground.

One is the fact that medieval warfare was in large part a ransom racket: you took noblemen prisoner in battle, and then their tenants had to put up enough money to buy them back. That's why there's so much said about the denying of prisoners: they were a perquisite of the king's. The other is the fact that Edmund Mortimer, Earl of March, has in some respects a better claim to the throne than Henry IV has, and though he is at first theoretically on Henry's side, he marries the daughter of the Welsh rebel Owen Glendower, and forms a rallying point of sorts for a plot against the House of Lancaster.

The conspirators are not an attractive lot: Northumberland, for example, the father of Hotspur, was a bully in *Richard II* and is a coward in this play: he was a traitor to Richard, then a traitor to Bolingbroke, and ends by betraying his own son. Worcester is sulky and insolent: Henry is compelled to assert his royal authority and send him offstage, and Worcester realizes that once he is distrusted by the king there is no turning back. The only attractive figure is Hotspur, who's already a legendary fighter and a logical leader of the conspirators—if only they can get him to shut up. But they don't trust him either, because Hotspur, however foolish in many respects, is at least ready to fight in good faith: he doesn't have a conspiratorial mind, and doesn't really understand what his colleagues are after, which is their own interests. Before long they have produced what for a Tudor audience would be one of the most terrifying of symbols, later to appear at the beginning of *King Lear*: a map, with proposals to divide the country into parts.

Prince Henry is mentioned in contrast to Hotspur in the first scene, and is said to be the same age as Hotspur, though historically Hotspur was twenty years older. In the second scene the Prince appears, with Falstaff. The Prince is the central figure of this and the next two plays, and it's a very careful planning that shows him from the beginning flanked with these two characters. Hotspur is a kind of parody brother and Falstaff a parody father: later in the play Falstaff actually puts on a dramatic subscene in which he plays the role of Prince Henry's father, and this scene displaces one that the Prince had already proposed, in which he would take the part of Hotspur and Falstaff that of Hotspur's wife. In this scene, too, the Prince represents Hotspur as answering, when his wife asks him how many he has killed today, "some fourteen," and before long we have Falstaff's story about his fighting with two men in buckram who expand eventually into fourteen. The comic symmetry has a serious side to it. The central and essential virtue for a king who's eventually going to win the battle of Agincourt is courage. According to an ethical system that goes back ultimately to Aristotle, a virtue is a mean between extremes, and the virtue of courage is a mean between cowardice at

one extreme and rashness or foolhardiness at the other. Falstaff represents
one extreme and Hotspur the other, little as that statement does justice to the
complexity of either.

Shakespeare's treatment of Hotspur's rhetoric is, even for him, an
extraordinary technical tour de force. To paraphrase a remark of Worcester's,
Hotspur says everything except the point of what he wants to say. "I profess
not talking," he says calmly later in the play, but he is certainly an
enthusiastic enough amateur. But he can't seem to give form or direction to
what he says, and as you listen to him—and of course you have to listen to
someone who hardly ever stops—a conviction begins to settle in your mind:
whatever his courage or other good qualities, this man will never be a king.
No one else in Shakespeare, not even the much later Coriolanus, who
resembles him in some respects, shows such energy in breaking away from
people. In the opening scene he gives us his brilliant portrait of the dandy
who professes to regret the invention of gunpowder: no great point in it,
except that it shows us how Hotspur divides people into the men who fight
and the anthropoids who don't. Later he comes on the stage reading aloud
from a letter—we never learn who wrote it. We learn only that the letter
urges caution, and Hotspur gets claustrophobia when anyone urges caution.

Then there is the hilarious scene in which Hotspur ridicules Owen
Glendower and his fantasies about the omens surrounding his birth. The
failure of Glendower to come to his aid at the battle of Shrewsbury clearly
has some connection with this. Again, Hotspur has no taste for music or
poetry—always a bad sign in Shakespeare—because he can't sit still long
enough to listen to them. We couldn't imagine him carousing in Eastcheap
with Falstaff and Poins: he'd be bored out of his mind in five minutes. His
obviously adoring wife addresses an eloquent and pathetic speech to him
about his neglect of her, but he's engaged in men's work and won't listen. In
the last act, brushing aside some letters for him, he complains:

> the time of life is short!
> To spend that shortness basely were too long
>
> (V.ii. 81–82)

Fighting is the one thing that does not bore him, and nothing that does not
lead to fighting is worth bothering with. His wife's name, incidentally, is
Kate: the historical Lady Percy was named Elizabeth, and Shakespeare's
main source calls her Eleanor. I don't for a moment think there's any
particular significance in Kate, but it would be highly characteristic of
Hotspur if in fact he were not quite sure what his wife's name was.

In contrast to Falstaff, who is all realism, Hotspur is a quixotic figure, as much in love with honour as Falstaff is detached from it. With many of his supporters abandoning him, and thinking that his glory will be all the greater with the odds against him, he goes into battle and is struck down by Prince Henry. His dying speech is the reverse of all the rest of his rhetoric, and says exactly and very economically what he means:

> O Harry, thou hast robbed me of my youth! ...
> But thought's the slave of life, and life time's fool;
> And time, that takes survey of all the world,
> Must have a stop. (V.iv. 76–82)

Most editors now follow the First Quarto for the second line, which gives a simpler reading: "But thoughts, the slaves of life, and life, time's fool." I don't question their editorial judgment, but if I were directing the play I'd insist on the Folio reading above. Going back to the ethic of the golden mean, of virtue as a middle way between extremes, we notice that the extremes have a good deal in common, and are less opposed than they look. Rashness or foolhardiness can be a form of cowardice, as any psychologist will tell you. And however absurd it sounds to associate Hotspur with cowardice, this speech indicates that all his life he has been running away from something, something that has a great deal to do with time and the way that time ticks away the moments of his youth, that all too brief interval when he can be still a first-class fighting man. We notice also the word "fool," apparently meaning victim, in the sense in which Romeo calls himself fortune's fool; a sense that will become very important in *King Lear*. The theme of time we must leave and pick up later.

Falstaff is so complex a character that it's hardly possible to make an unqualified statement about him, even that his name is Falstaff. His name was originally Oldcastle: when this gave offence, Shakespeare reverted to a very minor character introduced into what may well have been his first play, *Henry VI*. There a Sir John Falstaff comes running across the stage away from a battle; when asked with contempt if he will desert his great commander Talbot, he says: "All the Talbots in the world, to save my life." We note that this Falstaff is in a panic, something the Falstaff we know never is, apart from some very unreliable reports about him. The "cowardice" of Falstaff comes from a cool and reasonable approach to a situation full of hypocritical idealism: as is said of him by another character, he will fight no longer than he sees reason. As a result his cowardice is full of humour—something a mere panicky deserter never could have—and also very disturbing, because it calls into question a lot of clichés about honour and glory. His soliloquy on honour on the field of Shrewsbury must have seemed to many in the original audience about as funny a speech as had ever been spoken on a stage, because they accepted more of the idealism about honour, and for them the speech would probably have had far greater psychological release than for us. In one of the plays in Shaw's *Back to Methusaleh*, set in the future, a monument has been erected to Falstaff. It is explained that after a few experiences of warfare (even though this is early twentieth century, and before the atom bomb), it had been realized that cowardice was a major social virtue, and so a monument had been set up to the sage who discovered the fact. We're closer to that state of mind today than we are to the Elizabethan attitude, to say nothing of the medieval one.

To the kernel of the stage coward have been added a large number of other stage types. Falstaff is also a *miles gloriosus* or bragging soldier, who claims to have killed Hotspur; he is a parasite, a type deriving from Classical comedy, with the bottomless capacity for drink appropriate to a parasite (the point is made very early that his bills are paid by Prince Henry); he is a comic butt, someone to be played tricks on in order to see how he can wriggle out of them; he is a vice, a central figure of the old morality plays who acted as a tempter and stirred up complications, later someone with the role of starting a comic action going. Above all, he is a jester, whose outrageous boasts are his way of keeping the party lively: his two men in buckram grow into an astonishing number, but he is not a schizophrenic, as he would have to be to expect to be believed. In part two, after he meets Shallow, he soliloquizes: "I will devise matter enough out of this Shallow to keep Prince Harry in continual laughter the wearing out of six fashions."

Characters in comedy normally do not have enough scope to become counterparts of the great tragic heroes: Falstaff is the only comic character in Shakespeare who does, because his setting is a history play. The Falstaff of the comedy, *The Merry Wives of Windsor*, is a much smaller figure. But the Falstaff of the histories ranks with Don Quixote as an inexhaustible comic study, though for opposite reasons. Don Quixote clings to his idealistic and romantic hallucinations about the age of chivalry in a society which ignores them; Falstaff clings to a self-serving rationality and a prose rhythm, while all the noblemen bumbling in blank verse are, if equally self-serving, better at disguising the fact.

As long as Prince Henry's interest in him holds out, he seems invulnerable, but there are two weak spots in his armour. In the first place, he is Sir John Falstaff, knight, well enough known to have a rebel officer surrender to him because of his name alone. Consequently he is involved in the war game whether he wants to be or not, and is empowered to recruit soldiers for the war against the conspirators. Being a vice, he takes bribes to let the good recruits off and conscript only worthless ones: our sympathy for him goes down a good deal when he tells us complacently what he's done, but again his realism gives us a side to such warfare that the blank-verse history makers give little hint of. He speaks of the men he's collected as "the cankers of a calm world and a long peace," and defends their lean and beggarly appearance with the phrase "food for powder." What difference does it make whether a soldier has been a good or a bad soldier if he's dead? At the battle of Shrewsbury he tells us that of his hundred and fifty men about three are left alive, "and they are for the town's end, to beg through life." And while his exploits on the field of Shrewsbury are absurd enough, we may also remember that he is far too old to be on a battlefield at all, and is not, to put it mildly, in top physical condition. He's isolated also in a different and subtle way. I've spoken of elements in the action of a Shakespeare play that we don't see but know are there, like the sun in *Romeo and Juliet* and the moon in *A Midsummer Night's Dream*. In the histories we don't, except in film productions, see any horses, though we realize that horses are constantly carrying all the important people over the country and into battle. But we can't imagine Falstaff on top of a Horse.

His other weakness is his very real fondness for Prince Hal, who is, as he tells us early on, merely using Falstaff and the others as stooges for putting on an act of his own. In his opening scene he says to the Prince: "Thou hast the most unsavoury similes, and art indeed the most comparative, rascalliest, sweet young prince." There is no mistaking the genuineness of the affection in that tone: even the frigid Prince feels it occasionally, though never deeply. Falstaff is aware that his hold on Prince Henry is by no means secure, and this awareness increases as the two plays go on, driving him in the second part to make the very foolish move of writing the Prince a letter warning him against Poins, who, as the best of the Eastcheap lot, is the normal object of his jealousy. But even so we are told quite explicitly in *Henry V* that his public rejection by Henry has destroyed his will to live.

One of the sources for *Henry IV* and *Henry V* is an older play called *The Famous Victories of Henry the Fifth*, a messy dog's breakfast of a play that still helped to give Shakespeare a central idea for his own plays: that the popular appeal of a great king who conquered France would be immensely enhanced if he were presented first as a "madcap" Prince, associating with ordinary or low social types, getting into trouble with the law, and displaying the kind of undirected energy for which his later career provided an outlet. In this play Prince Hal tells us at the start that he is putting on a show very carefully designed for maximum effect, in which a reputation for being idle or even profligate will be suddenly reversed when he enters on his responsibilities. Throughout the play he seems utterly confident of his eventual success and his ability to take care of Hotspur as well: we may wonder what his confidence is based on, as whatever else he may be doing in Eastcheap, he is not getting much practice in fencing. Perhaps he already feels what comes out clearly in the imagery of *Henry V*: that he is on the rising side of the wheel of fortune, and so nothing can stop him. In this soliloquy, at the end of the second scene, two images are used that are important. One is the sun, which Henry will imitate when he rises from prince to king after having been sunk in the darker elements of his kingdom. Falstaff speaks of his group as "Diana's foresters, gentlemen of the shade, minions of the moon," which sounds like a parody of Oberon's wood in *A Midsummer Night's Dream*, and he urges the Prince, with unconscious irony, to make a place for the activities of the night when he becomes king. The other image is that of time, which emerges in the last line of the soliloquy: "Redeeming time when men least think I will."

As we'll be seeing at intervals all through, the role of time is always centrally important in Shakespeare. The tragic action normally cuts into time, and anyone who, like Hamlet, feels that there is no right time for him, and that the whole time of his activity is out of joint, can meet nothing but disaster. Macbeth often reproaches himself for acting a second too late, allowing someone crucial to escape his massacres by not seizing the exact moment. In comedy, time is usually a little more leisurely, sometimes taking a generation or so to work out its designs, as in *The Winter's Tale*. Prospero in *The Tempest*, in contrast, has studied astrology and knows when the right moment comes for him. For a king to be successful, a sense of timing is perhaps the most important ability he can have: in *Henry V* it is said of the new king, when he is about to invade France:

> Now he weighs time
> Even to the utmost grain.

The first remark Falstaff makes in this play is to ask Prince Hal what time it is, and he is told that such people as Falstaff, who sleep all day and drink all night, don't need to know the time. Falstaff is a time-blocking figure, someone who gets in the way of the movement of history. Hotspur's hair-trigger reactions also indicate that he has no sense of time, though for opposite reasons: he tends to jump his fences before they are there, and only in the enlightenment of his dying speech does he realize that life is time's fool, the plaything and often the victim of time.

Prince Henry himself is rather helpless when his father upbraids him for the manner of his life and tells him that he is simply being Richard II all over again. His plan of action is based on the crucial difference between the reputation of a prince, who is still technically a private citizen, and a king, a difference Richard did not take account of. Henry IV tells his son that when he was making his way to the throne he appeared very seldom in public and always with the maximum effect (this, we noted, is the opposite of what Richard II said about him, but something no doubt has to be allowed for selective memory). And clearly the Prince can't say: "Yes, but I'm going to be in a much stronger position than you—thanks I admit largely to you—and I'm putting on a far better act than you ever thought of." When this scene is parodied in the Eastcheap tavern, with Falstaff taking the role of the Prince's father and ending, naturally, with a plug for himself as the Prince's companion ("Banish plump Jack, and banish all the world"), the Prince answers, "I do; I will," and we realize that he means precisely what he says.

Prince Henry fits the general pattern of the play in that he is looking out primarily for his own interests: his companions are people to use and manipulate, and, as his father has already discovered, a king cannot afford real friends. The long scene in the Eastcheap tavern, Act II, Scene iv, begins with an episode I still find puzzling, but I think it has something to do with the same principle. The Prince enters laughing and perhaps drunk, telling Poins that he has become very popular with the drawers and servants of the tavern, who regard him as a good fellow and not proud like Falstaff, and one of them, named Francis, has offered him a gift of a pennyworth of sugar. There follows an elaborate practical joke on Francis, solely with the object of making him look a fool. After this has gone on for quite a while, Poins says: "What cunning match have you made with this jest of the drawer: come, what's the issue?" In other words: "What's so funny?" Francis has done nothing but try to express some affection for the Prince: his gift is not worth much, but it's the first rule of chivalry never to devalue a gift from a social inferior for that reason. The Prince does not answer Poins's question at all; he says:

> I am now of all humours that have showed themselves humours
> since the old days of goodman Adam to the pupil age of this
> present twelve o'clock at midnight.   (II.iv. 89–91)

The surface meaning of this is that he feels like indulging any fancy that has ever entered the mind of the human race. I think there may be something more being said: something to the effect that Prince Henry is very close to completing his "madcap prince" act, and that what he has got from putting it on is a sense of having soaked himself in every social aspect of the kingdom he is going to rule. He is becoming his entire nation in an individual form, which is symbolically what a king is. It is interesting though that this statement, a very important one if I've got it anywhere near right, comes in a scene that shows him pulling away from someone who is trying to appreciate him as a person.

It is true that the battle of Shrewsbury shows him in a much more sympathetic role: he gives what he thinks is the dead Falstaff an obituary speech that one might make about a dog that has been run over, but still there are traces of affection in it, and when Falstaff revives, with his preposterous claim of having killed Hotspur himself, he allows him to get away with it. Considering what Hotspur's opinion of Falstaff would have been, Henry's generosity comes close to a desecrating of Hotspur's body. The First Part of *Henry IV* is, in one of its aspects, the tragedy of Hotspur, and it ends with the triumphant survival of Falstaff. It is possible that Shakespeare had planned the rejection of Falstaff in a second play by this time. The historical material in the second part is thin enough to make it likely that a demand for more Falstaff was the main reason for the second part's existence, and Shakespeare must have known that his audience would find the scene of his public rejection a bit hard to take. Nonetheless, as the first part includes the tragedy of Hotspur, so the second part includes the tragedy of Falstaff, so far as Falstaff is capable of a tragic role.

2 Henry IV follows the same general outline as the first part; but it soon becomes clear that the Eastcheap group is heading for rapid disintegration. The first scene with Falstaff begins with Falstaff asking his page for the doctor's report on his urine; the third includes Falstaff's order "Empty the jordan." We feel that we are being physically pushed closer to Falstaff than we really want to get. Mistress Quickly is not so amiably chuckle-headed as before: Falstaff is still sponging off her, as he was in the first part, but her reluctance to pawn her plate to fill his clamorous belly has a genuine pathos, and the abortive lawsuit she brings has a kind of desperation. One gets the impression that Falstaff's supplies from the Prince are being cut down, and that it is much harder for him to support all his vices in the style to which they are accustomed.

Other characters indicate that the setting is not all good fun, clean or dirty. We meet Pistol, who is a familiar type of braggart soldier, but he is neither witty, nor, in Falstaff's phrase, a cause of wit in other men. Doll Tearsheet is fairly typical of the stage whores of the drama of the time, very tough-talking and belligerent and generally drunk. Even she is somewhat taken aback by Falstaff's lifestyle. When at the end of the play she is arrested and the beadle remarks "there hath been a man or two lately killed about her," we get a glimpse of underworld activities that no prince, however much of a "madcap" act he puts on, can afford to get mixed up with.

Similarly with others Falstaff meets. He is accustomed to feel that it doesn't matter what he does if his evasions afterward are sufficiently amusing, but such techniques do not work with the Chief Justice, nor with Prince Henry's younger brother John, who has about as much humour as the horse he rides on. Falstaff, in short, is beginning to feel the strain of a professional jester whose jokes no longer go over, apart from the fact that he does not stop with jokes. He spends time with Justice Shallow, the one fully realized character peculiar to this play, and the time extends, because each of them thinks he has something to gain from the other. But nostalgic reminiscences reminding him how old he is and how long it was since he was young are hardly what Falstaff wants to hear at this point.

In this play Henry IV is near his death: he is perpetually exhausted and he can't sleep. His great strength has always been in his ability to take short views, to do what has to be done at the time and not worry about the remoter perspectives. But in this play a long and desolate speech breaks out of him about how any youth, if he could see the entire pattern of time stretching out ahead of him, would simply lie down and die and refuse to go through with it. The nemesis of usurpation is working itself out: a good deal of the discussion between the king's party and the rebels consists of rehashing feuds and grudges that go back to the beginning of *Richard II*, or even earlier. The implication is partly that rebellion is, among other things, caused by a sterile brooding on history with the object, not of building up a future, but of reshaping the past. Meanwhile Prince Henry is very near the point at which he is to take over as king, and the wish for his father to die and change the scene is very close to his consciousness, as a conversation with Poins shows. In the meantime he is in a state of doldrums, anxious to break away from his madcap act, but still having to wait for his cue. His guideline is still "in everything the purpose must weigh with the folly," but the folly and the idleness are beginning to chafe. Eventually there comes the scene in which he is caught trying on his sick father's crown: one of the traditional episodes of the madcap prince saga that had to be included. His excuses when discovered sound lame—he has learned something from Falstaff but not enough—but then King Henry is dying and starved for affection, and he accepts the excuses with a certain wry amusement, mingled with hope.

Falstaff, though he has had many warnings that he will not be in as much favour with the new king as he thinks, pushes all the slights he has had out of his mind, and just as the impetuous Hotspur realizes at the moment of death that he has been running away from something, so the leisurely and heavily moving Falstaff plunges into a frenetic energy to get to the coronation of the new king and become the second-greatest man in the kingdom. Well, we know what happened to that dream. At the end of part one, on the battlefield of Shrewsbury, there is the greatest possible contrast

between all the ferocious fighting and the absurd antics of Falstaff with his
bottle of sack. But in the second part there seems a closer connection
between the rejection of Falstaff and the main historical action of the play, in
which Prince John gets the rebel army to disarm by a rather shabby and
obvious trick. The Archbishop of York, on the rebel side, remarks:

> we are all diseased,
> And with our surfeiting and wanton hours
> Have brought ourselves into a burning fever,
> And we must bleed for it.   (IV.i. 54–57)

Bloodletting was so standard a medical practice at the time that the analogy
carries on into the social body. But there is a crucial distinction, which the
Archbishop misses, between the bloodletting of civil war and of foreign war,
and this tough, gritty, cynical play ends with the expectation of very soon
invading France.

WILLIAM EMPSON

Falstaff

The theory that Shakespeare made Falstaff appear in his first draft of *Henry V*, so that our present text of that play is much revised and thereby confused, seems to be accepted now by most of the competent authorities; indeed to be regarded as the most positive result of Dover Wilson's very detailed work on the Falstaff trilogy, and therefore as the main support for a narrow view of Falstaff in general. I want in this essay to ask the reader to look at the whole position again. Whether Shakespeare changed his mind about *Henry V* is perhaps not very important, but it gives a definite point to start from; and I think it is time someone pointed out how very weak the evidence for this theory is.

To be sure, the evidence offered is imposingly various; from the Epilogue of *II Henry IV*, from some historical possibilities about censorship, and from the text of *Henry V* itself; but I think it breaks down all round. The relevant part of the Epilogue says:

> One word more, I beseech you. If you be not too much cloyed with fat meat, our humble author will continue the story, with Sir John in it, and make you merry with fair Katherine of France; where (for anything I know) Falstaff shall die of a sweat, unless 'a be already killed with your hard opinions; for Oldcastle died a martyr, and this is not the man.

From *Essays on Shakespeare*, edited by David B. Pirie. © 1986 by William Empson.

"For anything I know" and "if you want it" are a good deal more doubtful than what we are accustomed to nowadays in the way of advance publicity. Among Elizabethans it is not unique (e.g. the end of *Selimus*, for which the proffered Second Part seems not to have been wanted); but we need not suppose that Shakespeare was really feeling hesitant about whether these very popular plays were worth continuing. It seems likely that the Company, when it was forced to stop calling the buffoon of these plays Oldcastle, also had to promise to apologise before the public audience; some graceful bits of chat were therefore arranged, so as to drop in the apology with an air of casualness. In any case, the speaker disclaims knowing what the author will do, beyond the broad fact that the next part of the familiar story is being considered for a play; and the Company might not want to give away the secrets of the next production, even if Shakespeare had decided on them. Dover Wilson makes the valuable point that the Quarto order for the text of this epilogue shows it is two of them jammed together; the Folio editor merely altered the order to make the combination speakable. The first was spoken by someone responsible for the performance, perhaps the author, probably at Court, and the second by a dancer before he began his jig or what not; the second therefore need not be taken very seriously, and only the second includes this little advertisement. Dover Wilson says he cannot believe that the "jesting" apology about Oldcastle was "spoken on the stage while the matter was still dangerous", but I cannot see what he deduces from that; it seems to be a matter of months rather than years. As to the main point, I think Falstaff *is* quite prominently "in the play", though not in the cast, and indeed I think the new king's hard opinion, which Falstaff does die of, *is* a kind of "public opinion", so that there is no inconsistency at all. Of course this would be "stretching a point" if anyone gave it as an official explanation, but it is the kind of thing the Elizabethan mind would put up with, and the whole trick of this advertisement is to tease the audience by ostentatiously refusing to satisfy their curiosity. Shakespeare could have let it be spoken if he had already decided to kill Falstaff; it is as likely that he hadn't yet started on the new effort (one would expect he dallied till he knew he had to work fast); but either way it is no proof that he wrote out two whole versions.

Dover Wilson's argument in his edition of *Henry V* (1947) was that there was nobody to act Falstaff because Kemp had suddenly left the Company. I gather that this line of effort has now been abandoned. There was a Court performance of *I Henry IV* in 1600 (described as a private one, for the Flemish Ambassador), after Kemp is supposed to have gone, and the recent attempts to decide which actor took which part do not give it to him anyway. Kemp was a low comedian (a fine chap too), whereas one of the points you needed to make clear about Falstaff was that he was a scandalous gentleman; it doesn't seem Kemp's part at all. Besides, they would have to have some kind of understudy system. The argument has now moved to a more aristocratic ground, and we are told that Falstaff was removed from Agincourt because the descendants of "Fastolfe" influenced the censor. He was not suppressed altogether; the Ambassador could hardly be shown a play recently banned for libel, and Part II was printed in 1600, and indeed *The Merry Wives* (on this view) was brought out as an alternative to showing him at Agincourt. Dover Wilson suggests that the Company hid its embarrassment by *inventing* a story that the Queen asked to see him in love, and that Shakespeare could gratify her in three weeks. This was "convenient" for them, he thinks. I do not believe it could be done. Falstaff was a very prominent object, much the most successful Shakespeare character before Hamlet; some of this would be likely to leak out. The legend that the Queen commissioned *The Merry Wives* is recorded late and not worth much; it is evidence that the terrifying old woman had laughed at Falstaff, and that her moods were watched and remembered, but not much more. As negative evidence, however, it seems to me very strong; if she had allowed her underlings to suppress Falstaff, even in part, no "publicity" arrangement would be likely to get away with the opposite story. Besides, the "embarrassed" Company would just as soon have the truth leak out. And what about the treatment of a much more real Fastolfe in *Henry VI*? And why not deal with the new name firmly, as had been done to the previous name Oldcastle? All the same, peculiar things do happen, and the descendants of Fastolfe might have been just strong enough to keep him out of Agincourt, and to hush the suppression up, though not strong enough to suppress him elsewhere. If we found confusions in the text of *Henry V* which needed a very special explanation this theory might be plausible. But surely it is very gratuitous if we find none.

The textual arguments for revision, in Dover Wilson's edition, are as follows.

I. Pistol says at V.i.85 that he hears his Doll is dead of syphilis, so he has lost his rendezvous. I agree that the author ought to have put "Nell", and the actor had better say it, because the other word confuses us with another character. But the modern Damon Runyan slang happens to have been Elizabethan slang too; the slip was an easy one for the author to make. And I think there was an extra reason for making it here. The ladies were last mentioned in Act II; we learned that Pistol had married Mrs Quickly (Nell) and heard his express contempt for Tearsheet (Doll) as in hospital for syphilis; he had always skirmished with Doll (when on the stage with her) and had now become keen to stand by Nell, whose position was clearly more hopeful. There can be no point in assuming he has changed over without warning the audience. But we need not be surprised that Mrs Quickly got the disease too, and there is a deserved irony if Pistol, who talked brutally about Doll's trouble at the beginning of the play, finds at the end that the same applies to his Nell. Now, if Shakespeare meant this, both women were in his mind, and that is the kind of case where a hurried writer puts down the wrong word. It comes in the Quarto, supposed to be pirated by actors, not only in the Folio, but that need only be another of the depressing bits of evidence that Shakespeare never corrected the acting text.

Such is what I would make of it, but Dover Wilson deduces that the whole speech, and much else of the part of Pistol, was written for Falstaff, to whom Doll was last seen attached. Before erecting this mountain of conjecture I think he might have answered the note here in the Arden edition, which points out four other places where the text goes wrong over proper names; one of them calls the King of England "brother Ireland" (V.ii.2), and compared to that (which Dover Wilson believes to be a mistake in writing by Shakespeare, who must have been thinking about Essex, he says) I do not think a reasonable man need feel very solemn about these two dolls.

I also feel that, even if Shakespeare did first write this flabby blank verse for Falstaff and not for the now miserably deflated Pistol, we need not call in the machinery of censorship to explain why he changed his mind; if his first thoughts were so bad we had better keep to his second ones and be thankful. Maybe he did toy with the idea of taking Falstaff to Agincourt—he would feel the natural strength of any easy temptation—but we have no proof here that he wrote a whole draft of it.

II. The prologue to the second Act ends:

... the scene
Is now transported, gentles, to Southampton;
There is the playhouse now, there must you sit:
And thence to France shall we convey you safe
And bring you back, charming the narrow seas
To give you gentle pass; for if we may
We'll not offend one stomach with our play.
But, till the King come forth and not till then,
Unto Southampton do we shift our scene.

The next four scenes are in London, Southampton, London, and France, with the London ones describing first the illness and then the death of Falstaff. The final rhymed couplet, which follows another, whereas the prologues to the other four Acts all end with one rhymed couplet, seems a rather slack attempt to clear up a muddle and only succeeds in adding a contradiction (the Arden edition remarks, with psychological but perhaps not literal accuracy, that "the negative notion, being uppermost in his mind, thrusts itself in prematurely"). Dover Wilson deduces that the scenes about the death of Falstaff were added later. But he and the other people who hold this theory assume that comic scenes about Falstaff always existed in the play and had to be put somewhere, however different the first draft of them may have been. To prove that their position has been altered does nothing to prove that their content has been altered. It is rather curious, I think, that this simple fallacy is so convincing at first blush. You might perhaps argue that the dying Falstaff could not leave London, whereas the swashbuckling Falstaff could be shown in Southampton; but it would be almost necessary to start him off in London, if only for a farewell to the ladies. The first Act is just under four hundred lines long, and the average for the other four Acts, all a good bit longer, is just under six hundred. The technique of five "epic" prologues was new to Shakespeare, and obviously difficult to combine with his usual unbroken one; and all the Acts contain comic material except the first. Surely he might have tried to polish off Falstaff in Act I, and then found that the balance had gone wrong, as I think it would, and then corrected the second prologue rather casually. It seems to me equally possible that he had not thought of the solemn prologues as anything to do with the comedians, and had always intended a short banging first Act, and then pushed another couplet onto the prologue to Act II, of a baffling kind, merely because the Company objected that it didn't apply to them.

III. The first two arguments point out real confusions, but the third (for which Dover Wilson gives credit elsewhere) only marks a lack of understanding in the critics. The long scene IV.i, they say, must contain a huge interpolation. The King says he wants a council of lords at his tent, so they must come there "anon", but first he wants to think alone (this is at line 31); then he has three successive conversations in disguise with his troops; then a long soliloquy about how they don't understand his difficulties, because they have been saying that the King had no right to invade France and drag them into this hopeless situation (we must remember that they all expect death, and that the King has behaved well in refusing a separate escape); then Erpingham, who took the message before, comes back and says the lords are seeking him through the camp, and the King says they must be called back but adds graciously that he will be there before the messenger (this is about line 300); then all he does is to walk out to the audience and start off on another soliloquy—he is at last ready for his solitary prayer, and it is not at all hurried. A number of critics beside Dover Wilson have found this "awkward", therefore a mark of interpolation. The lords would find it awkward but the audience didn't; they thought it as clear as a bell. The sequence merely drives home the repeated argument of the previous plays that Henry had learned to be a good king by his experience of low life. Henry thought nothing of keeping the lords waiting while he talked to the troops; talking to the troops would even keep him from his prayers, but talking to experts on strategy never would. I do not believe that this very strong dramatic effect was an accidental result of enforced revision; I should be more inclined to call it playing to the gallery; and when Dover Wilson cannot see it he throws himself under serious suspicion, as an interpreter of Falstaff as well as of King Hal, because he is missing the whole popular story about the King he claims to rehabilitate.

Some other arguments for revision given by J. H. Walter in his article "With Sir John In It" (*MLR* July 1946) should perhaps he recognised here, but they seem to me unimportant. Fluellen doesn't use "p" for "b" in talking to Pistol (III.vi) but does so to Gower just afterwards, therefore the Pistol incident was added later (but he is on his dignity in talking to Pistol); we are promised "a little touch of Harry in the night" but don't get any of the fighting we expect, only morale-building (this seems to me an absurd objection; there was assumed to be much excitement in getting a stray contact with what Pistol calls "the lovely bully", and the morale for next day was more important than any skirmishing could be); in F though not in Q a comic capture by Pistol is impossibly made the first action of the battle (but if put later, it breaks the dramatic sequence); Fluellen at the beginning of Act V "relates to Gower an entirely fresh motive for his annoyance; it has no connection with Pistol's insults in III.vi" (Shakespeare always multiplies motives, and Pistol could be trusted to do the same; besides, Fluellen might not care to repeat the insults); at the end of this scene, in the "My Doll" speech, "Pistol's characteristic verse is completely absent" (of course it is; he is deflated and in soliloquy; is this Falstaff's characteristic verse, then?) and says he is old though, unlike Falstaff, he is not (he feels old); the Dauphin comes to the battle against his father's express orders (another detail to make his father look weak); there seems an intention to bring Henry and the Dauphin into opposition, but as it comes to nothing the Master of the Revels may have cut a degrading representation of royalty (then Shakespeare may have avoided going to such lengths as might have induced the Master of the Revels to make a cut); Fluellen was present when Williams told Henry about the glove, so ought to have recognised Williams later (but he is too excitable; the plot is not meant to be deep), and there is no reason why Henry should tell both separately to go and look for Gower (but it is only to make sure they meet and have an absurd quarrel; this bit of rough fooling, ending with tossing away some gold, is entirely "in character" with the Henry of the Falstaff scenes, and was very much needed to show him as the same man in his stern grandeur). I don't much like the play, and do not mean to praise it by defending the text; but the fashion for finding "joins" in the text has I think been carried to absurd lengths, though by people who agree with Dover Wilson rather than by himself, and I hope this tedious paragraph has proved it.

There is of course a reason why we find this struggle made to prove that Falstaff was meant to go to Agincourt. Dover Wilson, as I understand, was working on his edition of the Falstaff plays during the Second World War, and felt a natural irritation at any intellectualist fuss against a broad issue of patriotism. He felt that *Henry V* is a very good patriotic play, and the man Henry V is the ideal king, and Falstaff is a ridiculously bad man, and if you can't face that you had better wince away from the whole subject. Then when he came to carry out this programme he decided that the Victorian critics had put us all wrong about Falstaff by making a fuss about the report of Falstaff's death, at the beginning of *Henry V*; this had made them sentimentalise Falstaff. If it could be proved, then, that this description was only thrown in as a "job", to cheat the audience and hide a bit of truckling to high officials, then we need no longer smear false sentiment over him and (what is more) the modern royalist is safe in revering Hal as the ideal king. I agree that there has been some false sentiment about Falstaff, and it is a good thing to have the sturdy point of view of Dover Wilson tested out by a man who understands so well what tests it must pass. But he can't make it stand up; he is only flying from one extreme position to another; indeed, after stating his sentiment crudely, as I have just tried to do, I feel I can retort it back on him. When Dover Wilson winces away from recognising the positive merits of Falstaff, he is blinding himself to the breadth and depth of these plays, a thing which was recognised with great enthusiasm by their rough popular audiences at the time. What is really hard is to stretch one's mind all around Falstaff; he was felt to be a very rich joke, and one must never forget that in the course of argufying about him.

In trying to weaken the story of his death, Dover Wilson descends to such arguments as that "neither ague nor 'sweat' has anything to do with a broken heart", whereas when Henry IV dies the critic is eager to explain that apoplexy was not always due to over-eating but sometimes (as here) to cares of state. He jeers at the bad language in which Nym and Pistol, unsentimental characters one would think, echo the plain statement by Mrs Quickly, "the king has killed his heart", at which he dare not jeer. To be sure, their language is funny, and after Mrs Quickly's great description of his death they only say "Shall we shog?" like fleas. But they understand what has happened; the excuse for Hal made by Nym, "The King is a good king, but it must be as it may; he passes some humours and careers", is stuffed full of the obvious coarse sentiment about Hal which seems unable to enter Dover Wilson's mind. The idea is that he is like a race-horse in training; you must expect him to throw a rider. The hero is expected to kill his tutor, in fact it proves that the tutor had the real magical skill to produce a hero; we are to be reminded later that Alexander also killed his friend. It is no use for Dover Wilson to "play down" the death of Falstaff, because it was once for all "written up", and indeed he is in a logical dilemma there; how could the passage do what he supposes, swing over an audience resentful at being cheated, if they would only think it ridiculous? We can all imagine them taking it rather casually; it is Dover Wilson who needs to argue that they cried when Mrs Quickly brought out her comical remarks, as I daresay they did.

His attitude to the death, I think, could almost be called mean, which is very surprising from him, but one must realise that this comes from a conviction that the story demands reverence; that any idea of Shakespeare as "stating the case for Falstaff" should be met with indignation:

> Shakespeare plays no tricks with his public; he did not, like
> Euripides, dramatize the stories of his race and religion in order
> to subvert the traditional ideals those stories were first framed to
> set forth. Prince Hal is the prodigal, and his repentance is to be
> taken seriously; it is to be admired and commended ...

and so forth. It seems to me that, in this generous impulse of defence, he is rather underrating the traditional ideals of his race and religion. They do not force you to ascribe every grace and virtue to this rather calculating type of prodigal, merely because he defeated the French. So far from that, if you take the series as a whole (and here we are greatly indebted to E. M. W. Tillyard, another of these rather royalist critics), the main point of the story is that he was doomed because he was a usurper; France had to be lost again, and much worse civil wars had to break out, till at last the legitimate line was restored. The insistence on this is fierce in *Richard II* and both parts of *Henry IV*. Henry V has a very inspiriting kind of merit, and I think Shakespeare meant us to love him, though in an open-eyed manner; but the idea that Shakespeare presents him as an ideal king seems to me to show a certain lack of moral delicacy, which need not be described as a recall to the higher morality of an earlier world. And then again, it may be said that the audience were not thinking of such things; the intention of the series was a simple and patriotic one, whether "high" or not. But I should say that the popular story about the prodigal was itself complex (and by the way "Renaissance" not "medieval"), so that the whole of this defence for Hal is off the point—he did not need it. Of course I don't deny that there was plenty of patriotism about the thing, and that Shakespeare took that seriously, but it left room for other sentiments.

I think indeed that the whole Falstaff series needs to be looked at in terms of Dramatic Ambiguity, before one can understand what was happening in the contemporary audience; and I think that if this is done the various problems about Falstaff and Prince Hal, so long discussed, are in essence solved. Nor would this approach seem strange to Dover Wilson, who has done the most interesting recent work on the subject. Most of this essay has the air of an attack on him, but my complaints are supposed to show cases where he has slipped back into taking sides between two viewpoints instead of letting both be real. Slipped back, because on at least one occasion he uses explicitly and firmly the principle I want to recommend; and perhaps I will look more plausible if I begin with that illustration of it.

The question whether Falstaff is a coward may be said to have started the whole snowball of modern Shakespearean criticism; it was the chief topic of Morgann's essay nearly two hundred years ago, the first time a psychological paradox was dug out of a Shakespeare text. Dover Wilson, discussing the plot about the robbery in the first three scenes where we meet Falstaff, says that the question whether Falstaff sees through the plot against him, and if so at what point he sees through it—for instance, whether he runs away from the Prince on purpose or only tells increasingly grotesque lies to him afterwards on purpose—is *meant* to be a puzzle, one that the audience are challenged to exercise their wits over; and that this had an important practical effect (it is not a matter of deep intellectual subtlety of course) because you would pay to see the play again with your curiosity undiminished. The whole joke of the great rogue is that you can't see through him, any more than the Prince could. I think that Dover Wilson's analysis of the text here is the final word about the question, because he shows that you aren't meant to find anything more; the dramatic effect simply *is* the doubt, and very satisfying too. Dover Wilson is a rich mine of interesting points, and it seems rather parasitic of me to keep on repeating them as weapons against him; but it seems important to urge that the method he has established here should be tried out on adjoining cases.

However, I recognise that this approach is liable to become tiresomely intellectualistic; a man who takes it into his head that he is too smart to look for the answer, on one of these points, because he knows the author means to cheat him, is likely to miss getting any real experience from the play. Besides, the actor and producer have to work out their own "conception" of

Falstaff, in each case, and are sometimes felt to have produced an interesting or "original" one; it would be fatuous for the theoretical critic to say that they are merely deluding themselves, because there isn't any such thing. I do not mean that; the dramatic ambiguity is the source of these new interpretations, the reason why you can go on finding new ones, the reason why the effect is so rich. And of course there must be a basic theme which the contradictions of the play are dramatising, which some interpretations handle better than others; after planting my citadel on the high ground of the Absolute Void, I still feel at liberty to fight on the plains against Dover Wilson at various points of his detailed interpretation. But this way of putting it is still too glib. The basic argument of Dover Wilson is that the plays ought to be taken to mean what the first audiences made of them (and they took not merely a moral but a very practical view of the importance of social order and a good king). I agree with all of that, and merely answer that the reaction of an audience is not such a simple object as he presumed. No doubt he succeeds in isolating what the first audiences would find obvious; but we may still believe that other forces had to be at work behind Falstaff, both in the author and the audience which he understood, to make this figure as Titanic as we agree to find him; nor need we plunge for them deep into the Unconscious. The Falstaff plays were an enormous hit, appealing to a great variety of people, not all of them very high-minded, one would think. Obviously a certain amount of "tact" was needed, of a straightforward kind, to swing the whole of this audience into accepting the different stages of the plot. To bring out examples of this tact as evidence of the author's single intention, or of a single judgement which he wanted to impose on the audience, seems to me naive. So far from that, I think that on several occasions he was riding remarkably near the edge; a bit breathtaking it may have been, to certain members of the first audiences.

One cannot help feeling some doubt when Dover Wilson insists that Hal was never a "sinner", only a bit wild; especially when it becomes rather doubtful, as he goes on, what even the wildness may have consisted in. Not sex, we gather; it seems only old men like Falstaff go wrong like that. The same applies to drunkenness. Even the bishops in *Henry V*, Dover Wilson maintains, do not say that he has been converted, only that he has begun working hard (actually they say more); and even his father in reproaching him only speaks of sins in others which his wildness might encourage. Robbery, the reader is now to decide, he could not possibly have committed; to suppose that he even envisaged such a thing is to misread the whole play.

It is true that the early scenes of *I Henry IV* can be read as Dover Wilson does. I ought to admit this the more prominently because I said in my book *Pastoral* that "we hear no more" about the Prince's claim that he will repay the stolen money, which we do (III.iii.177). But after correcting this mistake I claim all the more that the dramatic effect is inherently ambiguous. Dover Wilson points out that we ought to consider the order of events on the stage, how the thing is planned to impress you; I warmly agree, but he only uses this rule for his own purpose. It is plain, surely, that we are put in doubt whether the Prince is a thief or not, at any rate in the early scenes; if you got a strong enough impression from those scenes that he was one, you would only regard the later return of the money as a last-minute escape from a major scandal (it has become possible for him because civil war has given him a well-paid appointment). No doubt, if you felt sure from the start that he couldn't really be one, the return of the money would act as laughing the whole thing off; but even so, the dramatist has put you through a bit of uncertainty about what he will ask you to believe. So to speak, an escape from a scandal is what happens to the audience, whether it happened to the Prince or not; and a dramatic structure of this kind assumes that at least some of the audience do not know the answer beforehand (in the old *Famous Victories*, for that matter, he simply is shown as stealing). It is therefore ridiculous, I submit, for a critic to argue heatedly that he has discovered the answer by a subtle analysis of the text. Such a critic, however, could of course turn round on me and say I am wrong to suppose it is "this kind of dramatic structure"; so far from that, he would say, he has shown the modern actor and producer how to make the play intelligible and coherent even to a fresh audience from the beginning. I therefore need to join in his labours, instead of calling them ridiculous; I need to show that the text is so arranged that the uncertainty can still not be dispelled even after the most careful study.

Among the first words of Falstaff, who is then alone with the Prince, he says "when thou art King, let not us that are squires of the night's body be called thieves of the day's beauty" and so on, and us is quite positively accepted by the Prince in his reply (whether for a joke or not) as including himself: "the fortune of us that are the, moon's men doth ebb and flow like the sea" and so on. Of course I am not pretending that this proves he is a thief; I give it as an example of the way the dramatist starts by making us think he may be a thief. The next point, as the jokes turn over; is a grave appeal from Falstaff: "Do not thou, when thou art King, hang a thief." Falstaff gets much of his fun out of a parody of moral advice, especially in these earlier scenes, and the point here must be that the Prince has no right to hang a thief because he is one himself. His reply (a very sufficient one) is that Falstaff will do it. Falstaff then inverts the obvious by upbraiding the Prince for leading him astray; he threatens to reform, and the Prince's answer is, "Where shall we take a purse tomorrow Jack?" Falstaff accepts this as if they are old partners in robbery, and is only concerned to defend his courage—"Zounds, where thou wilt, lad, I'll make one, an I do not, call me villain and baffle me." Poins now enters and announces a scheme for robbery, and when the Prince is asked if he will join he speaks as if the idea was absurdly outside his way of life—"Who, I rob? I a thief? Not I, by my faith." Falstaff has already assumed that the Prince knows this plan is being prepared ("Poins! Now we shall know if Gadshill have set a match"), and Poins is the Prince's own gentleman-in-waiting; however, Dover Wilson naturally makes the most of this brief retort:

> The proposal that the prince is to take part in the highway robbery is received at first with something like indignation, even with a touch of haughtiness, and only consented to when Poins intimates, by nods and winks behind Falstaff's back, that he is planning to make a practical joke of it.

The nods and winks are invented by the critic, of course (and printed in his text of the play), but they seem plausible enough; indeed the line, "Well, then, once in my days I'll be a madcap", reads like a rather coarse attempt to keep the respectable part of the audience from being too shocked. They are welcome to decide that the Prince is not really a thief after all. The point I want to make is that another part of the audience is still quite free to think he is one; indeed, this pretence of innocence followed immediately by acceptance (followed by further riddles) is just the way Falstaff talks himself. Poins then arranges the plot against Falstaff with the Prince, and finally the Prince makes his famous soliloquy, claiming that his present behaviour is the best way to get himself admired later on. I do not think that the words suggest he is doing nothing worse than play practical jokes on low characters. To be sure, the "base contagious clouds", the "foul and ugly mists", only *seem* to strangle the sun; you can still think the Prince innocent here; and he only describes his own behaviour as "loose". But then we hear about a reformation of a fault, And about an offence which must apparently be redeemed (though literally it is only time which must be redeemed). It seems to me that the balance is still being kept; you can decide with relief that surely after this he can't be a thief, or you can feel, if you prefer, he has practically admitted that for the present he is one! In one way, the doubt about the Prince doesn't matter, because the whole life he was sharing is displayed to us; but in another way, if a censorious man wants to claim this is a punishable libel against royalty, he will find that the text remains on a razor edge and never crosses it. This being what Shakespeare was clever enough to do, it is usual to "prove" that he must get off on one side or the other.

The more usual question about this soliloquy is whether it shows the

Prince as "callous and hypocritical", determined to betray his friends. Naturally Dover Wilson argues that it does not, because "it was a convention to convey information to the audience about the general drift of the play, much as a prologue did", and in any case at this stage of the play "we ought not to be feeling that Falstaff deserves any consideration whatever". I think this carries the "sequence" principle rather too far, if only because most people would know the "general drift" before they came; but I don't deny, of course, that the placing of this soliloquy is meant to establish Hal as the future hero as firmly a possible. Even so, I do not see that it does anything (whether regarded as a "convention" or not) to evade the obvious moral reflection, obvious not only to the more moralising part of the audience but to all of it, that this kind of man made a very unreliable friend. Surely the Elizabethans could follow this simple duality of feeling without getting mixed; it is inevitable that if you enjoy Falstaff you feel a grudge against the eventual swing-over of Hal, even though you agree that the broad plot couldn't be different. The real problems about the rejection do not arise here; we have no reason to presume it will come as a painful shock to his present friends (though "falsify men's hopes" may be a secret mark of the author's plan). I think a fair amount can be deduced about Shakespeare's own feelings for this kind of condescending patron; but in any case it was a commonplace of his period that the friendships of great men very often were unreliable. The whole thing seems to me in the sunlight, and for that matter the fundamental machinery seems rather crude, and perhaps it had to be to carry such a powerful conflict of judgement. There does not seem much for critics to disagree about.

Dover Wilson, however, feels that there is, because he wants to build up Hal as a high-minded creature of delicate sensibility. A brief scene with Poins (*II Henry IV*, II.ii) is made important for this purpose. We are told about Hal that:

> The kind of reserve that springs from absence of self-regard is in point of fact one of his principal characteristics, and such a feature is difficult to represent in dialogue ... We have no right to assume that Hal is heartless because he does not, like Richard II, wear his heart on his sleeve ... Why not ... give him a friend like Horatio to reveal himself? ... Shakespeare gives him Poins, and the discovery of the worthlessness of this friend is the subject of one of the most moving and revealing scenes in which the Prince figures. In view of all this, to assert as Bradley does that Hal is incapable of tenderness or affection except towards members of his own family is surely a quite unwarranted assumption.

Hal begins this scene by treating Poins with insolence, as one of the butts for his habit of contempt, and Poins answers (they have just got back from Wales as part of the civil war):

> How ill it follows, after you have laboured so hard, you should talk so idly! Tell me I how many good young princes would do so, their fathers being so sick as yours at this time is?

I can't see that this is an offensive retort; he is expected to keep his end up, nd there is not even an obvious insinuation that the Prince wants his father dead—he maybe being advised to recover favour. No doubt it could be acted with an offensive leer, but the usual tone in these scenes is merely a rough jeering. The Prince, however, becomes offended and says that his heart bleeds inwardly at his father's illness, but that he can't show it because he keeps bad company such as Poins. It seems a fair answer to this challenge when Poins says he would indeed think the Prince a hypocrite to show sorrow at the prospect of inheriting, "because you have been so lewd, and so much engraffed to Falstaff". "And to thee", says the gay Prince with his usual brutality. Now of course I agree that the scene is meant to tell the audience that Hal is starting to repent of his bad habits; it could not be more straightforward. It could be acted with a moody sorrow, but I don't think it need be; the main fact is that he is physically tired. But why are we supposed to think that he is "failed" by his friend in a pathetic manner, or shows affection to anyone not a member of his own family? The whole truth of this little scene, in its surly way, is to be so bare; it does nothing to put Poins in the wrong, and indeed lets him show a fair amount of dignity and good-humour; the Prince's feelings are dragging him away from his old companions, and no new fault of theirs needs to be shown. Surely Poins has much more difficulty than Hal in expressing delicate sentiments here; if he tried to condole with the Prince he would be rebuffed more harshly than ever. A production which made the Prince disillusioned at not getting sympathy would have to cut most of the words.

A more important argument of Dover Wilson for Hal is that it is extremely generous of him to let Falstaff get all the credit for killing Hotspur, especially because if Hal claimed his due he might become more acceptable to his father. Besides, he had promised his father he would kill Hotspur, and most men would feel their honour made the claim necessary. We are also told that the sudden fame thus acquired by the previously unknown Falstaff goes to his head and is the cause of the gradual nemesis which gathers throughout Part II. This seems to me a valuable idea, unlike the special pleading about the Poins scene, which would mislead an actor.

The trouble about the death of Hotspur, it seems to me, is that the story is deliberately left ambiguous, and we should not allow a learned argument to impose a one-sided answer. The lyrical language of Dover Wilson about the native magnanimity and high courtesy of the Prince, "which would seem of the very essence of nobility to the Elizabethans", really does I think bring out part of the intended stage effect at the end of the First Part, though the text is silent. The question is whether it is meant to go on reverberating all through the Second Part. To do the right thing at a dramatic moment is very different from going on telling an absurd and inconvenient lie indefinitely. Dover Wilson's view of the matter, I think, really would be picked on by spectators who preferred it that way, but other spectators could find quite different pointers. I do not want, therefore, to refute his view but to show that it is only one alternative, and I thus give myself an easy task.

The claim of Falstaff to have killed Hotspur is made to Prince Henry in the presence of Prince John, who says, "This is the strangest tale that e'er I heard." Prince Henry says:

> This is the strangest fellow, brother John.
> Come, bring your luggage nobly on your back.
> For my part, if a lie may do thee grace,
> I'll gild it with the happiest terms I have.

In Dover Wilson's edition, of course, "aside to Falstaff" has to introduce the last two lines. But I don't see Hal nipping about the stage to avoid being overheard by John, whom he despises; his business here is to stand midcentre and utter fine sentiments loud and bold. Just what lie was told, and what John made of it, we don't hear. It seems to me that the Second Part begins by throwing a lot of confusion into the matter, and that Dover Wilson merely selects points that suit him. At the start of the play three messengers come to the rebel Northumberland; the first with good news—the Prince has been killed outright and "(his) brawn,[1] the hulk Sir John" taken prisoner by Hotspur. Five other people are mentioned, but it is assumed that Falstaff was worth attention before he was believed to have killed Hotspur, and that even Hotspur has done well to capture him. The second messenger says that Hotspur is dead, the third that he was killed by the Prince. Dover Wilson admits this shows that the facts of his death "had been observed by at least one man", but adds that no other witness is quoted. But nobody at all, in the Second Part, says that Falstaff killed Hotspur. The King himself appears not to know that the Prince did it, says Dover Wilson; but the King has other things to talk about whenever we see him, and never implies that Hal can't fight. "The Lord Chief Justice grudgingly praises Falstaff's day's service at

Shrewsbury", says Dover Wilson, so he must think Falstaff killed Hotspur. He says that day's service "hath a little gilded over your night's exploits at Gad's Hill", which hardly fits a personal triumph over the chief enemy hero. Certainly people think he fought well somehow (perhaps because he got his troop killed to keep their pay); the joke of this is driven home in the Second Part when Coleville surrenders to him on merely hearing his name. But even Coleville does not say, what would be so natural an excuse, that he is surrendering to the man who killed Hotspur. What is more, Falstaff himself does not once say it, and he is not prone to hide his claims. Surely the solution of this puzzle is clear; Shakespeare is deliberately *not* telling us the answer, so that an ingenious argument which forces an answer out of the text only misrepresents his intention.

Consider how difficult it is for a dramatist, especially with a mass audience, to run a second play on the mere assumption that everybody in the audience knows the first one. On Dover Wilson's view, they are assumed to know that all the characters in the Second Part hold a wrong belief derived from the First Part, although the Second Part begins by letting a man express the right belief and never once lets anybody express the wrong belief. This is incredible. But if some of the audience are expected to *wonder* how the Prince's bit of chivalry worked out, their interest is not rebuffed; they may observe like Dover Wilson that Falstaff is getting above himself. In the main the theme is simply dropped; perhaps because some of the audience would not like the Prince to be so deeply in cahoots with Falstaff, perhaps because Shakespeare did not care to make the Prince so generous, but chiefly because it would only clutter up the new play, which had other material. The puzzle is not beyond resolution; it is natural to guess (if you worry about it) that the Prince waited till the truth came out and then said that Falstaff had been useful to him at the time—thus the claim of Falstaff did not appear a mere lie after the Prince had gilded it in his happiest terms, but had to be modified. This would have been the only sensible lie for the Prince to tell, and indeed Dover Wilson hints at it when he says people thought Falstaff had "slain, *or helped to slay*" Hotspur, which has no source in the text. You may now feel that I have made a lot of unnecessary fuss, when it turns out that I agree with Dover Wilson; but I think that his treatment ignores the dramatic set-up and the variety of views possible in the audience.

The next step in his argument is that Falstaff only becomes "a person of consideration in the army" because of the Prince's lies (whatever they were) about the Battle of Shrewsbury; "in Part I he is Jack Falstaff with his familiars; in Part II he is Sir John with all Europe". This is why he over-reaches himself; the final effect of the Prince's generosity at the end of Part I is that he is forced to reject Falstaff at the end of Part II. Now, on the general principle that one should accept all theories, however contradictory, which add to the total effect, this must certainly be accepted; it pulls the whole sequence together. But it must not be carried so far as to make Falstaff "nobody" at the beginning, because that would spoil another effect, equally important—for many of the audience. Falstaff is the first major joke by the English against their class system; he is a picture of how badly you can behave, and still get away with it, if you are a gentleman—a mere common rogue would not have been nearly so funny. As to the question of fact, of course, we are told he is a knight the first time he appears, and it is natural to presume he got knighted through influence; Shallow eventually lets drop that he started his career as page to the Duke of Norfolk. This is rather confusing now, as suggesting a social climb; but in those days to plant the boy in a great household gave him a good start in life, rather like the modern public school. The Stage History section of Dover Wilson's edition has some interesting hints, from both the eighteenth and twentieth centuries, to show that he has always been expected to be a gentleman; the dissentient voice is from a nineteenth-century American actor, who wrote a pamphlet claiming that he was right not to make the old brute a gentleman. Rather in the same way, I remember some American critic complaining that Evelyn Waugh shows an offensive snobbery about Captain Grimes, since he despises him merely for not being a real gentleman. So far from that, the whole joke about Grimes is that he is an undeniable public school man, and therefore his invariably appalling behaviour must always be retrieved by the other characters, though it always comes as a great shock to them. This English family joke, as from inside an accepted class system, may well not appeal to Americans, but in the case of Falstaff I think English critics have rather tended to wince away from it too.

Maintaining that he was nobody till after the Battle of Shrewsbury, Dover Wilson has to explain his presence at the council of commanders just before it, and says it was simply because Shakespeare needed him on the stage. This lame argument would not apply to the Elizabethan stage. At the actual council he only makes one unneeded joke; he is needed for talk with the Prince afterwards, in what our texts call the same scene, but the back curtain will already have closed on the royal coat-of-arms and so forth; Falstaff could simply walk onto the apron. He is at the council because that adds to the joke about him, or rather because some of the audience will think so. However, it is clear anyhow that the Prince brought him; the battle itself gives a more striking case of this line of argument from Dover Wilson. A. C. Bradley had argued that Falstaff shows courage by hanging around in the battle till the Prince kills Hotspur, and the reply has to be: "To establish his false claim to the slaying of Hotspur he must be brought into the thick of the fight." Surely this makes Shakespeare a much less resourceful dramatist than he is; even I could think of a funny device to trick the great coward into his great opportunity, after he had imagined he had found a safe place. Shakespeare does not "have to" give false impressions; and what we do gather from Falstaff is that he regards a battle as a major occasion for misusing his social position (e.g. "God be thanked for these rebels; they offend none but the virtuous"). I don't deny that those spectators who would resent the social satire are given an opportunity to evade it, and take him as the "cowardly swashbuckler" of the Latin tradition; but they aren't given very much. Over the crux at the start of the Second Part, I think, the indignant special pleading of Dover Wilson reaches actual absurdity:

> The special mention of [Falstaff's] capture in the false report of the battle that first reaches the ears of Northumberland ... are all accounted for by the indecent stab which the dastard gives the corpse of Hotspur as it lies stricken on the bleeding field.

To be sure, Falstaff "goes a bit too far" when he does that; it is his role. (By the way, the reason why we feel it so strongly is that the rebels have been made to look rather better than the royal family.) But really, how are we to imagine that the sight of Falstaff stabbing a recumbent Hotspur (in another play) made a messenger report that Hotspur was safe and Falstaff captured? No doubt almost any confusion can happen to a real messenger, but how can a dramatist expect his successive audiences to invent the extraordinary subtle confusion imputed here? The fact is, surely, that these pointers represent. Falstaff as already a prominent figure, though an embarrassingly scandalous one; they could easily be ignored by members of the audience who were using a different line of assumption, but they would give great assurance to members who started with this one.

The interesting thing here, I think, is that Dover Wilson is partly right; but in the next case I think he is simply wrong. Nobody, whichever way he took up Falstaff, was meant to think him too abject a coward even to be able to bluster. Dover Wilson refuses to let him drive Pistol out of the inn; chiefly, I suppose, because his theory needs Falstaff to be degenerating in Part II. At II.iv.187 Doll wants Pistol thrown out, so Falstaff says "Quoit him down, Bardolph", and Bardolph says "Come, get you downstairs", but Pistol still makes a threatening harangue; Falstaff then asks for his rapier (197) and himself says "Get you downstairs", while Doll says "I pray thee, Jack, do not draw"; then the Hostess makes a fuss about "naked weapons", then Doll says "Jack, be quiet, the rascal's gone. Ah, you whoreson little valiant villain, you", then the Hostess says "Are you not hurt i' the groin? Methought a' made a shrewd thrust at your belly"; Falstaff says to Bardolph, who must return, "Have you turned him out of doors?" and Bardolph says "Yea, sir, the rascal's drunk. You have hurt him, sir, in the shoulder"; Falstaff says "A rascal, to brave me!" and Doll in the course of a fond speech says he is as valorous as Hector of Troy. It is unusual to have to copy out so much text to answer a commentator. This is the textual evidence on which Dover Wilson decides that Falstaff dared not fight Pistol at all, and he actually prints as part of the play two stage directions saying that Bardolph has got to do all the work. It must be about the most farcical struggle against the obvious intentions of an author that a modern scholarly editor has ever put up.

This view of Falstaff is supported by a theory about Doll, rather obscure to me: "We have, I think, to look forward to 19th-century French literature to find a match for this study of mingled sentimentality and brutal insentience, characteristic of the prostitute class." I thought at first, not going further afield than *The Beggar's Opera*, that this meant some criminal plot for gain; but the audience could not know of it (this is the first we hear of Pistol), and I suppose it means that both she and Mrs Quickly like watching two men fight. The argument, therefore, is that she jeers at Falstaff for shirking the fight she had encouraged, so this proves he didn't fight. After Pistol has gone he boasts, "the rogue fled from me like quicksilver" and she answers (on his knee) "I'faith, and thou followedst him like a church." Dover Wilson has to push "aside" into the text before this remark and "sits on his knee" afterwards, before he can let it go on with her praise of his courage. She does not hide her remarks from him anywhere else. I take it she means that he followed like a massive worthy object, though too fat to do it fast; to find sadism here seems to me wilful. The same trick is used against Mrs Quickly in *Henry V*, II.i.36, over the textual crux "if he be not hewn now", which Dover Wilson refuses to change to "drawn"—"as Nym draws Q screams to her bridegroom to cut the villain down, lest the worst befall". But this frank blood-thirst is not at all in her style, and if it was she could hardly keep her house open. It seems that this picture of the ladies is drawn from the sombre vignette at the end of the Second Part, just before the rejection, when they are dragged across the front stage by beadles because "the man is dead that you and Pistol beat among you". Dover Wilson is breaking his own rules about the order of scenes, if he makes this imply that they were in a plot with Pistol at his first appearance.[2] What we do gather before his entry is that they are afraid he may kill somebody in the house, and know they will get into trouble if he does. He starts threatening death as soon as he comes, whether as a bawdy joke or not ("I will discharge upon her, Sir John, with two bullets"). Also Bell had just begun a pathetic farewell to Falstaff, who is going to the wars; she is cross at their being interrupted. Also she came on for this scene already elegantly unwell from too much drink. I need to list the reasons for her anger, because Dover Wilson comments on the line "Sweet knight, I kiss thy neaf" that Pistol "is ready to go quietly, but Doll will have thrown him out"—that is, she insists on having a fight. It is hard for Mrs Quickly to turn her own customers out, and Doll will be helping her to avoid serious danger if she can scare the bully away permanently; this, if anything, is what is underlined by the beadle scene, though by the time of *Henry V*, as we needn't be surprised, Pistol has become a valuable protector. Such is what I would call her motive, if I looked for one, but she may well simply be too drunk and cross to realise that he is already going quietly. Either way there is no need to drag in sadism.

Dover Wilson has still another argument from this scene to prove Falstaff's increasing degeneration. After Pistol has been thrown out the Prince arrives and eavesdrops on Falstaff, who is making some rather justified remarks against him, so that Falstaff again has to find a quick excuse; he says he dispraised the Prince before the wicked, that the wicked might not fall in love with him. "He now whines and cringes on a new note, while he is forced to have recourse to defaming Doll in turn, a shift which is neither witty nor attractive." To be sure, the words "corrupt blood" may imply that she has syphilis; it is only the editor's stage direction which makes him point at her, but the idea does give her a professional reason for displaying anger. He has long been saying he has it himself, so there doesn't seem any great betrayal in saying that she has it too (he does imply it, more gently a few lines later. In the next play she has to retire to hospital.) I imagine that the point of the joke is to insinuate that the Prince has it; thus it is too late to save him from the wicked, and too late for him to think he can cure himself by saying he has reformed. Falstaff needs to forestall being laughed at, as an ugly old man found making love. So he welcomes the Prince among his fellow-sufferers. The badinage in these circles is always a bit rough, and I don't deny that it is hard to know how you are expected to take it. But in this case we have an immediate pointer from an "aside" by Poins, who as usual is in a plot with the Prince against Falstaff. (By the way, this shows what nonsense it is to suppose that the Prince made a sudden pathetic discovery of the worthlessness of Poins only two scenes before, a decisive step in his life, we are to believe; they are on just the same footing as ever.) Poins says, "My lord, he will drive you out of your revenge, and turn all to a merriment, if you take not the heat." How could this be said if Falstaff was only whining and cringing, or even if he were picking a serious quarrel with the ladies? At the end of the scene, when he is called off to the war as an important officer (a dozen captains are knocking at every tavern door for Sir John Falstaff, sweating with eagerness—so says Peto, and Bardolph corroborates about the dozen; and however much the editor insists that this is only "a summons for neglect of duty" it still treats Falstaff as worth a lot of trouble in an emergency), both the women speak with heart-breaking pathos about how much they love him, and the text requires Doll to shed tears. If we critics are to call this a "calculated degradation", I do not know what we expect our own old age to be like. The truth is, surely, that we never see the old brute more triumphant; doomed you might already feel him, but not degraded.

However, I do not want simply to defend Falstaff against the reproaches of the virtuous, represented by Dover Wilson; it was always an unrewarding occupation, and even the most patient treatment of detail, in such a case, has often failed to convince a jury. I think, indeed, that Dover Wilson's points are well worth examining, being of great interest in themselves; but, what is more, I think many of them are thrown in with a broadminded indifference as to whether they fit his thesis or not. Some of them seem to me rather too hot on my side of the question, and this may serve to remind us of what is so easily forgotten in a controversy, that the final truth may be complex. For example, he has a fine remark on Mrs Quickly's description of Falstaff's death. She says she felt his feet, and then his knees, and so upward and upward, and all as cold as any stone. The only comment that would occur to me is that this dramatist can continue unflinchingly to insert bawdy jokes while both the speaker and the audience are meant to be almost in tears. Dover Wilson, taking a more scholarly view, remarks that the detail is drawn from the death of Socrates; the symptoms are those of the gradual death from hemlock. But whatever can he have intended by this parallel? Surely it has to imply that Falstaff like Socrates was a wise teacher killed by a false accusation of corrupting young men; his patient heroism under injustice, and how right the young men were to love him, are what we have to reflect on. I hope that somebody pointed out this parallel to Shakespeare; he did, I believe, feel enough magic about Falstaff for it to have given him a mixed but keen pleasure; but that seems as far as speculation can reasonably go. To make it an intentional irony really would be like Verrall on Euripides, and it would blow Dover Wilson's picture of Falstaff into smithereens. And yet, though it seems natural to talk like this, I am not certain; the idea that Falstaff was a good tutor *somehow* was a quite public part of the play, and might conceivably have been fitted out with a learned reference. He has a similar eerie flash of imagination about a stage direction in *Henry V*, where the heroes of Agincourt are described as "poor troops". He rightly complains that modern editions omit the epithet, an important guide to the producer; the story would be mere boasting if it did not emphasise that their victory was a hairbreadth escape after being gruelled. But then he goes on: "Did the 'scarecrows' that Falstaff led to

Shrewsbury return to the stage?" It seems rather likely, for the convenience
of a repertory company, that they did; but what can it mean, if we suppose it
to mean anything? What is recalled is the most unbeatable of all Falstaff's
retorts to Henry—"they'll fit a pit as well as better; tush, man, mortal men,
mortal men". Falstaff has just boasted that he took bribes to accept such bad
recruits ("I have misused the King's press damnably"—and the audience
would not think him a coward here, but that it took a lot of nerve to be so
wicked) and he boasts later that he got them killed to keep their pay (it is
before his success has "degraded" him) but this makes his reply all the more
crashing, as from one murderer to another: "that is all you Norman lords
want, in your squabbles between cousins over your loot, which you make an
excuse to murder the English people". This very strong joke could be
implied in *Henry IV*, as part of a vague protest against civil war, but to recall
it over Henry's hereditary claim to France would surely be reckless; besides,
the mere return of those stage figures could not carry so much weight. But I
believe that thoughts of that kind were somewhere in the ambiance of the
play, however firmly they were being rebutted; it is conceivable that Dover
Wilson here is being wiser than either of us know.

One gets rather the same effect, I think, from his remarks about killing
the prisoners at Agincourt, though here he is making a sturdy defence, not a
bold conjecture. The position is that the King comes out in IV.vi, "with
prisoners", and says his side has done well but must be careful; a pathetic
anecdote is told; then an alarum sounds, and the King immediately (without
enquiry) says:

> The French have reinforced their scattered men:
> Then every soldier kill his prisoners!
> Give the word through.

Dover Wilson insists that this has been misunderstood because the stage
direction "with prisoners" has regularly been omitted—it should be made
clear on the stage that there are more prisoners than captors. But this needed
to be said, not shown; the chief effect of bringing the prisoners onto the stage
could only be to make the audience in cold blood see the defenceless men
killed—indeed, that is clearly the reason why the editors left it out. He goes
on to argue, convincingly I think, that this incident was used in the
chronicles Shakespeare drew from as an example of Henry's power to
recognise a necessity at once, and that the French chroniclers do not blame
him for it, though Holinshed is apologetic. But we are concerned with the
effect on an audience, and here the very next words, which are from Fluellen
to Gower, say:

Kill the boys and the luggage! tis expressly against the law of arms, tis as arrant a piece of knavery, mark you now, as can be offert.

Gower remarks that *because* the Frenchmen escaping from the battle have killed unarmed boys in the King's tent *therefore* the King "most worthily hath caused every soldier to cut his prisoner's throat. O, tis a gallant king." These experts of course have just walked on for a new scene, and do not know, as we do, that it was Henry who started killing unarmed men, not the French. "Shakespeare, who might have omitted it", says Dover Wilson, "offers no apologies, but sets the device in a framework of circumstances which makes it seem natural and inevitable." This seems to me comic; the framework not only does nothing to make us think the killing of helpless people necessary but condemns it fiercely. (Even Dover Wilson reflects that it might be rather a waste of time, under a sudden counter-attack, if one hadn't got machine-guns.) Fluellen goes on to compare Henry in detail to Alexander the Big, mispronouncing it as PIG, and the final parallel is that as Alexander killed his friend Cleitus "in his ales and his angers" so Henry—well, he only turned Falstaff away, and wasn't drunk at the time. We have already seen Nym taking the same view—one must expect a hero to be ungrateful and violent; but this is a remarkable time to recall it. Henry soon comes back saying he is angry and again demanding that prisoners be killed; and even Dr Johnson, the patron saint of Dover Wilson's criticism, found it absurd that a man who had just killed all his prisoners should express anger by trying to kill them again. The Quarto of 1600, described by Dover Wilson as "a 'reported' version, probably supplied by traitor-actors, of performances—perhaps in a shortened form for provincial audiences—of the play as acted by Shakespeare's company", not only gives the whole prisoner sequence but adds a delighted "coupla gorge" from the coward Pistol, as he prepares to join in this really safe and agreeable form of warfare. He was already practising the phrase (almost his only acquirement in the French language) before he left London, so that it is firmly associated with his particularly sordid point of view; and if we are to believe that he is shown starting the massacre the play does everything it can to make the audience nauseated by such actions, even before it has them denounced by Fluellen. I do not see that Dover Wilson makes out his case at all (the question of course is not about the historical behaviour of the Prince, for whom the opinion of the French chroniclers is a weighty support, but about an effect on the Elizabethan stage). If we accept the text we must think (1) that Shakespeare's disgust against Henry explodes here, (2) that Henry's treatment of Falstaff is recalled as part of a denunciation of his brutality and deceitfulness in general, and (3) that Shakespeare, in his contempt for his brutal audience, assumes that nobody will realise what he is doing. I agree with Dover Wilson that this vehement picture is improbable; I want the conflict of forces in the play to be real, but not secret and explosive in this way.

Surely there is an easy escape from the dilemma, which must have been suggested before. Shakespeare first followed the chroniclers about Henry's decision, without making any accusations against the French; then he felt this made Henry look too brutal and "got round it", just as he contradicted the statement of Holinshed that Henry sacked Harfleur. Instead of saying that Henry started killing unarmed men he said the French did; this propaganda device is familiar nowadays—you do not simply ignore the story against your side, in case it is floating in the minds of your hearers, but contrive to plant it on the other side. This required adding both Fluellen's remarks and Henry's speech about being angry, but cutting only the single line "Then every soldier kill his prisoners." We have then to suppose that the Company ignored the omission mark, not seeing the point of it, and that the actor of Pistol added his usual gag. We are making them pretty stupid, and assuming that Shakespeare didn't much bother over what they did with his texts; but Dover Wilson is among those who have made a strong case for thinking so. Now, after making the incident more reasonable in this way, I still think that Shakespeare must have been in a mixed frame of mind when he wrote this comic speech of Fluellen, as part of a plan to make Henry appear milder than he was. Saving Henry's face was getting to be rather an effort, surely. I do not mean that Shakespeare was secretly opposed to his work, still less that he was trying to insinuate a criticism of Henry for the wiser few; I think he felt it a duty to get into the right mood for the thing, and could manage it, but found he had to watch himself, and go back and correct himself—any author who has done propaganda knows this frame of mind. Such at least is what I would make of it, but I am not certain that the view of Dover Wilson, so much more startling than he realises, is not the true one.

Where the possibilities are so complicated, I think, a critic needs to hold on to the basic material, the *donnée*, as Dover Wilson advises. But one also needs to realise that this story of a prodigal who became a hero was already very rich when Shakespeare took it over or "cashed in on it"; it was the most popular part of the History series and carried a variety of implications, all the more, because it was taken easily as a joke. To re-plan the trilogy on the basis of leaving some of them out, and that is really what Dover Wilson is up to, is sure to mislead; also I find it odd of him to claim that a historical point of view is what makes him treat Falstaff as medieval rather than Renaissance. Of course this does not make me deny that the medieval elements are still there. Falstaff is in part simply a "Vice", that is, an energetic symbol of impulses which most people have to repress, who gives pleasure by at once releasing and externalising them. His plausibility is amusing, and his incidental satire on the world can be accepted as true, but what he stands for is recognised as wrong, and he must be punished in the end. Also (as a minor version of this type) he is in part the "cowardly swashbuckler", of the Latin play rather than the Miracle Play, whose absurdity and eventual exposure are to comfort the audience for their frequent anxiety and humiliation from "swashbucklers". As part of the historical series, he stands for the social disorder which is sure to be produced by a line of usurpers, therefore he is a parallel to the rebel leaders though very unlike them; the good king must shake him off in the end as part of his work of reuniting the country. Also I think there is a more timeless element about him, neither tied to his period in the story nor easily called Renaissance or medieval, though it seems to start with Shakespeare; he is the scandalous upper-class man whose behaviour embarrasses his class and thereby pleases the lower class in the audience, as an "exposure"; the faint echoes of upper-class complaints about him, as in the change of his name, are I think evidence that this was felt.[3] For these last two functions, cowardice is not the vice chiefly required of him. But surely we have no reason to doubt that there were other forces at work behind the popularity of the myth, which can more directly be called Renaissance; something to do with greater trust in the natural man or pleasure in contemplating him, which would join on to what so many critics have said about "the comic idealization of freedom". I think it needs putting in more specific terms, but I don't see that Dover Wilson can be plausible in denying it altogether.

The most important "Renaissance" aspects of Falstaff, I think, can be most quickly described as nationalism and Machiavellianism; both of them make him a positively good tutor for a prince, as he regularly claims to be, so that it is not surprising that he produced a good king or that his rejection, though necessary, could be presented as somehow tragic. The Machiavellian view (no more tied to that author then than it is now, but more novel and shocking than it is now) is mainly the familiar one that a young man is better for "sowing his wild oats", especially if he is being trained to "handle men". The sort of ruler you can trust, you being one of the ruled, the sort that can understand his people and lead them to glory, is one who has learned the world by experience, especially rather low experience; he knows the tricks, he can allow for human failings, and somehow between the two he can gauge the spirit of a situation or a period. The idea is not simply that Falstaff is debauched and tricky, though that in itself made him give Hal experience, and hardly any price was too high to pay for getting a good ruler, but that he had the breadth of mind and of social understanding which the

Magnanimous Man needs to acquire. This is very unmedieval, seems a lower-class rather than an upper-class line of thought and is, of course, militantly anti-Puritan, as we can assume the groundlings tended to be, and Falstaff can be regarded as a parody of it rather than a coarse acceptance of it by Shakespeare, but surely it is obviously present indeed I imagine that previous critics have thought it too obvious to be worth writing down—there was no need to, till Dover Wilson began preaching at us about his Medieval Vice and his Ideal King. After rejecting Falstaff Henry continues to show the popular touch and so forth that Falstaff taught him; indeed, *Henry V* limits itself rather rigidly to describing the good effects of this training, for example in his treatment of the troops and of the Princess.

In looking for the basic legend about King Hal, before Shakespeare took it over and invented Falstaff to illustrate it, we are fortunate to have *The Famous Victories of Henry V*, published in 1596 but probably a good deal older. It is a vigorous and worthy object (too often recalled with contempt, I think); very much "in the school" of Shakespeare, even if the school taught Shakespeare and not he it, especially in the power to make homely but heart-piercing jokes. There is no single line in Shakespeare about Henry as strong and funny, granting that the Prince is somehow loved, as "I dare not say he is a thief, but he is one of those taking fellows". Maybe it is a kind of luck for the author that the pun on "taking" is still obvious, but it is a kind of luck he has often; the style is very direct. However, there is no great need here to praise it; the question is what Shakespeare accepted and what he altered.

Here we come to the main point, which I fear I have approached too slowly. Henry V was considered the first national King of England, the first who wasn't really a Norman, speaking French, and modern historians agree in so far as he was the first King of England to use the English language for his official correspondence—as would easily be learned by anyone in a position to look up the documents. The only dates one seems to need are that Agincourt was in 1415 and Chaucer died in 1400; we may imagine that the real Henry only accepted something which had happened, but the legend gave him the credit for it. Obviously, they thought, he refused to do his French lessons; he must have hung about the pubs with somebody like Falstaff, and decided, very properly, not to learn anything except what he learned there. That is why you get so much fuss about the French language in *Henry V*, whereas the plays usually ignore any language problem. The basic point of Henry's first soliloquy, saying that he will be more admired later because he is despised now, is not a cynical calculation to betray his friends but a modestly phrased reassurance that he is learning how to be a national king. All this made a much more serious defence of Falstaff, in the mind of a realistic spectator, than any romantic idea that he had improved the

Prince by showing him low life; to have made the monarchy national was a decisively important thing, however absurdly bad Falstaff was otherwise, however much he needed to be rejected;[4] and, for that matter, the story does not need us to suppose that Henry was very good to start with, either. The whole trilogy about Falstaff and the Prince, I think, becomes painfully confusing, because your sympathies are torn between two bad characters, unless you regard it as showing how a useful development occurred; then it can be enjoyed freely.

Some critics have suggested that Shakespeare privately loved Falstaff but, like the Prince, betrayed him in public or when taking an official view of affairs; no doubt that feeling was somehow present, for many of the audience as well as for Shakespeare; but even from a political angle Falstaff stood for something valuable—I do not deny that it seemed absurd to say so, but one felt there was "something in it". Nor was this sentiment at all furtive, because it fitted so naturally into the official Tudor propaganda. That the Tudors were the first really national dynasty was a regular plank in their propaganda. Henry fitted in, apart from using the English language, because like them he was partly Welsh, and the claim is made for him several times in *Henry V*. The Tudors were supporting their doubtful right to the throne (as Tillyard pointed out in *Shakespeare's History Plays*) by a claim that their Welsh ancestors were the real British line, with magical virtues about them, involving Brutus and King David of Jerusalem himself, and anyhow older than the Saxon invaders let alone the Norman ones. I suspect that the Elizabethans did not take this line of talk as solemnly as they sometimes pretended, and it is mixed up here with a more rational desire to forget old quarrels so that the island can be united; but antiquarian arguments were serious to them—for that matter, the scholarly rediscovery of how to read Anglo-Saxon legal documents was one of the things that cut off Charles I's head. I suspect that Shakespeare was giving the Government, as well as the popular audience, a great deal of what they wanted, so much that they would put up with some things they didn't want (it is hard to see why else the Company escaped after the performance of *Richard II* for the Essex rebels); perhaps his apparent subservience to the Tudor Myth, which anyhow came from a genuine horror of civil war, worked out as giving him more freedom. In any case, it was not mere rhetoric at the beginning of *I Henry VI*, when the characters were bemoaning the death of Henry V, to make them say:

England ne'er had a King until his time.

This was an idea that the audience had already taken into its head. He held a position rather like that of John the Baptist; he was the forerunner of the

Tudors. I realise that this is a bit remote from the needs of a modern producer, because he cannot get it across to his audience, but it does I think remove the suggestion of false sentiment against which Dover Wilson very understandably revolted.

One tends now to think of the wooing scene of Henry with Katherine, at the end of *Henry V*, as a sickeningly obvious bit of film dialogue; the good young millionaire democrat can immediately melt the fastidious aristocratic foreign beauty by the universal power of his virile or earth-touching mode of approach. Dr Johnson and Voltaire did not find it sickeningly obvious but implausibly low; Henry could not have been such a hayseed, they thought, even if Katherine could have liked it. Shakespeare did not invent the incident; there is a shorter and less aggressive version of it in *The Famous Victories*, and one might argue that his epilogue to *II Henry IV* promises the audience that the expected scene will be treated fully. I suspect that all later examples of it are derived from the Hal Legend, so that it is a specific invention, like matches; but at the start it had to have a positive point, not merely its later rather mysterious background of democracy or something. It was a kind of hyperbole to suppose that the Norman Prince could not talk his own language to his Norman bride (instead of making the end of the play flabby, as Dr Johnson thought); and he was rationally admired for the incapacity because it proved he had changed his allegiance. There is also an idea that only his wild oats, or only Falstaff, could have taught him this; but the main idea is the patriotic one. Also, even here, the audience is not expected simply to "identify" themselves with Hal; his boasts about what a fine fighter his son by Katherine will be are bound to strike a chill, because everybody knew that Henry VI was going to be the final disaster for his usurping line. Dover Wilson points out in his notes that there is "an irony" here, but does not seem to consider what an irony is used for. Even in his triumph Hal could only be a forerunner of the real British Tudors.

We tend to forget that the rising power of England, in Shakespeare's time, was still rather embarrassed to have been so long ruled by an invading dynasty who spoke French; but that is only because the English are good at forgetting such things. *Henry V* itself has one or two memories of the Norman Conquest which have been neglected; I only noticed them myself when looking over the text after seeing the British wartime version of the play, to find where the cuts stood out. One would expect that the rougher propaganda of earlier days had left in some damaging admissions, but that the national hero had at any rate been patriotic all right. But when Henry is answering the French Ambassador who brought the insulting tennis balls something much odder turns up. He boasts that he will conquer and rule France, his proper heritage as a Norman, and in answering the Dauphin's jeer at his life he says he naturally lived like a beast when he had only England to live in:

> We never valued this poor seat of England,

but he will live in an entirely different way when he has got hold of the much more valuable bit of property called France. Critics, so far as they attend to this, placidly call it irony; and no doubt a contemporary of Shakespeare could take it that way too. Nor is it then flat, because a patriot should always regard his country as weak but heroic, certain to win but only certain because of its virtues. But surely it would be a natural reflection to many in the first audiences that a feudal lord really did think of a country like this, without any irony. Surely it is odd, when the dramatist clearly wants to make the hero patriotic, that he gives the audience such a very strong and plausible case where he isn't. It seems to me riding very near the edge, in that audience, to make the ever-popular Hal say (may I repeat what Dover Wilson's Ideal King said),

> We never valued this poor seat of England.

Of course I willingly agree that the answer is merely the familiar one of dramatic suspense; this remark comes early in the play, and by the end of it we have got Hal being almost shamingly homey; if he can't talk French, he obviously can't move as a feudal lord from London to Paris. Also it is rather an odd kind of dramatic suspense, because the audience already knew that Henry wasn't this kind of feudal lord; it was only a kind of playing at saying the tactless thing. But it would be very noticeable to the audience, and the author did not mean it to be thrown away at once by the nods and winks at the audience which Dover Wilson is so fond of inserting in his stage directions. That Hal turned out to be the first "English" king, unlike his ancestors, was to be presented with drama, and the dramatist gives it a certain violence (though of a kind which could be explained away) by recalling the doubt which would have appeared real to a fifteenth-century audience, and perhaps did not appear very unreal to a sixteenth-century one either.

You cannot call it far-fetched of me, in looking at this play, to argue that the English were conscious of having been ruled by the French, because the Dauphin is made to say it very firmly about the English lords:

> Shall a few sprays of us,
> The emptying of our fathers' luxury,
> Our scions, put in wild and savage stock,

Spirt up so suddenly into the clouds,
And overlook their grafters?

The Duke of Bourbon follows with the line

Normans, but bastard Normans, Norman bastards,

a comment on the English aristocracy which has more carrying power in the
theatre than on the printed page. Soon after, the Dauphin reports that "our
madams" say the cross-breeding has made the English lords more virile than
the French ones. It is all rather coarse propaganda, but there is no doubt
what it means. One must remember that Queen Elizabeth herself was felt to
have done a fair amount to exclude the older aristocracy from power, and
surround herself by lords of her own creation.

The answer of the play to the surprise of the Dauphin is that the British
islands were becoming united and therefore strong; the idea is not simply
that the English were determined to enslave the French, because of a very
obscure argument about the rules of succession among Norman conquerors.
This "jingo" aspect of a superficially rather coarse play (rightly described by
the Germans around 1914 as "good war reading") is a bit embarrassing, and
I think it is mostly removed if you remember a political background which is
not part of the text. The English had been in doubt during the sixteenth
century whether to have military adventures in Europe or to compete with
Spain in adventures for new worlds. Elizabeth's father had made a fool of
himself in Europe, which could not be said publicly, but Elizabeth herself
had quietly and penuriously shown a preference for new worlds; it would not
appear recklessly unpatriotic, even in *Henry V*, to insinuate that there was
something to be said for her policy. Indeed, this was the only possible line of
expansion; if the English had kept France, a modern reader is likely to reflect,
they would soon have been ruled from Paris; and for that matter if they had
kept America (later) they would soon have been ruled from Washington—
the two great losses secured national independence. I am not saying that
Shakespeare was wise about this controversy, or even right (he seems
remarkably little interested in new worlds, apart from some good jokes
against them in *The Tempest*; however, in the *Merchant of Venice* he can see the
romance of making London a world trading centre like Venice all right); only
that this was the context of political controversy in which he was building up
his enormously popular stage machine. After all, the only claim of Hal to
France is that he is a Norman not an Englishman, and almost the only thing
he is praised for is learning to be an Englishman not a Norman. Shakespeare,
I think, felt that one ought to be patriotic and yet that one needn't pull a long

face about not ruling France; the international angle was all right somehow, though one had better keep on the fence a bit, whereas the danger of civil war at home wasn't. In the middle of his play of conquest, therefore, he can cheerfully let Hal admit to God that he has no right to conquest, and only beg for the escape of these particular devoted troops (who have been questioning the rights of the war):

> Not today, O Lord,
> No, not today, think not upon the fault
> My father made in compassing this crown,

This is the most genuine thing Henry ever says (some critic argues that even now he was trying to cheat God over the deal, if you look into the facts about his offer of chantries, but that is off the point I think); and we are to regard it as accepted by God, therefore successful in saving these troops; but it does not, of course, remove the doom from Hal himself or from his usurping lineage, or even perhaps from the Norman-English claim to rule France, and he never prays for any such enormous thing. I would not want to sentimentalise the Prince, but "Not today, O Lord" really is a noble prayer when you realise how harshly limited he knows it to be; he is hardly praying for anybody except the individual troops he has just been talking to. (Naturally it was cut from the wartime film production.) And by being genuine there (as I understand the feeling) he gets not only what he asked but a magical extra gift, never known to himself but worth celebrating for ever, as he says the battle itself will be; not the conquest of France but the gradual unification of his own islands. They still had to go through a terrible slow mill, because God grinds down small; the Wars of the Roses had still to come after his early death; but Hal deserved his moment of triumph because he had shown the right way or at any rate seen things in their right proportions, before his time. That is the "religious" or "patriotic" feeling about Hal (one can hardly say which), and I feel it myself; it is a real enough thing, though grand claims need not be made for it. On this view, of course, the play isn't interested in conquering France, but in showing a good leader getting troops from different parts of the islands to work together in a tight corner and a foreign place. You may feel that this is an absurd amount of whitewashing of the play's motive, and I don't deny that the obvious appeal was the simple drum-and-trumpet one; what I maintain is that there was a controversy about these questions of foreign policy, and the play had to satisfy the less simple-minded spectators too. For that matter, Shakespeare had made Henry's father talk with almost comic cynicism about how he would use foreign aggression, or a crusade, or something, to avoid civil war; and the one thing in politics that Shakespeare really did regard seriously was civil war. I am not imputing to him an idea which could not have come into his head.

I ought now to say something about the introductory scenes of the play which give the reasons for the war, though I can say little. The clergy first make clear that the war is to their own interest and then recite Henry's technical claim to the French throne at great length. (Modern historians, as I understand, consider that Henry had no decent reason for attacking France:, except possibly the one that Shakespeare made his father give.) The wartime film handled this, rather ingeniously, by keeping us in the play-house at the beginning and turning this recitation into farce, guying old-world techniques rather than anything else. It is hard to imagine how the first audiences took it; one must remember they were well accustomed to hearing sermons. Dover Wilson's attempts to save the face of the clergy do not seem to me worth a reply, but he is right in insisting that the recitation did not seem dull, as it does now; not, however, as he thinks, because everybody took it for granted. I imagine that Shakespeare was rather ostentatiously not making up anyone's mind for them.

Assuming then that the legend about Hal and the value of his tavern life had this rather massive background. I want now to say something about the interior of Falstaff; that is, not anything which was kept secret from the first audiences, but how it was that Shakespeare's incarnation of the legend could be felt intuitively as a very real character, whom one was curious to know more about; as evidently happened. The eighteenth-century Morgann, if I may avoid appearing too "modern" at this point, has some piercing remarks about the interior of a stage character in general, and how the impression of it is built up; but is mainly concerned to say about Falstaff (after using this idea to explain how we feel he isn't a coward though he appears one) that his deeper interior is more sordid than we are encouraged to recognise, though we still somehow know it. This interior of Falstaff, rather hard to get at for most of us, is also sharply lit up by some remarks of Dr Johnson; and one could wish that Dover Wilson, who is rightly fond of pointing out that later critics have not had the firm good sense of Johnson, had profited by his master here. It is not surprising that Johnson speaks with confidence about this sort of life, because he had observed it; he could say without absurdity that he regretted not having met Falstaff. Also he himself was a man of startling appearance; a pugnaciously and robustly amusing talker, who regularly conquered but never won anything that mattered, a hero of taverns, fretted by remorse which Falstaff makes much play with if nothing more), starved of love, unwilling to be alone. He has several comments such as that "a man feels in himself the pain of deformity"; "however, like this merry knight, he may make sport of it among those whom it is his interest to please". If we compare this with the struggles of Dover Wilson to prove that Falstaff was a Medieval Vice, with no interior at all, surely the truth of Johnson stands out like a rock. The picture of him as driven on by an obscure personal shame, of an amoral sort, has several advantages, I think. Wyndham Lewis has written well about his incessant trick of "charm", his insistence on presenting himself as a deliciously lovable old bag of guts, helpless but able to make a powerful appeal to the chivalry of the protector; one needs to add that this curious view of him made a sharp contrast to his actual wickedness—that was the joke; but both sides of it are really present. He clamours for love, and I do not see why Dover Wilson should ignore it. I made a mistake in my *Pastoral* from assuming that this line of talk was concentrated upon the Prince; in *I Henry IV*, II.ii—"If the rascal have not given me medicines to make me love him, I'll be hanged; it could not be else—I have drunk medicines", it must be Poins, not the Prince, who is supposed to have administered the love-philtre. Poins has just told the audience (though not Falstaff) that he stole the horse whose loss creates all this amorous tumult (because Falstaff is too fat to walk) and Falstaff was shouting for Poins; to be sure, the Prince is the only person yet spoken to by Falstaff in this scene, and the Prince's usual claim to innocence has put him under suspicion—the actor could drag the words round to apply to the Prince, as I first thought, and Falstaff can hardly know which of them stole it. But even Falstaff could hardly say of the Prince, "I have forsworn his company hourly any day these two and twenty years, and yet I am bewitched by the rogue's company." The historical Hal vas about sixteen here; the stage one might be regarded as twenty-two, so that Falstaff had forsworn his company since he was born, but this would be rather pointlessly absurd, and the natural view is that it applies to his (presumably older and steadier) gentleman-in-waiting. It is a rather startling cry, and comes early while the character of Falstaff is being defined to the audience; I take it the idea is that he regularly expresses love towards the young men who rob for him, and that this is a powerful means of leading them astray—it is a proud thing to become the favourite of such an expert teacher. For that matter Fagin in *Oliver Twist* is always expressing love to flatter the Artful Dodger and suchlike; even a member of the audience who hated Falstaff from the beginning would recognise that this bit of the machine had to be there, as a normal thing. It doesn't make very much difference whether Falstaff said it about Hal or Poins. The only thing that still puzzles me here is the recurrence of the number twenty-two, which probably means some private association of Shakespeare's. When the Prince says he has repaid the money gained by robbery he adds that he has procured Falstaff a charge of foot (they can all get their faces straight, now that civil war has loosened the purse-strings) and Falstaff says: "I would it had been of horse. Where shall I find one that can steal well? O for a fine thief, of the age of two and twenty or thereabouts. I am heinously unprovided." The numbers regularly have a magical claim; consider the repeated thousand pounds; these twenty-two years of the young thief seem to me like the laborious number-magic in *Hamlet*, designed to prove that the First Gravedigger was appointed on the day of Hamlet's birth and has been waiting there ever since for an arrival never before seen but now due. I don't suppose the number twenty-two was meant to tell the audience anything.

Returning to Falstaff's heart, I think there is a quick answer to the idea that the old brute had no heart, and therefore could not have died of breaking it. If he had had no heart he would have had no power, not even to get a drink, and he had a dangerous amount of power. I am not anxious to present Falstaff's heart as a very attractive object; you might say that it had better be called his vanity, but we are none of us sure how we would emerge from a thorough analysis on those lines; the point is that everybody felt it obvious that he had got one—otherwise he would not be plausible even in attracting his young thieves, let alone his insanely devoted "hostess". I daresay that the wincing away from the obvious (or from Wyndham Lewis's account) which I seem to find in recent critics is due to distaste for homosexuality, which is regarded nowadays in more practical terms than the Victorian ones; the idea of Falstaff making love to the Prince, they may feel, really has to be resisted. But surely Johnson gives us the right perspective here; Falstaff felt in himself the pain of a deformity which the audience could always see; no amount of expression of love from Falstaff to his young thieves would excite suspicion on that topic from the audiences, not because the audiences were innocent about it, but because they could assume that any coming thief (let alone the Prince) would be too vain to yield to such deformity. I agree that a doubt here could not have been allowed, but there was no need to guard against it. A resistance to it should not prevent us from noticing that Falstaff is rather noisily shocked if young men do not love him. It is as well to take an example from near the end of Part II, where on Dover Wilson's account there should be practically nothing left in him but degeneration. He complains about Prince John (IV.ii.85), "this same young sober-blooded boy doth not love me, nor a man cannot make him laugh", and goes on in a fairly long speech to claim that he has taught Prince Hal better humanity. This is easily thought ridiculous because it is almost entirely a praise of drink, but the mere length presumes dramatic effect; and drink was presumed to teach both sympathy and courage (it is the culmination of these two ideas in a "heart", of course, which make it rather baffling to discuss what kind of heart Falstaff has); and we have just seen Prince John perform a disgusting act of cowardly treachery. This detail of structure, I think, is enough to prove that at least the popular side of the audience was assumed to agree with Falstaff. Indeed, if you compare Hal to his brother and his father, whom the plays describe so very unflinchingly, it is surely obvious that to love Falstaff was a liberal education for him.

It is hard to defend this strange figure without doing it too much. May I remind the patient reader that I am still doing what this essay started to do, trying to show that Falstaff from his first conception was not intended to arrive at Agincourt, because the Prince was intended to reach that triumph over his broken heart. The real case for rejecting Falstaff at the end of Part II is that he was dangerously strong, indeed almost a rebel leader; Dover Wilson makes many good points here, and he need not throw the drama away by pretending that the bogey was always ridiculous. He is quite right in insisting that the Prince did not appear malicious in the rejection, and did only what was necessary; because Falstaff's expectations were enormous (and were recklessly expressed, by the way, to persons who could shame him afterwards); the terrible sentence "the laws of England are at my commandment, ... and woe to my Lord Chief Justice" meant something so practical to the audience that they may actually have stopped cracking nuts to hear what happened next. The small capital would be entered by the mob for a coronation, and how much of it Falstaff could raise would be a reasonable subject for doubt; he could become "protector" of the young King; once you admit that he is both an aristocrat and a mob leader he is a familiar very dangerous type. The "special pleading" of Dover Wilson here, that the King only gave him honour by sending him to the Fleet Prison, a place where lords were put in temporary custody while waiting for enquiry before the Privy Council and such like, instead of treating him as a common criminal, seems to me off the point; he really was important enough for the Fleet Prison, both in the eyes of the imaginary fifteenth-century and the real sixteenth-century audience. Dover Wilson argues, rightly I think, that Henry shows a good deal of forbearance in his conditions to Falstaff, so far as one can interpret them; but one must remember that the King and the dramatist both had to show forbearance, for just about the same reasons, and facing a similar mob. I do not mean that either of them privately wanted to be hard on the old man, only that they both had to get through a public event. As to why Shakespeare's play had a casual Epilogue, for some performances, saying "maybe Jack will bob up again some time", it is not hard to imagine that he might need to send his audience away in a good temper by having that said. So much so, indeed, that it is not evidence of his real intentions; maybe he had suddenly become so important that he had to lie like a Foreign Office. In the same way, Henry had to get rid of Falstaff with unquestionable firmness but without any suspicion that he had behaved with malice, because a rising in favour of Falstaff was just what he needed to avoid. A bit of political understanding, I think, is enough to make this problem transparent.

However, to say that the rejection has to be done firmly if done in public is not to say that it need be done so at all. The real case against Hal, in the reasonable view of A. C. Bradley, is that he was dishonest in not warning Falstaff beforehand that he would have to reject him after coronation, and still more in pretending on that occasion that Falstaff had misled him. Their separation, says Bradley, might have been shown in a private scene rich in humour and only touched with pathos; a remark which shows how very different he would like the characters to be. Dover Wilson answers that *Falstaff* makes a public rejection necessary; the Prince "first tries to avoid the encounter, begging the Lord Chief Justice to say for him what must be said. But Falstaff will not allow it ... Though under observation (the Prince) falters and finds it difficult to keep up", etc.; and the Prince could not have warned Falstaff at a convenient time, because "Shakespeare has been busy since Shrewsbury manoeuvring the former friends into different universes between which conversation is impossible". One is often baffled by a peculiar circularity in the arguments of Dover Wilson. This may be an adequate defence for Hal, though his claim that he was misled still looks unnecessarily shifty; but it cannot also be a defence for the dramatist; indeed, I think it brings into a just prominence the fact that Shakespeare wanted, and arranged, to end his play with this rather unnerving bang. By the way, Dr Johnson called it, so far from a bang, "a lame and impotent conclusion", and poor Dover Wilson has to argue that his master is only complaining at the absence of a final heroic couplet. He argues against a phrase of Bradley, that Hal was trying "to buy the praise of the respectable at the cost of honor and truth", that the word *respectability* had not been invented (but the *thing* is visible enough here) and that the change in Hal is "an instance of the phenomenon of 'conversion'" (this does not join well onto his previous arguments that Hal was never really a sinner). None of this, I think, is adequate ground for doubting what seems obvious, that Shakespeare was deliberately aiming at a rather peculiar dramatic effect, imposing considerable strain, as most critics have felt whether they accepted it or not. The inherent tension between the characters is given its fullest expression and then left unresolved; as G. K. Chesterton remarked, this really is a "problem play", whereas the plays so called in the nineties were simply propaganda plays—a man might fully recognise the merits and importance of Henry V, and still doubt, without the dramatist trying to decide for him, "whether he had not been a better man when he was a thief". Of course, the play is not obtrusively a problem, because it simply tells a popular story, but to do that so strongly brings out what is inherent in it, and the apparently coarse treatment may involve profound or at least magical thinking. There seems room for the suggestion of J. I. M. Stewart, that Henry was felt to require before he arrived at Agincourt the mana which came from sacrificing the representative of a real divinity, or a tutor of heroes.

After imposing decent enough conditions on Falstaff, Henry sweeps out with the remark that the Lord Chief Justice must "perform the tenor of his word", and this is at once interpreted by the Chief Justice throwing Falstaff and all his company into the Fleet Prison; perhaps only till the mobs have dispersed, as Dover Wilson suggests. Neither he nor any other critic that I have seen discusses what would happen to Falstaff when he got there; a thing which would seem obvious to the audience but cannot to us. Surely it is likely that he would be smashed by the Fleet Prison. It assumed the prisoner to be a rich landowner who could toss money away before he got out, and it examined his sources of money and encouraged creditors to speak up. Lords at Elizabeth's court were commonly ruined if they were sent to the Fleet, living as they did on a speculator's market, and it is hard to see how Falstaff would do better. As for what are almost his last words, "Master Shallow, I owe you a thousand pound", which Dover Wilson calls "*the* last word", they are certainly a last boast, and I warmly agree that Shakespeare did not want to send the old boy off the stage whining and appearing broken, or even telling too much truth for that matter—nor did the King. But I think a contemporary spectator would reflect that, although ready money would be a great help to Falstaff "and his company" in the Fleet, it wouldn't take them at all far. And indeed, when the next play shows Falstaff dying as a free man in the tavern, I think this person might reflect that the King must have bought him out, paying off Shallow as well as the others. I would like to have a ruling from a historian on the point, but I suspect that the last boast of Falstaff was only just enough to get him off the stage.

I have next to argue that he was sure to die. Surely we have all met these strong old men, fixed in their habits, who seem unbreakable ("wonderful" as people say) till they get a shock, and then collapse very suddenly. He is over seventy, because he was breaking Scogan's head at the court gate fifty-five years ago; and his pox has been emphasised. The shock given to him is very severe all round; it does not matter whether ambition or love or his pleasures mattered most to him, he had lost them all, and had also lost his *mystique*; his private war against shame had been answered by public loathing of a kind which no tongue could get round; even his "company" would be reproaching him and jeering at him. As against this, which seems ordinary human experience, we have Dover Wilson arguing *both* that he was a study in increasing degeneration *and* that "the last thing Shakespeare had in mind" when he wrote the Epilogue of Part II "was a sad death for his fat knight", who was needed as a comic at Agincourt. Now, a certain amount of petty criminality can reasonably be shown among the troops at Agincourt, where it is punished fiercely, but does Dover Wilson mean that a searching picture of the third degree of degeneration would have fitted comfortably into the scene of national triumph? It seems rather hard on the Prince; who would also, I think, prefer not to be in danger of unbeatable comic criticisms from his old tutor at such a time. The idea that the text has gone wrong, I submit, comes from not seeing the story in the round; to have brought Falstaff to Agincourt would have thrown a serious jam into the gears of a rather delicate piece of machinery. But there again, it is rather too glib to talk in this technical way about the necessities of the playwright; what he manages to get out of them is an effect of truth. Given the two characters, that was the way it would have to end.

I want finally to consider what the plays meant to Shakespeare himself, as apart from the audience; there is no very definite conclusion to be expected, but one ought not to talk as if an achievement on this scale has no personal backing. It seems that Shakespeare, though of course he won his position in the Company much earlier, already perhaps from the *Henry VI* sequence, odd as it appears now, made his decisive position out of Falstaff. Not merely as a matter of money, which was very important, but also as a matter of trust from the audience, the triumph of Falstaff made possible the series of major tragedies; it was not merely an incident to him. I pursued the subject of the personal background to Falstaff in my *Pastoral* (pp. 102–9), and want to remark that I still believe what I said there, though this essay is concerned with something rather different. Indeed I think that to understand the many-sidedness of the legend he was using makes it more plausible to think he felt his own experience to be an illustration of it. I proved, I think, that the first soliloquy of the Prince, assuring the audience that he was going to abandon his low friends, is drawn almost line by line from the Sonnets trying to justify the person addressed. It seems inherently probable that the humiliation of Shakespeare's dealings with his young patron, which one can guess were recently finished, would get thrown into the crucible in which the Prince's friends had to be created. Falstaff looks to me like a secret come-back against aristocratic patrons, marking a recovery of nerve after a long attempt to be their hanger-on. But this was not done coarsely or with bad temper; the whole triumph of the thing, on its intimate side, was to turn his private humiliation into something very different and universally entertaining. I have been arguing that Falstaff is not meant to be socially low, even when he first appears, only to be a scandal to his rank; whereas Shakespeare of course had only a dubious profession and a suspect new gentility. There are warnings in the Sonnets that friendship with Shakespeare is bad for the patron's reputation, though we hardly ever get an actual admission of inferior social status (we do in the "dyer's hand"); he would rather talk obscurely about his "guilt". Snobbery, I think, had always seemed more real to him than self righteousness, and even in the Sonnets we can see the beginning of the process that turned player Shakespeare into Falstaff, not a socially inferior friend but (what is much less painful) a scandalous one. Nobody would argue that the result is a life-like portrait of Shakespeare; though he must have known how to amuse, and talks in the Sonnets with a regret about his old age which was absurd even for an Elizabethan if he was then under thirty-five, and undoubtedly was what they called a "villainist" tutor, the type who could give broad experience to a young prince. The point is not that he was like Falstaff but that, once he could imagine he was, he could "identify" himself with a scandalous aristocrat, the sufferings of that character could be endured with positive glee. I am sure that is how he came to be liberated into putting such tremendous force into every corner of the picture.

APPENDIX

Since writing this in Peking, I have poked my nose into texts of the chroniclers, translator of Livius, Hall, and Holinshed, and the modern historian J. H. Wylie (*Reign of Henry V*). I find the subject is so confusing that one can hardly accuse the play of departing from history at all. It should be reported that the sources of Shakespeare do not strike one as devoted to patriotic whitewash. Perhaps their chief difference from the play is that they have more about money.

Thus critics often say that Shakespeare made Henry look more merciful by falsely denying that he sacked Harfleur; there is a bit of suppression of truth, but Henry did not sack it. He took care not to let his soldiers kill, rape, and burn; that is what Shakespeare makes him warn Harfleur against, and save it from. He did mulct the town very heavily, and he sent away "2000 of the poor and the women and children of every rank to save them from the soldiers"—so says Wylie, who argues that he meant in the end to replace the whole population by English settlers. Wylie does however report that the French at the time were surprised by his mercy (in the case of this particular town, where he may have had special plans). A John Falstaff was made lieutenant of captured Harfleur; so that is where Falstaff really went, of course he didn't go to Agincourt. To have to reject such entirely typical material must have given keen regret to the dramatist; but I am sure he never wrote it down; it would have been quite off the rails. The chronicler Hall says "the goods in the town were innumerable which were all prey to the English", but Wylie says you could keep your goods if you took an oath of allegiance to Henry. I am not clear what this involved in its turn.

In the same way, it is a possible point of view about the killing of the prisoners at Agincourt that Henry was chiefly interfering with his officers' ransom money. Holinshed says it was annoying for the French commanders to have French soldiers loot the English camp, because they were no longer trying to win the battle—"very many after were committed to prison, and had lost their lives, if the Dolphin had longer lived". He goes on to say how dolorous and terrible it was for Henry to order the killing of prisoners, but he seems to leave room for a suggestion that Henry meant "I can't afford profiteers here; you must destroy this property you have been collecting; the thing is getting out of hand." According to the modern Wylie, Henry when giving this order specifically excluded the killing of any Dukes or Earls, because they would be his own share of the ransom money. This detail does not appear in the chroniclers, and perhaps they did suppress that much as removing a possible source of credit for him.

Before nerving myself to approach the real confusions of history I looked up the great disintegrator J. M. Robertson on the killing of prisoners at Agincourt. As one would expect, he says that this bit of the play was written by three or four fools each of them quite indifferent to what was done by the others. In a case like this, where there really is something wrong, one can read him with much sympathy. But he also says a thing which I think shows an entirely wrong assumption. He denounces the speech of Henry to Harfleur, warning the citizens what a loot really means; the sickening cruelty of the threat, he says, is only made tolerable by an excuse disgraceful if true, that Henry had no control over his own army. Are these the heroes so soon to be exalted at Agincourt? and so forth. This highminded nineteenth-century point of view cannot survive a glance at the chroniclers, who did think it rather clever of Henry to manage not to let his troops behave appallingly. Shakespeare is keeping to the truth in expressing that ("Show mercy to them all"); but he might naturally become uncertain, as he read on, about how much truth he ought to put into this play.

J. M. Robertson, discussing the speech (IV.vii) which begins with that noble line

I was not angry since I came to France

—it came over with great moral beauty in the film, because it means that no personal disaster could make him angry, only the suffering of children— points out that he says nothing whatever about these children. He says that the horsemen on yon hill offend his sight, therefore he orders a deceitful message to be sent to them, that if they attack he will kill his prisoners; whereas the audience knows that he has killed them already. That is, he hasn't been able to become gloriously angry before, because only now has he had enough blood to get drunk on it. This is really interesting criticism, because it shows what a knife-edge the great effects have to balance on. But it is none the less absurd; the intention is obviously the highminded one, that Henry was justly angered by an enemy atrocity, and was driven by it into a questionable reprisal. A critic does not have to be a whitewasher to think this, indeed he can say that the appeal to the gallery is coarse and false; but he must still recognise that Henry is repeatedly praised because he gave as much attention to a low-class Englishman (let alone a child) as to a Norman aristocrat, and also because he never boasted about the highminded motives which actually decided his behaviour. This, surely, is what makes us decide what we expect the passage to mean.

Robertson supposes three superimposed versions, none of them by Shakespeare. The first tried to alter the famous killing of prisoners into a mere threat (this desire for mercy is absurdly ascribed to Marlowe); the second gave the real story but did not bother to reconcile it with the threat; the third added the remarks of Fluellen and Gower, also presumably the two earlier soliloquies of the Boy, not bothering to remove any contradictions but meaning to suggest that the killing of the prisoners was a highminded reprisal. Passages are given to the different authors on grounds of style as well as logical coherence. Now Robertson's arguments from style are exposed to a fundamental objection, not unlike the objection to his argument from morality. The style of Shakespeare itself was very variable all along, even though, or perhaps because, he is the outstanding case of an author who kept on "developing" his style. It seems to me obvious that he could imitate the style of Marlowe whenever he thought that style would be suitable, because it is such a definite thing to imitate; and it is suitable here. As to the King of France, it is ludicrous to "prove" by a laborious count of double-endings that he can't be Shakespeare's; because Shakespeare wanted to make this character sound weak. J. H. Walter may be right in saying that the censor would have been annoyed if even a foreign royalty had been shamed, but Shakespeare could display the weakness of this man merely by giving him plenty of double-endings. Robertson really did have a good ear, and is very acute in other matters; one ought to read him for the incidental truths which he buried in his rather tragically irrelevant programme.

The strength of Robertson having driven me to the historians, I was impressed to find that they destroyed his case at once. The position is at once more puzzling and more natural than he had supposed. The entire layout of this rather subtle confusion about the prisoners is already present in Holinshed; that is, first the prisoners are killed, then Henry threatens to kill them, then we simply hear that the French have killed the boys in the camp. We need not invent three totally non-co-operative authors, who surely must have annoyed the actors bitterly, if we only want to know why the author of a History Play copied down what the chronicler said. We do, on the other hand, have to wonder why it was done so very tactlessly, in an age which expected tact about kings. *Henry V* as it stands gives such a bad impression of Henry that it is literally never acted, even nowadays, whereas the chroniclers give a reasonably good impression of him. A literary critic is not being fussy if he tries to explain why this occurred.

Holinshed says very little about anybody's motives, and I think he gives a better impression of Henry than Shakespeare does merely because, by telling more of the truth, he gives you the right timing. He says that, when the King heard the outcries from the lackeys and boys who had run away from the French spoiling of the English camp, he thought there was a danger of a second battle in which the mass of prisoners taken might be dangerous to his own army, so he ordered them to be killed at once, "contrary to his accustomed gentleness". When this lamentable slaughter was over (it was pity to see) the Englishmen disposed themselves in order of battle, ready to abide a new field; and at once they had a fresh onset to handle, from a separate group who had all that day kept together. After this had been won, the King saw that the French were again thinking of assembling for further battle, so he sent them his famous threat, and they parted out of the field and he made every man kneel down while they sang *Non Nobis Domine*. Holinshed introduces this part of his story with the doubtful phrase "Some write that ...", but he puts in the margin "a right wise and valiant challenge of the king". The opinion of a whitewasher would not be worth attention, but Holinshed has a sturdy enough morality; he has clearly decided that this action prevented further slaughter. His account does at least remove the combination of absurdity and meanness which made Dr Johnson say "he shows he is angry by threatening to kill his prisoners after he has killed them already"; in Holinshed there is enough lapse of time to let Henry get some fresh live prisoners. The stage always hurries things up, and here the most disgraceful part of the story is an accidental result of that.

In the same way, the idea that the killing of the prisoners was a just reprisal need not have been presented as an obvious delusion of the absurd Fluellen. According to Wylie, though later French historians rubbed in the barbarity of Henry at Agincourt, even his fiercest French critic at the time, though denouncing the carnage at Caen, did not blame him here. Two unexpected things were going on, as one need not be surprised to learn, which Henry could not have known to be independent of one another. I am rather doubtful how to interpret the learned Wylie when he says that the battle was as much arranged beforehand as a modern sports event; even there one can have large technical surprises, and I presume he does not mean to deny that Henry had planned one. What we were told at school, that the English long-bow-men won the battle by a trick, which was also what Shakespeare's audience had been told in *The Famous Victories of Henry V*, does not seem to get much attention from Wylie; but I presume he is only wincing away from the obvious. I am sure he is right about the general tone of the affair. The looting of the English camp, he says, was outside the rules, from the point of view of both sides; the looters seized Henry's crown and other holy objects, and raised a shout with *Te Deum* which meant that they had got hold of the King's magic again. Meanwhile the Duc de Brabant, who by bad timing had missed the earlier slaughter, was coming in with a fresh army for which the English hadn't been prepared, so the English couldn't again arrange the choice of ground for their new technical trick about archers. As I understand Wylie, the French not only blamed the looters as a matter of course but positively cursed the Duke for making his uninformed attack when the main event was over, thus causing death to a number of persons already captured whose status deserved attention. Hall says that the French blamed the looters for Henry's killing of the French prisoners, whereas Holinshed doesn't; but I have been impressed by the scholarly arguments that Shakespeare must have read all the sources, including some which were unpublished when he wrote, and if this is so the differences are unimportant. One can well believe that Government officials were willing to show him unpublished documents, at the price of a little briefing about how to take the right line on this tricky but important topic.

May I summarise my position: if you suppose that the single line "Then every soldier kill his prisoners" was marked by Shakespeare as cut when he altered his plan but somehow got into the printed texts, then you get a consistent treatment of the story. There is no way to tell whether Shakespeare decided to make these changes in the story about the prisoners while in solitude or because the censor ordered him to do it, because either case would leave just the same marks on his text. As to the pirated First Quarto, which gives a still more shocking treatment at this point, you must remember that the story was well known and that some audiences might prefer to have the treatment shocking. On the other hand, if you insist on making Shakespeare intend to retain this one line, you make Shakespeare thrust on the audience an epigrammatic and bursting hatred of Henry; the line if thrown back into the rather complicated treatment has the effect of giving Henry the comic fierce hard-to-beat wickedness of the Jew of Malta. I think a critic has to choose between two alternatives here.

I need also to explain the motives of the editors of the First Folio, who restored the line "Then every soldier kill his prisoners." I fancy they thought, rightly enough, that they had done their duty if they gave the printer, or had copied for him, their treasured original manuscript of the play. If they remembered a censorship of twenty years ago they would be rather pleased to beat it when it no longer mattered, and the line was universally known to be true to history; besides, it had sometimes been delivered, as we can presume from the first Quarto. The peculiar dramatic effect of it would not now bother them. I may now claim to have given intelligible and tolerable motives, though not specially good ones, to all the characters concerned in these queer bits of printing, as any theory about them needs to do.

NOTES

1. *Brawn* suggests the wild boar, a strong and savage creature, honourable to hunt, though the fatted hog is not quite out of view. A similar ambivalence can be felt I think in the incessant metaphors of heavy meat-eating around Falstaff compared to "one halfpennyworth of bread to this intolerable deal of sack", where it is assumed (already in Part I) that the drunkard has no appetite.

2. I see that in his edition of the *Merry Wives* (1921) Dover Wilson was already assuming (with joviality, as at correct though spirited behaviour) that Henry V had ordered the women to be thrown into jail the moment he got hold of power, before Pistol could get back from telling Falstaff that Henry IV was dead. I should have thought that this could only be invented by someone who hated Hal bitterly. The dramatic point of the scene, surely, is that the ordinary processes of law are going firmly on. Pistol rushed off to Falstaff because he had got into trouble, and both he and the women assume wrongly that Falstaff can clear it up. We are not asked to suppose that the new King is indulging immediate private malice against these humble characters.

3. The objection by one family to the name Oldcastle is merely natural. But there is evidence from stage directions that Falstaff's gang once had several members bearing such prominent names that they all had to be suppressed (e.g. Dover Wilson's *II Hen. IV*, note on II.ii). If this is true, Shakespeare was showing a good deal of nerve; it looks as if he felt in such a strong position with the censor that he threw in extra names merely to let the censor take them out before the real bargaining started. I don't quite believe in this picture, but his position must have been fairly strong to carry the Company through their performance of *Richard II* for the Essex rebels.

4. The fact that Oldcastle was a Lollard, therefore a forerunner of the National Church, indeed a "martyr", might come into the earlier stages of the growth of the legend—Henry while his father lived made a friend of Oldcastle, and this could be regarded as "national" behaviour. But it must have come to seem remote from the popular story, because Shakespeare cannot have wanted to run up against it, and his apology gives a convincing impression of surprise at finding the knight was a Puritan.

PAUL M. CUBETA

Falstaff and the Art of Dying

Once the historical myths and dramatic concerns of *The Henriad* served by Falstaff's comic vision have been resolved by his legendary repudiation, Falstaff the character can no longer exist: "Reply not to me with a foolborn jest" (Shakespeare, *2H4* V.v.55).[1] On that command to silence, the newly crowned king has destroyed his fool and jester. Falstaff could undergo a mock-magical death and resurrection at the end of *1 Henry IV*, and he essentially "dies of a sweat" at the end of *2 Henry IV*, when he races recklessly to Westminster Abbey "to stand stain'd with travel, and sweating with desire to see" Hal newly crowned (V.v.24–25). But Falstaff the man cannot be dismissed or lie forgotten in Fleet Prison, abandoned by king and playwright. The Shakespearean investment in the saving grace of that comic spirit in his Lancastrian world has been too great. And so in *Henry V* he redeems Epilogue's promise in *2 Henry IV* to continue the story "with Sir John in it" (Epi., 28) with a vividly realized, yet non-existent death scene, both comic and pathetic, private and demonstrated, dedicated to the spirit of Falstaff the man.

Never allowed securely to grasp this protean giant even when his comic imagination and ironic vision die, the audience participates in the immediacy and intensity of the deathbed scene but not by observing those who stand at Falstaff's bedside. Simultaneously the audience is kept at double distance

From *Studies in English Literature SEL 1500–1900*, 27, no. 2 (Spring 1987). © 1987 by *SEL Studies in English Literature 1500–1900*.

from the mystery of Falstaff's dying thoughts. Instead of a sentimental farewell in the cold, pragmatic Lancastrian world, Shakespeare seeks instead a resolution in which tragedy and comedy, doubt and belief, clarity and confusion are bound in a manner historically appropriate, morally satisfying, and psychologically dazzling. The theatrical gamble of creating a character by not creating him, of giving him life by destroying him yields the most memorable scene of the play.

To achieve the dense texture of this recollected deathbed scene, Shakespeare does not turn to his usual source for things even vaguely Falstaffian in *The Henriad—The Famous Victories of Henry V* (1598). In the life of Falstaff, Shakespeare has embodied rituals, folk tales, conventions, festivals as familiar to an Elizabethan audience as those he may now be suggestively recalling in the medieval and Renaissance tradition of *ars moriendi*, or the art of dying. To design a coherent structure and meaning to Falstaff's dying moments of introspection and memory, which appear as merely broken, delirious fragments, Shakespeare may also give Falstaff the occasion to attempt a private meditation on his life in the manner of a Renaissance meditation for Wednesday night.

Reported in an intensely moving yet uncertain retelling, Falstaff's mode of dying is as mysterious and as hauntingly perplexing as any circumstance in his life. The only words directly attributed to him, the great inventor of language, are "God, God, God!" (*H5* II.iii.19). But what this punster, this parodist and unparalleled player with the rhythms of spoken language means or what tone the repetitions are spoken in is not ours to hear. The challenger of the moral, social, political, and religious values on which civilization rests dies with a word, the Word, on which pun cannot prevail. Like his heart, which Pistol avers, was "fracted and corroborate" (II.i.124), the scene recollecting Falstaff's death is a kind of transitory memorial moment, broken, unfocused, contradictory, unchronological and impossible to recreate for even their listeners by his bedside mourners, who are then about to be swept up into events in France and propelled to their own deaths.

For the old man's allegedly delirious dying moments as told by a grieving companion whose control of the English language was never firm, Shakespeare needed some kind of intelligible inner structure not available to him in the limited theatrical possibilities of an undramatic scene of dubious recollection. All that is really necessary to complete the exposition of the Falstaff story is Pistol's opening declaration and exhortation, "for Falstaff he is dead, / And we must ern therefore" (*H5* II.iii.5–6). The flexible strategies of the meditative exercises on *ars moriendi* allow Shakespeare the undergirding of a coherent traditional structure familiar to a Renaissance audience, with its fascination for deathbed scenes. Thus he can both shape rhetorically the dramatized design of the brief scene of companionable reminiscence and give meaning to the interior monologue and meditation of the dying Falstaff. Not rheumatic, as the Hostess suggests, he is also not incoherent, only seeming so in her narrative. In this shaky account, Shakespeare illuminates for his theater audience thoughts and intentions which even in happier times Falstaff could not always share with these companions. Yet Falstaff's voice must now be the Hostess's, hopelessly literal-minded and completely antithetical to his own.

Falstaff's mocking pledges of repentance, comically counterpointing Lancastrian political guilt, may at the hour of his death, no longer counterfeited, be transformed into another attempt at reformation. But this one is more ambiguous than those extending from Hal's first soliloquy promising to redeem the time to his father's dying plea for divine forgiveness: "How I came by the crown O God forgive" (*2H4* IV.v.218).[2] By prince or whore Falstaff is constantly reproached to repent, to remember his day of reckoning. His friends often sound as though they were repeating the conventional pieties of Thomas Lupset in his *Waye of Dyenge Well* (1541) or Robert Parsons's *The First Booke of the Christian Exercise, Appertayning to Resolution* (1582), in which chapter 8 is entitled "The daye of deathe Of what opinion and feelinge we shalbe, touching these matters, at the tyme of our deathe,"[3] or Gaspar Loarte's *The Exercise of a Christian Life* (1579). The moral exhortations Loarte insistently makes are typical:

> take then a zelous and feruent desire to line a new here after, and striue to get other new behauiours, & to liue far otherwise than thou hast done tofore.... Eschewe al occasions of sinne, especially the companie of wicked men, but muche more of women, such as may prouoke thee to noughtines, and geue thee loose and lewd example.... Thou must flye suche places where God is customably offended, as be dising houses, tauernes, daucing schooles, and such like.... Thou must take hede of al excesse in eating, drinking, sleping and clothing, and indeuour thy self to obserue a mediocritie and temperance in eche of them.[4]

These books of Renaissance meditation, among others, Catholic and Protestant, published in numerous editions in fifteenth- and sixteenth-century England, all explored like good-conduct books the ways in which the devout or those whose faith was more fragile should prepare for a final reckoning.[5] The admonitions of sin, death, and judgment were so common as Renaissance homilies that an English audience could have warned Falstaff as well as Hal or Doll. "Live now as you will wish to have lived when you come to that sorrowful day" is the kind of exhortation that runs through Parsons's *First Book*. He would find a curious moral ally in Doll: "when wilt thou leave fighting a' days and foining a' nights, and begin to patch up thine old body for heaven?" (*2H4* II.iv.231–33). Hal, newly crowned, is only more austerely puritanical in chastising the Falstaff he abandons: "Leave gormandizing, know the grave doth gape / For thee thrice wider than for other men" (V.v.53–54).

For Falstaff, playing the penitent is a subject for infinite amusement. In plays which find their moral center in redeeming the time, repentance, reformation, and reckoning, Hal and Falstaff can counterpoint their pledges. "I'll so offend, to make offense a skill, / Redeeming time when men think least I will" (*1H4* I.ii.216–17) is Hal's first promise to himself and to the audience as he rationalizes his manipulation of his tavern friends both to learn about the potential corruption of fleshly indulgence and to prepare for a public apotheosis in good time. The language may be spiritual, but the hours of study, more active than contemplative, are more for his brilliant political future than for the salvation necessary for his eternal life. For Falstaff, on the other hand, the language of moral reformation in *1* and *2 Henry IV* carries economic, not political or spiritual ambiguities. Hal, ironically amused, notes the rapidity with which Falstaff transforms his pledge to "give over this life, ... and I do not, I am a villain, I'll be damned for never a king's son in Christendom" (*1H4* I.ii.95–97) into a plan to take purses at Gadshill: "I see a good amendment of life in thee, from praying to pursetaking" (102–103). Falstaff's instant moral defense is that it is "no sin for a man to labor in his vocation" (104–105). His pun on *vocation* as profession and religious conversion is echoed at Shrewsbury when Hal tells Falstaff to prepare for battle and say his prayers, for he "owest God a death" (V.i.126). Falstaff's rejoinder picks up the homophonic pun on *debt*, as he is determined that this is not the day to prepare to die well or at all: "'Tis not due yet. I would be loath to pay him before his day" (127–28). Let those who value honor do so. "A trim reckoning" (135). Playful language then can redeem all moral questions.

One of the deliberately unresolved mysteries of *The Henriad* is whether Falstaff does finally make a good end, for we have only the Hostess's not unbiased judgment that "'A made a finer end, and went away and it had been any christom child" (*H5* II.iii.10–12). An audience comes to this scene after another one of public confession and repentance so carefully orchestrated that the broken and uncertain fragments of Falstaff's only private meditation are made more resonantly convincing. Scroop, Cambridge, and Gray, trapped into confessing their treason and sentencing themselves to death, seem relieved that they have been caught. Each in turn thanks God for "the discovery of most dangerous treason" (II.ii.162), asks for divine and monarchial forgiveness, and seem almost to parody the assertion of Lupset and others that in *ars moriendi* "this dyenge well is in effecte to dye gladlye":[6]

> Cam[bridge:] But God be thanked for prevention,
>   Which [I] in sufferance heartily will rejoice,
>   Beseeching God, and you, to pardon me.
>   (158–60)

The traitors, "poor miserable wretches" (178), are borne off to their execution at the moment when Falstaff also dies, betrayed by his king, who, says the Hostess, "kill'd his heart" (II.i.88). The perspectives of betrayer betrayed, parodied and balanced, continue as a Lancastrian legacy from the time of Bolingbroke and Northumberland in *Richard II*.

For a brief interlude, almost outside the time of *Henry V*, as Henry dispatches his traitors and exultantly moves to France "to busy giddy minds / With foreign quarrels" (*2H4* IV.v.213–14), Shakespeare elusively distances the dramatic scene of Falstaff's death by recessing it into an interior moment, a scene-within-a-scene and then within that a memory-within-a-memory. Those last friends of Falstaff—Hostess, Boy, Pistol, Nym, and Bardolph—try to recapture Falstaff's deathbed hour as a last memory. But so equivocal is their disagreement that an audience cannot even be sure who was there besides the Hostess, the Boy, and Bardolph. Nym has heard another account of Falstaff's death: "They say he cried out of sack" (II.iii.27). But who are these anonymous bedside witnesses whose story is as quickly challenged as are the contradictory reports of those who now botch the telling of their witnessed accounts? The distorted perspective of each seems finally to return the memory of Falstaff only to the security of the theater audience which can only intuit the manner of his death.

The design of the scene that is played is constructed from ambiguities of time, imagery, and theme inherent in the history plays: order/disorder, bawdy/sentimental, innocence/experience, youth/age, physical/spiritual, salvation/damnation, time/sea, life/death. Falstaff's dying like his living remains beyond precise description or adequate dramatization, imbedded in the structure of its telling. The Hostess, as the primary witness, does not herself understand the import of her account. In the confusion, distancing, and failure of Falstaff's last story lies its dramatic achievement.

To the extent that there are facts, they suggest that an emaciated Falstaff developed a sudden sweat and a high fever and died shortly after midnight. Although delirious, he seemed aware that he was on his deathbed.

He apparently saw a flea on Bardolph's nose and said it was a black soul burning in hell. He inveighed against sack and prostitutes whom he called devils incarnate. He talked about the Whore of Babylon. He fumbled with his sheets, smiled at his fingertips, apparently mumbled something about green fields, called out "God" three or four times. As his feet grew cold, he asked the Hostess for more bedclothes and died.

If Falstaff is making a determined effort to die well by attempting a deathbed repentance, it is one only his Maker could be sure of. No character has been advised more insistently to remember his end, nor promised more persistently to do so when the time was right. Yet at the moment of Falstaff's dying the Hostess urges upon him as a dubious theological comfort not to think of God: "I hop'd there was no need to trouble himself with such thoughts yet" (II.iii.21–22). Her words express Falstaff's long-standing determination to postpone any day of spiritual reckoning. Nonetheless, Falstaff may be attempting a meditation in the Renaissance manner of *ars moriendi*, perhaps as broken and as incomplete as the narrated account of it. Whether spiritually efficacious or not remains beyond the limits of the play. But the dramatic, ritualistic, and psychological appropriateness of such a spiritual moment fulfills the design of Falstaff's creation and existence.

The paradoxical symmetry of Falstaff's life has always been mythic, not realistic,[7] as it embodies rituals, folk tales, and festivals. For a man who lives out of all time, the hours of his birth and death are recorded as nowhere else in Shakespeare. As he tells the Chief Justice, "My Lord, I was born about three of the clock in the afternoon, with a white head and something a round belly" (*2H4* I.ii.187–89). Born allegedly an old, fat man, he dies "ev'n just between twelve and one, ev'n at the turning o' th' tide" (*H5* II.iii.12–13) like a "christom child," newly christened and now shrouded in his white baptismal clothes. From corrupted old age he moves in death to appearing as an innocent child, even as the play returns to the first time an audience saw Falstaff as he emerged at noon from bed in *1 Henry IV*. The first mythic definition of Falstaff is reenforced in his death scene. It is, as Hal says, superfluous to ask Falstaff the time of day, for he has nothing to do with these symbols of order, political responsibility, or personal self-discipline. It is also superfluous to ask the Hostess how she could have been certain when high tide occurred on the Thames that last night. Like the fertility festival and the ritual games of the purged scapegoat, this moment is haunted by an aura of folklore and superstition. It was an old English belief, according to Sir James Frazer, held along the east coast of England that most deaths occur as the tide ebbs, a natural "melancholy emblem of failure, of weakness, and of death."[8] An audience would not have known which turning of the tide, or which twelve and one without a sense of the symbolic rightness that would remove the verbal ambiguity of the Hostess's sense of time and tide. The death of the dubiously legitimate king, Henry IV, who dies repentant in the Jerusalem Chamber as the Thames "thrice flowed, no ebb between" (*2H4* IV.iv.125) parallels that of player-king Falstaff, who once mocked him for Hal's amusement in Eastcheap and now dies in Eastcheap no longer playing penitent. These balanced moments suggest again Christian rituals intertwined with folk tales, from the death of newly christened babies to those of kings and errant knights.[9]

If the Hostess, forgiving soul, believes that Falstaff is in Arthur's bosom, she is secure in her belief that Falstaff has not been judged and damned. It makes little difference whether she means the Christian heaven of Abraham's bosom as defined in Luke 16:22 or the pagan heaven of King Arthur's Avalon. And if Henry IV's belief in the prophecy that he would die in Jerusalem on his "voyage to the Holy Land, / To wash this blood off from my guilty hand" (*R2* V.vi.49–50) can be accommodated by a quibble on Jerusalem Chamber, the Hostess's malapropism should be no less certain in its intent. Falstaff has always been more a practitioner of his view of *ars vivendi* than *ars moriendi*, so if the conduct of his life has been at best morally ambiguous, then its appropriate ending would be spiritually uncertain. Medieval and Renaissance meditative rituals serve both arts for him. At Shrewsbury he prefers catechisms on honor and comic resurrections that leave the body intact; rather than the grinning honor of dead Sir Walter Blunt, he declares, "Give me life, which if I can save, so" (*1H4* V.iii.59–60). Salvation is a matter of preserving the body in time present. When at Eastcheap he promises, "I must give over this life, and I will give it over" (I.ii.95–96), the words would suit a Puritan preacher better than does their context in the midst of battle. "But to counterfeit dying, when a man thereby liveth, is to be no counterfeit, but the true and perfect image of life indeed" (V.iv.117–19).

One of Falstaff's most agile verbal games is that in his profane parody of the language of *ars vivendi* he plays a secular *ars moriendi*. As Hal tells Poins, "He will give the devil his due" (I.ii.119). He constantly protests his fear of damnation, of being corrupted by Hal even if he were a saint; he delights in refuting the charge that he is "that villainous abominable misleader of youth, Falstaff, that old white-bearded Sathan" (II.iv.462–64). He wishes, he says, that he could have been a puritan weaver so he could sing penitential psalms. He declares to the Chief Justice that he lost his voice "hallowing and singing of anthems" (*2H4* I.ii.189–90). Whether he is playing Lord of Misrule, Antic, Miles Gloriosus, Comic Satan, or Corrupter of Youth, his archetypal roles make a travesty of the traditional posture of the penitent who must think of his sins and prepare for the hour of his dying.

Robert Parsons indeed writes his *First Booke of the Christian Exercise* for readers "so carelesse, or so carnallie geeuen" that like Falstaff they would hardly do more than glance at his opening pages. He asks, therefore, only for their patience while he tries to persuade them of the error of their ways and so to move them to the "necessarie resolution, of leauinge vanities to serue God."[10] Falstaff knows Parsons's text—and Lupset's, Bunny's, and Luis de Granada's—and quotes them as liberally and as cavalierly as he does Scripture, whenever they accommodate his chameleon-like purposes of serving himself while pleasing a prince in whose earthly kingdom he has hopes of long-lasting reward. He will paraphrase a meditative counselor like Parsons to share a moment of self-mockery with his prince: "What are thow the better now to haue liued in credit with the world? in fauour of princes? exalted of men?"[11] No Renaissance leader of devotional meditation would have had the imagination to concoct for a deathbed repentance the moral inventory available to Falstaff: lying, cowardice, avarice, vanity, gluttony, drunkenness, sloth, thievery, misusing the king's press, fornication. But their ponderous spiritual guides would also have neglected to point out the love and loyalty, the wit and imagination, and the comic genius that redeem Falstaff's living.

If Falstaff's deathbed scene were simply to conclude a dissolute life as Hal, his brothers, or the Chief Justice would have it, Falstaff would fall to his prayers and seek the grace Henry urges in his repudiation of him—"How ill white hairs becomes a fool and jester!" (*2H4* V.v.48). What for Luis de Granada is a metaphor of consequence for a wasted life has been Falstaff's whole reality in Eastcheap, but the Shakespearean dramatic moment of Falstaff's dying will not yield transparent spiritual conclusions to Luis de Granada's easy rhetorical questions:

> If a waiefaringe man, hauinge but one farthinge in his purse, shoulde enter into an inne, and placinge him selfe downe at the table, shoulde require of the host to bringe in Partridges, Capons, Phesauntes, and all other delicates, that maie be founde in the howse, and shoulde suppe with verie great pleasure, and contentation, neuer remembringe that at the last there must come a time of accompt: who woulde not take this fellowe, either for a iester, or for a verie foole? Now what greater folie or madnes can be deuised, than for men to gene them selues so looselye to all kindes of vices, and to sleepe so sowndlie in them, without euer remembringe, that shortly after at their departinge out of their Inne, there shall be required of them a verie strayt and particular accompte of all their dissolute and wicked lyfe?[12]

If Falstaff denies Luis de Granada's economic and moral premises, which are also at the heart of the Lancastrian political enterprises, his dying moments are brilliantly poised between accepting and rejecting those spiritual conclusions.

The undramatized scene of Falstaff's death has been ruthlessly anticipated in *2 Henry IV* as his voice modulates from robust, zesty parody to a genuine fear of encroaching death—"Peace, good Doll, do not speak like a death's head, do not bid me remember mine end" (*2H4* II.iv.234–35). At his end he appears to be a shrunken, dying old man, no longer the maker and embodiment of vital language and consummate comic actor. No longer wittily supporting his role-playing as the devil incarnate, his language, incoherent and disconnected, is reduced to conventional religious platitudes, traditional pieties, and pleas for more blankets. No longer able to hide behind the fantasies of invented language, he cannot counterfeit kings of England nor play Lord of Misrule. He cannot turn diseases to self-serving commodity or spiritual utility. And he is no longer "the cause that wit is in other men" (I.ii.10).

As a great performer in need of an audience, Falstaff has never before had an introspective or meditative moment which might be called personal. His soliloquies on honor in *1 Henry IV* or on sack in *2 Henry IV* are essentially public moments, the comedian indulging himself with the theater audience rather than his stage audience. Only in a play in which he does not exist and on his deathbed does Falstaff have a ritualistic moment of meditation in which he is only partly aware of those around him and in which his mind turns inward and backward in memory.

Just before his death Falstaff may meditatively engage what Ignatius Loyola calls "seeing the spot," recalling the scene upon which one is meditating with the immediacy of actually being present in it.[13] This conventional "composition of place," which begins a meditation, would invoke the first of the "three powers of the soul"—memory, understanding, and will.[14] Falstaff may remember a romantic moment when he picked flowers in a green meadow, although the text remains as brilliantly insecure as the telling of the babbling. That lost innocence bears no resemblance to other memories recollected in Shallow's orchard of those nights when old classmates recall having heard the chimes at midnight. Other reminiscences are also unambiguous emblems of his life—sack and women; but those memories seem now touched with the recognition of some kind of moral or spiritual understanding, the second stage of the meditative process. Now Falstaff no longer cries out for sack but against it, and he calls the women of Eastcheap "dev'ls incarnate" (*H5* II.iii.31–32). The Hostess's well-meaning denial, based on the fact that he "could never abide carnation" (33), was repudiated from the first when Falstaff admits that he would enjoy the sun only if it were "a fair hot wench in flame-color'd taffata" (*1H4* I.ii.9–10). The identification of his whores with the Whore of Babylon may suggest that Falstaff is thinking of the Apocalypse in Rev. 17:3–6: "and I saw a woman sit upon a scarlet colored beast.... And the woman was arrayed in purple and scarlet colour." Or perhaps as a dubiously reformed Puritan he is attacking the Catholic: Church, as Edmund Bunny would have him do in his meditation. The Hostess's possible pun on "rheum" for Rome—"but then he was rheumatic" (*H5* II.iii.38)—may reinforce the allusion without clarifying Falstaff's "understanding." Seeing a flea land on Bardolph's nose may be only the last flicker of the endless jokes at his expense—"his face is Lucifer's privy kitchen" (*2H4* II.iv.333)—or a deathbed prophecy of Bardolph's impending sacrilege and punishment.

Is Falstaff like Hal seeking a reformation that will glitter o'er his fault as he tries without parody to redeem the time? The fragmented and disconnected structure of his last words, the ambiguity of his observations, and the malapropisms of the Hostess deny resolution as Falstaff may drift to the third and final step in the meditative process, the engaging of the affections, or the will, which traditionally concludes with a colloquy. A meditation on *ars moriendi* would appropriately end in an invocation or prayer to God. And Falstaff calls out to God. But what does he mean? Is this only a feverish cry of fear? Is he trying to make an act of contrition and asking for divine forgiveness? Is this the cry of a man who believes that he has been abandoned by God—as by friend and king—in his last hour? Is one perhaps to hear an elusive echo of Christ's last words on the Cross, a moment Renaissance spiritual advisors urged for deathbed meditations; as, for example, Thomas More in *Four Last Things*: "But whan the poynt approched in which his sacred soule shold depart out of his blessed bodye, at that pointe he cryed loude once or twice to his father in heuen"?[15] Luis de Granada in his *ars moriendi* exercise for Wednesday night would be secure in his spiritual interpretation of this colloquy, but Shakespeare's audience is denied that certainty:

> And as well herein, as in the other thinges, thou hast to consider what great greiffe and anguishe of mynde the sycke person shall then abide in callinge to minde his wicked and synfull life: and how gladly he wishethe at that time that he had taken a better waie: and what an awstere kinde of lyfe he woulde then determine to leade, if he might have time to doe the same: and how fayne he woulde then enforce himselfe to call vpon almightie God, and to desier him of helpe and succour. Howbeit the verie paine, greife,

and continuall increasinge of his sickenes and death will scarcely permitte him so to doe.[16]

The Hostess is equally certain that she knows, but she urges Falstaff to get his mind off death and an afterlife. This, the only time any one tells Falstaff not to worry about his end, physical or spiritual, would be an ironic comfort, indeed, if Luis de Granada's precepts were attended to:

> The first stroke wherewith death is wont to strike, is the feare of death. Suerlie this is a very great anguishe vnto him that is in loue with his lyfe: and this forewarninge is such a great greife vnto a man, that oftentimes his carnall friendes doe vse to dissemble it, and will not haue the sicke man to beleue it, least it shoulde vexe and disquiet him: and this they will doe sometimes although it be to the prejudice and destruction of his miserable sowle.[17]

The Hostess's spiritual purposes may be a miscalculation, but this is her finest moment, not just in the innocence of her double entendres, the humor of her verbal blunders, or her sentimental recollecting of Falstaff's death. If ever there was a woman who had been sorely abused and put upon and "borne, and ... been fubb'd off" (*2H4* II.i.34), it is she who has been victimized by Falstaff, who has indeed "handled" her most outrageously. Yet at the end she loves and comforts, forgives by forgetting. There is in her a Christian charity starkly missing in Falstaff's monarch. Her ministrations may also be reminiscent of those of Socrates' friends at the onset of the death of their companion, condemned as another alleged villainous, abominable misleader of youth and a threat to the established political order: "I put my hand into the bed and felt them, and they were as cold as any stone; then I felt to his knees, and so up'ard and up'ard, and all was as cold as any stone" (*H5* II.iii.23–26). At the beginning of his "Remembrance of Death" in *Four Last Things*, Thomas More recalls Plato's account of Socrates' death in the *Phaedo*—"For some of the olde famous philosophers, whan thei wer demaunded what facultie philosophy was, answerd that it was the meditacion or exercise of death"—and then urges us to "fantasy" our own death in a detailed vision that may bear resemblance to some of the Hostess's recollection: "lying in thy bedde, ... thy nose sharping, thy legges coling, thy fingers fimbling, ... and thy death drawyng on."[18] Even if Shakespeare is recalling More, the unintended bawdy is characteristically the Hostess's own in gesture and simile. Falstaff's stones are cold. Desire no longer outlives performance, as Poins once ridiculed the old man. And his nose, now as sharp as a pen, makes Falstaff's gloriously hyperbolic epithets of Hal—"you starveling, you [eel]skin, you dried neat's tongue, you bull's pizzle, you stock-fish" (*1H4* II.iv. 244–45)—an inverted echo mocked by death, which has finally dethroned surrogate king and father.

The Hostess's vivid recollection of the approaching coldness of death suggests the unrelenting descriptions constantly set out by Loarte, Parsons, Bunny, and Luis de Granada as they urge one to meditate on the moment of dying with a calculatedly precise enumeration. If Shakespeare had their admonitions in mind, he has transformed the macabre and morbid into a bittersweet and humorous account worthy of Falstaff's vital comic spirit. He has detached the spiritual implications and left instead only the poignant corporeal reality, as the scene moves from meditation and remembrance to those who witness or learn of the event with limited understanding and qualified affection. As Parsons lugubriously imagines the inevitable moment:

> Imagine, what the violent mortyfiinge of all the partes together will doe. For we see that first the sowle is driuen by death to leaue the extreamest partes, as the toes, feete and fyngers: then the legges and armes, and so consequentlye one parte dyeth after an other, vntill lyfe be restrained onlye to the harte, which holdeth out longest as the principall parte, but yet must finallye be constrained to render it selve.[19]

Not so, however, with Falstaff. His heart was fracted and corroborate and killed first.

This final creating of a character thematically and dramatically dead at the end of *2 Henry IV* is thus theatrically and structurally achieved through a transformation of an *ars moriendi* meditation composed of the fragments of the disintegrating comic world of *The Henriad*. It is a memorial to a real and mythic character whose essential ambiguity remains as mysteriously allusive in dying as in living. The Shakespearean mode of dramatization is far more affective in its indirectness than any threatening exhortation of a Renaissance spiritual counselor. For us who are invited to meditate on Falstaff the loss of Falstaffian life leads to a diminution of theatrical richness. Consolation is not to be found in any recognition that Falstaff tried to die well.

In the Hostess's disjointed narrative it is possible that some in Shakespeare's audience might recall some of the popular block wood cuts of the *Ars Moriendi* that circulated in hundreds of editions and unknown numbers of copies throughout the fifteenth and sixteenth centuries.[20] In the Editio Princeps an emaciated Moriens lies naked in bed with a blanket pulled up to his waist and his arms extended over it. He is variously surrounded by friends, family, servants, doctors, and nurses as well as grotesque little demons.[21] Such an engraving precedes Luis de Granada's Wednesday night meditation on *ars moriendi* in *Of Prayer, and Meditation*. To a Renaissance audience the realistic and the symbolic, the mythic or the allegorical could co-exist in art and could perhaps be recalled in this traditional mode as a model for the moment that Shakespeare is dramatizing through narration. The Hostess is surely an attentive nurse; Boy, a loyal young servant. Bardolph would have made a good devil; he has been advised of that often enough. Possibly at the end the shrunken Falstaff might, in addition to all his other mythic and traditional roles, unwittingly adopt that of Moriens. But whereas Moriens is shown to have died well as his soul, a young child, leaves his mouth and ascends, we are left only with the Hostess's sentimental assurance of Falstaff's "finer end."

The Hostess's lament brings only a brief truce to erstwhile companions who were at swordpoints earlier that evening. Falstaff's memory now yields to their economic self-serving calculation and suspicion even before the scene is over. By the day of Agincourt his name is forgotten. Swept up in the nationalistic fervor of war against France, this ironic band of brothers shogs off to turn a profit in a world where thievery and whoring have at least moral and mortal consequences. Nym and Bardolph are hanged by order of the King, and Nell dies disease-ridden "i' the spittle / Of a malady of France" (V.i.82–83). And there is none to mourn their passing who would argue that they died well.

NOTES

1. Quotations are taken from *The Riverside Shakespeare*, ed. G. Blakemore Evans (Boston: Houghton Mifflin, 1974).

2. For a persuasive exploration of the parallelisms in the *Henry IV* plays and the two historical tetralogies, see Sherman H. Hawkins, "*Henry IV*: The Structural Problem Revisited," *SQ* 33 (1982):278–301.

3. The work of the English Jesuit Parsons was modified by the Puritan Edmund Bunny in *A Book of Christian Exercise* (1584), but with his admonitions on the Christian necessity for repentance in preparation for death virtually unchanged.

4. Gaspar Loarte, *The Exercise of a Christian Life*, trans. James Sancer (pseudo. Stephen Brinkley) (Rheims, 1584), pp. 8–10.

5. When Caxton translated in 1490 the early fifteenth-century anonymous Latin *Tractus* as the *Ars Moriendi*, or the *Crafte of Dying Well*, he was making available a text that was to become immensely popular over the next two centuries. For a full discussion of the tradition of *Ars Moriendi* in England during the sixteenth century, see Nancy Lee Beatty, *The Craft of Dying: A Study in the Literary Tradition of the 'Ars Moriendi' in England* (New Haven: Yale Univ. Press, 1970), chs. 2 and 4. See also Louis L. Martz, *The Poetry of Meditation* (New Haven: Yale Univ. Press, 1954), pp. 135–44, and Sister Mary Catharine

O'Connor, *The Art of Dying Well: The Development of the Ars Moriendi* (New York: Columbia Univ. Press, 1942).

6. Thomas Lupset, *The Waye of Dyenge Well* (London, 1541), fol. 11v.

7. *Morgann's Essay on the Dramatic Character of Sir John Falstaff*, ed. William Arthur Gill (London, 1912), p. 184.

8. Sir James Frazer, *The Golden Bough* (New York: Macmillan, 1942), abridged edn., pp. 34–35. Noted in J. I. M. Stewart, *Character and Motive in Shakespeare* (London: Longman, Green, 1949), p. 137.

9. Philip Williams, "The Birth and Death of Falstaff Reconsidered," *SQ* 8 (1957):362.

10. Robert Parsons, *The First Booke of the Christian Exercise* (Rouen, 1582), pp. 8, 9, 14, 25, and passim.

11. Parsons, p. 107.

12. Luis de Granada, *Of Prayer, and Meditation*, trans. Richard Hopkins (Paris, 1582), fol. 188r. An English edition was published in London in 1592.

13. "Thou must understand, that they are in such wise to be meditated, as though they happed euen in that instant before thine eyes, in the selfe same place where thou art, or within thy soule: or otherwise imagining thou were in the very places where suche thinges happed, if haply this waies thou shalt feele better deuotion" (Loarte, p. 67).

14. W. H. Longridge, *The Spiritual Exercises of Saint Ignatius of Loyola* (London: Robert Scott, 1919), pp. 52–57.

15. *The Workes of Thomas More ... wrytten by him in the Englysh tonge*, ed. William Rastell (London, 1557), p. 78.

16. Luis de Granada, fols. 183v–84r.

17. Luis de Granada, fol. 190r.

18. Rastell, pp 77–78.

19. Parsons, p. 102. Edmund Bunny's account (*A Book of Christian Exercise*, [London, 1584], p. 90) is essentially the same. Luis de Granada (fol. 184r) is no less explicit in his urging our attention:

> Consider then also those last accidentes, and panges of the sicknes, (which be as it were messingers of death) how fearfull and terrible they be. How at that time the sicke mans breast panteth: his voyce waxeth hoarce: his feele begynnge to die: his knees to waxe colde, and stiffe: his nostrels ronne out: his eies sincke into his head: his countenance looketh pale and wanne: his tonge faultereth, and is not able to doe his office; finally by reason of the hast of the departure awaye of the sowle out of the bodie, all his senses are sore vexed, and troubled, and they doe vtterlie leese their force, and virtue.

20. O'Connor, pp. 114–71. Of nearly 300 extant copies of block books, Sister Diary Catharine saw sixty-one of the *Ars Moriendi* in twenty-one printings from thirteen distinct sets of blocks. The series of eleven block prints depicting Moriens's deathbed temptations were printed in England by Wynkyn de Worde in the early sixteenth century and were copied and modeled with many adaptations in costume and character until Shakespeare's day, but always, as in the Wednesday night illustration in Luis de Granada's *Of Prayer, and Meditation*, with Moriens at the heart of each print in each set.

21 In block cut I, a demon with a long nose hooked upward leans menacingly over Moriens. In VIII there is a representation of the mouth of hell, signified by flames with three figures writhing in agony. In IX the long-nosed demon appears with another devil pointing to a cellar where a boy is stealing a jug of wine from one of four casks—memories

of past pleasures now to be forsaken? In X a man extends a scroll to Moriens "Ne intendas amicis"—"Do not concern yourself with your friends," *The Ars Moriendi*, ed. W. Harry Rylands (London: Wyman and Sons, 1881).

EDWARD TOMARKEN

Morality in Henry IV

Samuel Johnson is surely the most revered moralist of English literature, yet his ethical pronouncements on Shakespeare alienate modern critics. One of the most regularly cited passages in this regard is the section of the *Preface* where Johnson accuses Shakespeare of sacrificing virtue to convenience, that is, of neglecting opportunities for promoting piety and decency. Most modern commentators, on the other hand, admire Shakespeare for refraining from such obtrusive lectures. At his best, however, Johnson the moralist is not didactic, not in favor of tedious declamations on virtue and vice, but concerned with an ethical dimension that is inherent in the structure of the work of art. *Henry IV* is particularly exemplary in this regard because it is approached by Johnson in moral and by moderns in political terms. Understanding the basis of Johnson's moral position throws new light on a section of the *Preface* that is traditionally seen as manifestly didactic and reveals how an ethical interpretation of *Henry IV* relates to modern commentary. Specifically, Johnson's moral view bears upon Shakespeare's political position, suggesting how the critic's ethical decision can contribute to the modification and undermining of ideology, to what Laclau and Mouffe have called the "democratic hegemony" of orthodox political theory. My conclusion is that we need to recognize the ethical dimension basic to literary criticism because literary analysis relates to ideology by way of morality.

The innovative elements of Johnson's Shakespeare criticism become

From *Samuel Johnson on Shakespeare: The Discipline of Criticism.* © 1991 by Edward Tomarken.

apparent when the *Preface* is treated as a preface to the *Notes*. Studies of the *Preface* in isolation have made clear that most of its ideas are derivative.[1] But Johnson's traditional generalizations also serve to summarize and bolster innovative readings of the plays found in the *Notes*. Such eclectic moments in literary criticism are not mere aberrations of interest only to those concerned about the specific text, but are of general significance for literary criticism and theory. One of the reasons for the emergence of new literary methodologies and the modification of ideologies is the inadequacy of old terminology for communicating an innovative interpretation. Johnson's reading of *Henry IV* moves beyond the limitations of didactic criticism and raises a new kind of question for modern Shakespeareans.

Prominent in terms of the discipline of criticism is the need to study literary theory in relation to textual analysis. For Johnson, the *Preface* represents his attempt to theorize about his practical findings in the *Notes*. Like most critics, he had to formulate his innovative interpretations in traditional terms that were becoming inadequate because of new insights such as his own. For the history of literary criticism such practical breakthroughs are crucial, since they are often the points of transition between different theories and ideologies.

FALSTAFF IN CONTEXT

The following passage from the *Preface* is immediately recognized as exemplary of the critic often called the great moralist: "His [Shakespeare's] first defect is that to which may be imputed most of the evil in books and in men. He sacrifices virtue to convenience, and is so much more careful to please than to instruct, that he seems to write without any moral purpose" (7:71). The *Notes* to *Henry IV* conclude with a summary statement, the last paragraph of which uses similarly didactic terms: "The moral to be drawn from this representation is, that no man is more dangerous than he that with a will to corrupt, hath the power to please; and that neither wit nor honesty ought to think themselves safe with such a companion when they see *Henry* seduced by *Falstaff*" (4:356; 7:523–24). Johnson believes that Shakespeare's purpose is to disclose the dangers of being seduced by the kind of person Falstaff represents. By implication, if Henry is vulnerable, who, however honest or intelligent, is safe from the wiles of a Sir John? In this sentence, Johnson begins to distinguish himself from his contemporaries. Since the Restoration, critics had discussed Falstaff apart from the other characters and the action of *Henry IV*. Johnson, it should be noticed at the outset, is interested, not merely in Falstaff, but in his relation to Prince Hal and, by extension, to the audience.

Johnson's contemporaries discussed Falstaff as if he were a drama in himself. In 1698, Jeremy Collier could not disguise his delight that "the admired Falstaff" goes off in disappointment: "He is thrown out of Favour as being a *Rake*, and dies like a Rat behind the Hangings. The Pleasure he had given would not excuse him. The *Poet* was not so partial as to let his Humour compound for his Lewdness" (*SCH* 2:88).[2] Collier's didactic position enables him to avoid deciding why we feel attached to a rake who deserves to be punished for his lewdness. But Johnson does not see the matter in these simplistic terms and therefore feels obliged to explain the positive as well as the negative side of this great comic character. His explanation needs to be cited in its entirety, because, in my view, it has not been surpassed:

> But *Falstaff* unimitated, unimitable *Falstaff*,, how shall I describe thee? Thou compound of sense and vice; of sense which may be admired but not esteemed, of vice which may be despised, but hardly detested. *Falstaff* is a character loaded with faults, and with those faults which naturally produce contempt. He is a thief, and a glutton, a coward and a boaster, always ready to cheat the weak, and prey upon the poor; to terrify the timorous and insult the defenceless.... Yet the man thus corrupt, thus despicable, makes himself necessary to the prince that despises him, by the most pleasing of all qualities, perpetual gaiety, by an unfailing power of exciting laughter, which is more freely indulged, as his wit is not of the splendid or ambitious kind, but consists in easy escapes and sallies of levity, which make sport but raise no envy. It must be observed that he is stained with no enormous or sanguinary crimes, so that his licentiousness is not so offensive but that it may be borne for his mirth. (4:356; 7:523)

This statement stands apart in its own day, accounting in very penetrating terms for the attractive qualities of Falstaff without in the least diminishing his faults. Other eighteenth-century critics chose to defend or attack Falstaff, emphasizing either his rejection by Henry V or his ability to captivate the audience. The latter position reached its culmination in Maurice Morgann's defense of Falstaff's "cowardice" on the battlefield. Although Morgann's essay appeared after Johnson's edition of *Henry IV*, the debate about Sir John began much earlier (*SCH* 6:164–80).[3] In 1709, Nicholas Rowe admitted that the great Shakespearean comic figure was a "Thief, Lying, Cowardly, Vainglorious, and in short every way Vicious." Nonetheless, he found the rejection of Sir John difficult to accept, for the playwright has given his character "so much Wit as to make him almost too agreeable; and I don't know whether some People have not in remembrance of the Diversion he had formerly afforded 'em, been sorry to see his Friend *Hal* use him so scurvily when he comes to the Crown in the End of the Second Part of *Henry IV*" (*SCH* 2:195).[4] Similarly, Charles Gildon, in 1710, found the Falstaff of the second part less diverting than that of the first part: "Tho the Humour of *Falstaff* be what is most valuable in both these Parts yet [it] is more excellent in the first, for *Sir John* is not so Diverting in the second Part" (*SCH* 2:248).[5] In 1733, William Warburton, on the other hand, focused upon Hal, not Falstaff, and applauded Henry's final judgment of his drinking friend: "The *King*, having shaken off his Vanities, in this Scene reproves his old Companion Sir *John* for his Follies with great Severity. He assumes the Air of a Preacher ... bids him seek after Grace ... and leave gourmandizing" (*SCH* 2:534).[6] Warburton believes that this final judgment of Falstaff has been prepared for since the first act, when the prince, in soliloquy, establishes a clear distinction between himself and the knight. For Warburton, Falstaff is a minor character in a drama about the development of a prince into a king. In this respect, however, Warburton is in the minority. Most eighteenth-century commentators considered Falstaff to be the main character. In 1744, for instance, Corbyn Morris wrote a "Character of Sir John Falstaff," which, he admitted, was "chiefly extracted from the *first Part of Henry the IVth*": "Sir *John Falstaff* possesses Generosity, Cheerfulness, Alacrity, Invention, Frolic and Fancy superior to all other Men. The *Figure* of his *Person* is the Picture of Jollity, Mirth, and Good-nature, and banishes at once all other Ideas from your Breast; he is happy himself, and makes you happy.... If you put all these qualities together, it is impossible to *hate* honest *Jack Falstaff* If you observe them again, it is impossible to avoid *loving* him" (*SCH* 3:125–26).[7] In 1756, John Upton asserted that the two parts of the play must be seen as separate, a position that permitted avoidance of the problem of the rejection of Falstaff in the second part of *Henry IV*.[8]

When Johnson set about editing *Henry IV*, two related issues had been contested for some time: whether Falstaff finally deserves our praise or blame, and whether the two parts of the play should be seen as separate entities.[9] Indeed, Johnson refers in his notes to Rowe, Gildon, and Upton as well as to Warburton, indicating his awareness of both sides of the debate. His reply to Upton is most pointed: "Mr. Upton thinks these two plays improperly called *the First* and *second parts of Henry the Fourth*.... These two plays will appear to every reader, who shall peruse them without ambition of critical discoveries, to be so connected that the second is merely a sequel to the first; to be two only because they are too long to be one" (4:235; 7:490). Johnson refuses to avoid the thorny problem of Falstaff's place in the body politic by separating the first part from the second part in which Hal turns upon Sir John. Instead of resorting to character criticism, Johnson faces this issue by locating Falstaff in context. At the same time he is not content, as is Warburton, to see Hal's "imitate the sun" soliloquy (1:2, 190–212) as satisfactory preparation for Henry V's turn upon the companion of his princely days. In order to understand this matter in its full complexity we must first consider Warburton's position. In a part of Theobald's *Preface* now attributed to Warburton, the following attitude toward Hal's soliloquy is set forth.

> And our Poet has so well and artfully guarded his Character from the Suspicions of habitual and unreformable Profligateness that even from the first skewing him upon the Stage, in the first Part of Henry IV, when he made him consent to join with *Falstaff* in a Robbery on the Highway, he has taken care not to carry him off the Scene without an Intimation that he knows them all, and their unyok'd Humour; and that, like the Sun, he will permit them only for a while to obscure and cloud his Brightness, then break thru' the Mist when he pleases to be himself again, that his Lustre, when wanted, may be the more wonder'd at. (*SCH*, 2:479)[10]

Johnson would probably not have known that this portion of Theobald's *Preface* was by Warburton, but he did respond to a more cryptic manifestation of this attitude in his comment on Warburton's note to a line in Prince Hal's soliloquy in act I.

> PRINCE HENRY. So, when this loose behaviour I throw off.
>   And pay the debt I never promised;
>   By how much better than my word I am,
>   By so much shall I falsifie men's hopes;
>   Just the contrary. We should read FEARS. WARBURTON.

Johnson comments on Warburton's note as follows: "To *falsify hope* is to *exceed hope* to give much where men *hoped* for little. This speech is very artfully introduced to keep the Prince from appearing vile in the opinion of the audience; it prepares them for his future reformation, and, what is yet more valuable, exhibits a natural picture of a great mind offering excuses to itself, and palliating those follies which it can neither justify nor forsake" (4:123; 7:458). Warburton implies that only those who have a negative view of the prince, those who have "fears" rather than "hopes" for him, misguidedly believe that he will not be able to disassociate himself from

Falstaff. Johnson sees the matter in more complex terms. The audience is prepared for the prince's reformation while at the same time shown that he willingly participated in and enjoyed the follies of Falstaff and his other drinking companions.

Johnson has thus radically altered the kind of question raised by *Henry IV*. Realizing that Hal is attracted to the world of Falstaff while knowing from the outset that such a companion cannot be acceptable to a king, we understand that Shakespeare is interested not in the characters as individuals but in the context of their friendship. Thus, those of Johnson's predecessors who, like Gildon or Morris, focused upon Falstaff or who followed Warburton in centering upon Hal are equally far from the mark. Johnson stands alone in his own century in refusing to separate the character of Falstaff from the play of which he is a part and in resisting the notion that *Henry IV* is a play about Henry V.

Although a number of his contemporaries claimed that we cannot but love Falstaff, Johnson asserts that in both parts of the play Sir John uses his inimitable wit and humor to evade responsibility for his folly. And while others of his contemporaries argued that Prince Hal never becomes seriously involved in the episodes at the tavern and at Gadshill, Johnson attends to Hal's actions as well as his words and sees that Henry V is right to repent of the activities of his youth. But if in these respects Johnson was alone in his own time, he has much company in the present day. Few now discuss Falstaff separately or assert that Prince Hal only appears to be partaking in the pranks of the subplot. Johnson speaks to our age, placing Falstaff firmly in the context of *Henry IV*.

Indeed, it is probably for this reason that the only comic scene in *1 Henry IV* that Johnson does not like—where Hal seems to imply that he will later reward Francis for serving out his indenture time (2.4)—involves an attempt to prepare for Hal's taking the throne (4:152-53, 7:468). Johnson is the first to consider how the drama shapes our attitude toward Falstaff and leads us to a conclusion about the development of Prince Hal. Who would deny that these are the central questions? While using the didactic terminology that led his contemporaries to defend or attack Falstaff, Johnson steers a middle course, facing issues that still concern us two centuries later.

THE POLITICAL QUESTION

Even if modern commentators address the same issues as Johnson, they arrive at different conclusions: Johnson's position, properly understood in its own terms, raises a serious problem for modern critics. Present-day commentary on *Henry IV* is for the most part divided between two schools of thought that date back to the middle of this century. Some, like John Dover Wilson and E. M. W. Tillyard, believe that Hal's final rejection of Falstaff shows that Henry is ready to assume his responsibilities as sovereign of the realm. Others, such as John Danby and A. P. Rossiter, accept that it is politically expedient to reject Falstaff but find it difficult to accept in human terms: if Henry V has finally become a perfect Machiavellian monarch, he has done so at the cost of turning upon the manly sympathy of his princely days. Tillyard defends his view in the following terms: "The structure of the two parts [of *Henry IV*] is indeed very similar. In the first part the Prince is tested in the military or chivalric virtues.... In the second part, the prince prove[s] his worth in civil life" by accepting the rule of the Lord Chief Justice and rejecting his old companions.[11] For Tillyard, the rejection of Falstaff is the key moment in the play, an act that unifies the two parts of *Henry IV* because it represents the "Elizabethan standards" of political and social life. But Clifford Leech finds problems with this position: "When one is interpreting a Shakespearian play, one is always in danger of being reminded that Shakespeare was an Elizabethan, that the assumptions and standards of judgment were therefore different from ours.... But he was also a human being with a remarkable degree of sensitivity.... We do him, I think, scant justice if we assume that he could write complacently of Prince John of Lancaster, and could have no doubts about Prince Hal."[12]

This difference of opinion remains unresolved. In 1983, Harold Toliver wrote in defense of Tillyard's position, and Harry Levin reformulated the opposing view.[13] The twentieth-century debate concerns the political significance of the rejection of Falstaff: should the historically informed audience regard Henry V's commands at the end of the play as right and proper under the circumstances or as expedient but heartless?

Although employing moral terminology, Johnson makes plain that the ethical issue is closely related to the historical and political purport of the drama. At the outset, internal evidence is cited for the assertion that Shakespeare "designed a regular connection of these dramatic histories from *Richard the Second* to *Henry the Fifth*" (4:109; 7:453), and Johnson reproduces Theobald's notes at the beginning of both of these plays and for all the other histories, explaining that the action of the drama refers to actual historical events. These notes are not included in the Yale edition of Johnson's *Notes to Shakespeare* because Johnson left Theobald's comments unchanged. But, as is made clear in the *Preface*, Johnson left without comment only those notes of his predecessors that he regarded as important and with which he agreed. Further evidence that Johnson is aware of the play's political message appears in his comments on Hotspur and the other rebels. The note to Hotspur's famous boast to "pluck bright honour from the pale fac'd Moon" begins with

Warburton's attack on Gildon and Theobald, who characterized this speech as madness. Rather, Warburton asserts, it is "sublime" and comparable to the words of Eteocles. Characteristically, Johnson remains independent of both these positions, equally wary of seeing Hotspur either as a madman or as a tragic hero: "Though I am far from condemning this speech with *Gildon* and *Theobald* as *absolute madness*, yet I cannot find in it that profundity of reflection and beauty of allegory which the learned commentator [Warburton] has endeavoured to display.... The passage from *Euripides* is surely not allegorical, yet it is produced, and properly, as parallel" (4:133–34; 7:462).

Although not accepted without reservation, Warburton's comparison of Eteocles and Hotspur does demonstrate that Hotspur should not be dismissed as a madman. Few modern critics would contest this assessment, for Hotspur overreaches himself in refusing to accept his place in the body politic. Johnson evidences a similar sensitivity to the political implications of personality in his comment on the other leaders of the rebellion. In act I, when Worcester first mentions the conspiracy against the king, Johnson explains: "This is a natural description of the state of mind between those that have conferred, and those that have received, obligations too great to be satisfied" (4:137; 7:463). This personality conflict is seen as a result of the political dilemma of the play: having been helped by nobles like Worcester to a crown that he could not acquire without their aid, Henry IV must expect that they will object to his absolute rule over them.

THE COMIC SPIRIT OF FALSTAFF

The Falstaff–Prince Hal relationship functions as part of a play about the development of a Tudor monarch. Johnson's first note suggests how personal and historical/political matters are intertwined. Concerning King Henry IV's complaint about the wildness of his son, Johnson points out that this element of Hal's personality had been anticipated in *Richard II*, an indication that Shakespeare "designed a regular connection of these dramatick histories" (4:109; 7:453). Another note on this same scene goes one step further, placing a moral as well as a personal issue firmly in the political context. Henry IV asserts that he wishes to pursue the "holy wars," occasioning Johnson's discussion of whether the Crusades were a right and proper pursuit for a Christian, a passage that concludes with the observation that since the Muhammadans had set out to destroy them, the Christians were obliged to defend themselves. Here Johnson considers the Crusades, an event that appears to be only tangentially related to the play, because he wishes to prevent the king's remark being taken as merely a political ploy, a pious platitude useful for impressing his subjects. Rather, he suggests that the playwright wanted the audience to intermingle religious and moral considerations with political problems, to feel some sympathy for a monarch who comes to regret the means by which he came to power. King Henry IV's sincere and truly Christian remarks help prepare us for the remorse he is to feel later on. Throughout his notes on the history plays, Johnson points out the necessity of understanding how the characters relate to the historical context. Near the beginning of *Henry V*, he remarks: "At this scene begins the connection of this play with the latter part of *King Henry IV*. The characters would be indistinct, and the incidents unintelligible, without the knowledge of what passed in the two foregoing plays" (4:383; 8:536).

But with the entrance of Falstaff a different sort of editorial comment appears, one of several notes that dwell on Sir John's language. Johnson goes to great lengths to explain Falstaff's humor; indeed, nearly half of the notes for the play, approximately sixteen of the thirty-six pages in the Yale edition, are devoted to explaining the jokes and quips between the knight and his companions, a fact that is even more remarkable when one recalls Johnson's remark on Shakespeare's puns in the *Preface*: "A quibble was to him the fatal Cleopatra for which he lost the world, and was content to lose it" (7:74).[14] This sentence is often cited as an example of Johnson's limited understanding of Shakespeare's language, but it is usually misleading to separate Johnson's theory from its application. In the editing of *Henry II*, he labored continually with quibbles. For instance:

> PRINCE HENRY. Thou judgest false already: I mean,
>   thou shalt have the hanging of the thieves, and so become
>   a rare hangman.
> FALSTAFF. Well, *Hal*, well; and in some sort it jumps
>   with my humour, as well as waiting in the Court, I
>   can tell you.
> PRINCE HENRY. For obtaining of suits?
>
> *Suit*, spoken of one that attends at court, means a *petition*; used
> with respect to the hangman, means the *cloaths* of the offender.
> (4:118; 7:456)

In this instance, Johnson's explanation helps us understand the precise way in which the prince is deflating his drinking companion. Hal implies that his friend is as unlikely to be involved in any ceremony at court as in one on the gallows. The suggestion that Falstaff belongs in neither place, both being too extreme, is to be kept in mind when we come to the conclusion.

But Johnson's sensitivity to Shakespeare's language is not restricted to the conversation of Falstaff or to the use of the pun. At the first entrance of Hotspur, Johnson explains the connotation of the image of the "Severn's flood," which was so "affrighted" that it "ran fearfully among the trembling reeds" (1.3.104–5). Previous commentators had censured this passage as nonsense, for it represents a "stream of water as capable of fear." But Johnson explains that "*Severn* is here not the *flood*, but the tutelary power of the flood, who was frightened, and hid his head in *the hollow bank*" (4:129; 7:461). Characteristically, Johnson's aversion to puns does not prevent his careful analysis of language in order to clarify the important ideas of the play. Johnson is anxious to make sense of Hotspur's words so that the reader can distinguish the rebels' from the king's party in subtler terms than those of sanity and insanity. Johnson's analysis of the language of these characters leads to an important, if subtle, distinction between Hotspur and Hal. Percy is seen as one able to do much but who would do more than he is able. The prince, by virtue of his relationship with Falstaff, is implicated in the folly of humorous role-playing and merry quips, indicative of the flexibility and capacity for change of a "great mind."[15]

The self-defeating nature of Hotspur's ability is an early focal point. In the third scene of act I, when the conspiracy is first mentioned, our attention is directed to Hotspur's response to what he most wants to hear: "*Worcester* gives a dark hint of a conspiracy. *Hot-spur smells it*, that is, *guesses it. Northumberland* reproves him for not suffering *Worcester* to tell his design. *Hot-spur*, according to the vehemence of his temper, still follows his own conjecture" (4:136; 7:463). Hotspur's vehemence does not permit him to pause even as the conversation turns to his own obsession. The limitations of this rugged soldier are seen in the conversation of the conspirators, who must wait for Hotspur's enthusiasm to subside before they can get down to the details of the uprising.

Although different from his fiery counterpart, Hal is not seen in wholly flattering terms. For example, the prince at the tavern (2.4.12) characterizes himself as "no proud Jack, like Falstaff, but a Corinthian." A modern editor glosses the last word of this line in the following complimentary terms: "a boon companion.... Corinth was noted for gay dissipation." Johnson is much less flattering: "a wencher" (4:151; 7:467). In *Richard II*, Johnson characterizes King Henry V by referring to "his greatness in his manhood" and to the "debaucheries in his youth" (4:92; 7:450). Further reference to the distinction between these two characters is provided by the immediately preceding note in *1 Henry IV*, which concerns Hotspur's conversation with Lady Percy. While the prince revels in low comedy, Hotspur sets his military duty above the love of his wife.

Refusing to gloss over Hal's failings, Johnson nonetheless fosters our sympathy with and understanding of the personable qualities that distinguish him from Hotspur. Hal's reflections on Hotspur are paraphrased by Johnson for purposes of clarity: "That is, *I am willing to indulge myself in gaiety and frolick, and try all the varieties of human life. I am not yet of Percy's mind,* who thinks all the time lost that is not spent in bloodshed, forgets decency and civility, and has nothing but the barren talk of a brutal soldier" (4:155; 7:469). In fact, near the end of *Henry V*, Johnson chastises Shakespeare for contradicting the nature of this distinction, which has been established in preceding dramas: "I know not why *Shakespeare* now gives the king nearly such a character as he made him formerly ridicule in *Percy*. This military grossness and unskilfulness in all the softer arts, does not suit very well with the gaieties of his youth, with the general knowledge ascribed to him at his accession, or with the contemptuous message sent him by the *Dauphin*, who, represents him as fitter for the ballroom than the field, and tells him that he is not to *revel into dutchies*, or win provinces *with a nimble galliard*" (4:479; 8:565). We gradually come to realize that Hal is a fuller human being than Percy: as Hotspur ignores his own domestic duties in his military obsession, the prince can be expected to respond to the full range of womankind, from wench to lady.

Hal is most notably to be distinguished from Hotspur in his association with Falstaff. Johnson gives his highest praise to the scene (2.4) where Falstaff takes the part of the king and admonishes the prince for his errant ways:

> FALSTAFF. *Harry,* I do not only marvel, where thou spendest thy time, but also how thou art accompanied; for though the camomile, the more it is trodden on, the faster it grows, yet youth, the more it is wasted, the sooner it wears.

> This whole speech is supremely comick. The simile of camomile used to illustrate a contrary effect, brings to my remembrance an observation of a later writer of some merit, whom the desire of being witty has betrayed into a like thought. Meaning to enforce with great vehemence the mad temerity of young soldiers, he remarks, that *though* Bedlam *be in the road to* Hogsden, *it is out of the way to promotion.* (4:166; 7:472–73)

This digression, a rarity in Johnson's edition, serves to illustrate a linguistic abuse, a form of bathos, a trope that at once advances and subverts the speaker's purpose. Of course, Falstaff deliberately turns the trope upon himself, and that is why the scene is supremely comic. In fact, we are invited by our editor to pause over this particular comic moment, because it epitomizes what Johnson means by Falstaff's humor as consisting "in easy escapes and sallies of levity, which make sport but raise no envy" (4:365; 7:523). As the player-king, the knight scolds the prince in "high-flown" style—modern editors trace the camomile image to Lyly's *Euphues: Anatomy of Wit*[16]—which, in calling attention to itself, distracts our attention from the main purpose of the speech, saving the prince from some embarrassment about the question of "how thou art accompanied."

Falstaff's humorous skill here is of the sort that will not excite envy because he turns it upon himself and thereby allows Hal an easy escape. The authority of the player-king is, to some extent, undermined by his misuse of euphuistic rhetoric. Not simply a humorous character, Falstaff demonstrates that his inimitable comic spirit derives from his ability to see how others view him. He knows that the king finds him an unsuitable companion for his son, that the son accepts the justice and the humorlessness of his father's attitude, and that the audience enjoys the skill with which he plays upon these perspectives.[17]

This portrait of Sir John reveals not only the complexity of his sense of humor but also a side of his disposition that is often neglected. In the third scene of the third act, Bardolph abuses his drinking companion in obvious physical terms, telling Falstaff that he is so fat as to "needs be out of all compass." The knight's reply—"thou art the knight of the burning lamp"—elicits the following comment from Johnson: "This is a natural picture. Every man who feels in himself the pain of deformity, however, like this merry knight, he may affect to make sport with it among those whom it is his interest to please, is ready to revenge any hint of contempt upon one whom he can use with freedom" (4:188; 7:478). Johnson wants us to see genuine anger on the part of the knight; for a moment, the vulnerable man is revealed behind the clown's mask. The full picture of Falstaff, including his vulnerability to insult, is important to Johnson for two reasons. It will be a factor in Hal's final rejection of him and will also serve as a reminder that Falstaff in anger, as in enjoyment, is aware of how he appears to others. The point to be emphasized at this stage is that it is precisely this comprehensiveness of response, this broad range of human awareness, that accounts for the prince's and our attraction to Falstaff.

Yet Johnson provides no excuses for Falstaff on the battlefield. On the contrary, he is seen in contrast to the courageous prince. Explaining the famous image in which Vernon describes the prince and his comrades riding off to battle as "all furnisht, all in arms, all plum'd like estridges, that with the wind, baited like eagles, having lately bath'd" (4.1.97–99), Johnson remarks that "a more lively representation of young men ardent for enterprize perhaps no writer has ever given" (4:199; 7:482). Falstaff, on the other hand, is described, not in the sublime terms of lively enterprise, but in terms of sheer cowardice, which he inadequately disguises as a joke. On the battlefield, when Sir John hands Hal a bottle of sack in place of a pistol, Johnson, unlike Maurice Morgann, does not attempt to excuse the knight's behavior.[18] Instead, he points to the comic way Falstaff tries to cover up or pass over his own cowardice.

> FALSTAFF. If Percy be alive, I'll pierce him.

> *Falstaff* takes up his bottle which the Prince had tossed at his head, and being about to animate himself with a draught, cries, if *Percy be alive I'll pierce him*, and so draws the cork. I do not propose this with much confidence. (4:222; 7:487–88)

Johnson speculates tentatively about this pun to make clear that Falstaff quibbles about the name of the enemy and pierces no more than a bottle of sack, while, in battle with Percy, Hal risks his life. In this way, we notice that the prince is beginning to pursue a way of life different from that of Falstaff.

THE ATMOSPHERE OF *2 HENRY IV*

Johnson records the change in the atmosphere in the second part of the play in a comment on Northumberland's acknowledgment of the death of his son Percy and his decision to join the rebellion.

> NORTHUMBERLAND. But let one spirit of the first-born Cain
>   Reign in all bosoms, that each heart being set
>   On bloody courses, the rude scene may end,
>   And darkness be the burier of the Dead!

> The conclusion of this noble speech is extremely striking. There is no need to suppose it exactly philosophical; *darkness* in poetry may be absence of eyes as well as privation of light. Yet we may remark, that by an ancient opinion it has been held, that if the human race, for whom the world was made, were extirpated, the whole system of sublunary nature would cease. (4:242; 7:493)

Remarking on the ancient belief in the possible return of chaos and old night, Johnson stresses the poetic expression of Northumberland's personal grief and desire for revenge. It is a commonplace among modern critics that, unlike

1 Henry IV, the second part is marked by an increasing sense of decay, corruption, and the questioning of authority. Johnson apparently agrees. Similarly, important historical and political information is contained in a note on Lord Bardolph's speech (1.3.36–62). Here Johnson refuses to accept Pope's emendation, which was adopted by Theobald, Hammer, and Warburton. The problem is that in Pope's version Lord Bardolph recommends no delay, while, in the original, he cautions against haste. Siding with Johnson against Pope and the others, most modern editors offer a paraphrase (without acknowledgment of their debt to Johnson) of his explanation of this passage, which A. R. Humphreys labeled "the chief crux of the play."[19] Johnson is the first to realize that the uprising must be seen to be hurried, for the substantial political charge against the rebels is not that their claims were unjustified but that they acted before exhausting all alternatives to war.

Most of Johnson's notes, however, are devoted to explaining the puns and jokes of Falstaff, Hal, and their retinue at Mistress Quickly's inn, for the humor of these characters represents for Johnson significant entertainment. In the last act of *Henry V*, Johnson remarks: "The comick scenes of the history of *Henry* the fourth and fifth are now at an end, and the comick personages are dismissed.... I believe every reader regrets their departure" (4:474; 8:563). But in *2 Henry IV*, the reader is made aware of a change in tone. When Falstaff addresses Hal as "a bastard son of the King's," Johnson remarks that "the improbability of this scene is scarcely ballanced by the humour" (4:283; 7:503). Unlike the scene in part 1 (3.3.85ff.) where Falstaff also abuses the prince, which Johnson characterized as a "merry dialogue" (4:193; 7:480), this scene lacks the deft sense of humor we expect of Falstaff. Particularly improbable here is Falstaff's insulting of the king, something he carefully avoids in the previous scene. It seems to me that Johnson is assuming that an eighteenth-century audience, like an Elizabethan one, would tolerate the knight's abuse of the prince, his drinking companion, but not of the king. Aside from the breach of decorum, this remark manifests Falstaff's insensitivity to his public spectacle, his blindness to the negative impression he is making upon others. Yet, as we have seen, his great comic genius resides in precisely such an awareness. Johnson suggests that in preparing the way for the rejection of Falstaff, Shakespeare sacrifices the most important element of one of his greatest creations, Falstaff's ability to turn his sense of humor against himself.

JOHNSON AND MODERN CRITICS

However, there are major differences between Johnson and present-day critics concerning Falstaff. Although they may disagree about the proper attitude to the end of the play, contemporary commentators agree that Falstaff changes in the second part and becomes less likable, his humor being darker and more corrupt. The knight's treatment of Shallow and Silence (3.2) is now generally regarded as shabby. Clifford Leech goes so far as to suggest that "we have come to wonder whether there is ultimately much to choose between Falstaff and Prince John."[20] For Johnson, on the other hand, the difference between these two characters must never be obscured. With regard to the gulling of Justice Shallow, Johnson explains that Shallow's description is equivalent to admitting that he "is King Arthur's fool" (4:301; 7:506–7). We are reminded that Shallow, as his name suggests, is a low character and a fool; the implication is that if Falstaff had not taken advantage of him, someone else would have. Indeed, Falstaff himself says as much.

> FALSTAFF. If the young Dace be a bait for the old Pike, I see no reason in the law of nature but I may snap at him.

> That is, *If the pike may prey upon the dace, if it be the law of nature that the stronger may seize upon the weaker,* Falstaff *may with great propriety devour* Shallow. (4:302–3; 7:507)

For Johnson, the devouring of Shallow is natural to Falstaff, who, we recall, was characterized as one who preys upon the weak; this behavior represents no change in Falstaff. Far from condoning the knight's actions on the battlefield or toward Shallow, Johnson sees each as cowardly and worthy of punishment; they are both, however, to be distinguished from major crimes. Prince John's action at Gaultree is described in unmistakably Johnsonian terms: "It cannot but raise some indignation to find this horrible violation of faith passed over thus slightly by the poet, without any note of censure or detestation" (4:317; 7:512). Moral outrage is expressed here because this breach of trust, while it may have been necessary for political purposes, represents a cold and calculated act of deception and inhumanity.

We may be tempted here to apply the passage from the *Preface* cited at the beginning of this chapter and conclude that Johnson required a didactic interjection. But the condemnation of Prince John should be understood in the larger context of Johnson's overall view of the drama. In neglecting to condemn the action of Prince John at Gaultree, Shakespeare obscures the difference between Falstaff and Prince John, namely, that the former's humanity makes him appealing to us in spite of his folly and vice. Prince John, on the other hand, remains unmoved by the humor of the fat knight. And both Falstaff and Johnson are mindful of this fact.

FALSTAFF. Good faith, this same young sober blooded Boy doth
not love me; nor a man cannot make him laugh.

Falstaff speaks here like a veteran in life. The young prince did
not love him, and he despaired to gain his affection, for he could
not make him laugh. Men only become friends by community of
pleasures. He who cannot be softened into gaiety cannot easily be
melted into kindness. (4:320; 7:513).

Able to deceive others without a pang of conscience, this young prince is
incapable of responding to Falstaff. Indeed, his crime seems to be defined by
this inability. For Johnson, a man capable of gaiety would be too gentle, too
kind to treat his fellow human beings as did Prince John at Gaultree. And in
spite of his continual sloth and cowardice, few believe Falstaff capable of such
an act. For this reason Johnson asserts that Falstaff "is stained with no
enormous or sanguinary crimes." Crime involves the active betrayal of one's
humanity; folly and vice, the result of passivity and self-indulgence, involve
serious errors but not what Johnson calls "malignancy."

Prince Hal, on the other hand, comes finally to take his place
somewhere between the warm but self-indulgent Sir John and the cold and,
at times, unscrupulous Prince John. For Johnson, the play should conclude
in a manner that does justice to the distinction between these three
characters. To say that he is dissatisfied or even deeply disappointed is an
understatement. The resolution occasions a most uncharacteristic
exclamation from a critic who is widely praised for his judiciousness and
common sense: "I fancy every reader, when he ends this play, cries out with
Desdemona, O most lame and impotent conclusion" (4:355; 7:522). The reference
is to Desdemona's protest at Iago's indiscriminately negative characterization
of women. What disturbs Johnson about the end of this play is not Hal's
change in attitude toward Falstaff but his sending him to the Fleet. Indeed,
so far as I can ascertain, Johnson is the first to attend to the fact that the
judgment of Falstaff involves two separate and different punishments. With
regard to the first decision, the banishment of Falstaff from court, Johnson
has no difficulty: "Mr. *Rowe* observes, that many readers lament to see *Falstaff*
so hardly used by his old friend. But if it be considered that the fat knight has
never uttered one sentiment of generosity, and with all his power of exciting
mirth, has nothing in him that can be esteemed, no great pain will be
suffered from the reflection that he is compelled to live honestly and be
maintained by the king, with a promise of advancement when he shall
deserve it" (4:353; 7:521).

Rowe and those who adopted his position are being warned not to be sentimental about Falstaff. Unlike many eighteenth-century critics, Johnson has no objection to a moderate punishment of Falstaff, particularly if its aim is to reform the knight, who, as we have seen, is viewed as a "thief and a glutton, a coward and a boaster." Although likeable, Falstaff should not be esteemed, and therefore am attempt to encourage this comic genius to reform his way of life is admirable. But sending Falstaff to the Fleet disturbs Johnson: "I do not see why *Falstaff* is carried to the Fleet. We have never lost sight of him since his dismission from the king; he has committed no new fault, and therefore incurred no punishment; but the different agitations of fear, anger, and surprise in him and his company, made a good scene to the eye; and our authour, who wanted them no longer on the stage, was glad to find this method of sweeping them away" (4:354; 7:522).

What could Falstaff have done to deserve imprisonment, what new crime could he have committed in the twenty lines of text that elapsed since he was banished? Shakespeare wanted first to show the knight's consternation at his punishment and then to clear the stage quickly of this bulky distraction. A convenient stage device, the imprisonment of Falstaff undermines the careful distinction developed in the play between crimes of weakness and those of malice, between Falstaff and Prince John, with Prince Hal poised between the two.

The issue at hand may become clearer by comparing Johnson's view of the conclusion to that of a modern editor. The new Arden edition cites with approval the words of its predecessor, which appeared in 1923. The following passage constitutes the Arden position for the last half century: "Falstaff's ultimate disgrace and punishment have gained for him much undeserved commiseration; the punishment ... temporary imprisonment in the Fleet and banishment from court—was not exceptionally severe. Queen Elizabeth inflicted similar sentences upon favourite courtiers and court ladies who incurred her displeasure. To Shakespeare's contemporaries, the King's treatment of Falstaff would not appear harsh."[21] In taking the two punishments as one, in inextricably linking the banishment and the imprisonment, these twentieth-century editors beg the question. When the king forbade his friend within ten miles of his person, is there any indication that this punishment was felt by "Shakespeare's contemporaries" to be insufficiently harsh? Moreover, are we to believe that to Elizabethans there was no appreciable difference between banishment and incarceration?

Most modern commentators are not interested in the distinction between the two punishments because they follow Shakespeare himself, who, as Johnson points out, wants to sweep the Falstaffians from the stage in order to focus upon the political figures, the Lord Chief Justice, Prince John, and King Henry V, those who represent the power and might of the Tudor dynasty. But even in political terms, the conclusion is lame and impotent. What sort of a ruler is a king who makes no distinction between crimes worthy of imprisonment and vices deserving of exile? To return to Tillyard's position, what sort of respect is aroused by a king who first banishes a man and then a moment later allows his Lord Chief Justice to imprison him? Or, to return to the opposition to Tillyard represented by Leech, is it satisfactory to say that the audience understands the necessity of imprisoning Falstaff but cannot agree with Prince John's pleasure at the removal of all the Falstaffians, all those who inspired our merriment throughout both parts of the play and who constitute the "people" of the play? The difference between Johnson's reading of the play and that of these modern critics is that the former formulates himself in moral terms and the latter ignore him, restricting themselves to historical and political terms. But my contention is that Johnson points to a personal/moral issue that is inseparable from the historical/political dilemma of *Henry IV*.

Johnson's objection to the conclusion of *Henry IV* is not essentially didactic: he is not castigating Shakespeare for a lack of declamatory speeches concerning the appropriate vices and virtues. Rather, Johnson employs moral terms to characterize a problem about the form of the conclusion. Once understood in structural, not didactic, terms, this position raises a new question for modern Shakespeareans. What kind of political doctrine is represented by a Tudor dynast who is incapable of distinguishing between vice that arises from malice and that which springs from frailty? Johnson's objection points to the neglect of the ethical dimension inherent in the modern political view of the conclusion.

The manner in which Johnson's moral position impinges upon the modern political one can be seen by considering Stephen Greenblatt's most recent version of his essay on *Henry IV* and *Henry V*; entitled "Invisible Bullets." A founder of the "new historicists," who employ historical investigation to locate materials that at once advance and undermine the established political position, Greenblatt demonstrates that Thomas Harriot's "Brief and True Report of the New Found Land of Virginia" (1588) provides a model for a concept of political language that is both orthodox and subversive. Greenblatt applies this model to *Henry IV* and *Henry V*. The conflict between these two elements is more marked in certain circumstances: "This exposure is most intense at moments when a comfortably established ideology confronts unusual circumstances, when the moral value of a particular form of power is not merely assumed but explained." But the difficulty with these explanations is "not that they are self-consciously wicked ... but that they are dismayingly moral."[22] Since morality exposes but also covers up the problem, Greenblatt turns to

linguistic analysis. But, as we shall see, he finds the same difficulty that
Johnson located in moral terms.

Turning to the protagonists, Greenblatt asserts that "Hal is a juggler,"
a conniving hypocrite, and that the "power he both serves and comes to
embody is glorified usurpation and theft." As a "juggler" he is finally
identified with the playwright himself. The problem is that Hal will
eventually become the king, the orthodox establishment, and must therefore
juggle with the subversive nature of Falstaff: "This staging of what we may
term anticipatory or proleptic parody is a major structural principle of
Shakespeare's play. Its effect is not ... to ridicule the claims of high
seriousness but rather to mark them as slightly suspect and to encourage
guarded skepticism," a skepticism that is finally rejected with the
imprisoning of Falstaff.[23] Greenblatt concludes by considering the end of
Henry V, the "language lesson" that Hal gives the French princess, the very
same scene that troubled Johnson so much that he concludes his remarks on
Henry V by pointing out that "the great defect of this play is the emptiness
and narrowness of the last act" (4:487; 8:566). Although the result is "the
apparent subversion of the monarch's glorification," Greenblatt points out
"it is not at all clear that *Henry V* can be successfully performed as
subversive." The dramas are thus seen to end with an ambiguous
combination of orthodoxy and subversion. But, for Greenblatt, the
subversive element only becomes apparent to modern audiences when they
are provided with the appropriate historical, linguistic materials, which point
up the double-sided aspect of Elizabethan political language. "There is
subversion, no end of subversion, only not for us."[24] Yet Johnson
experienced the same phenomenon, though he couched it in moral terms,
examined structural properties, and was unlikely to have been familiar with
the historical materials referred to by Greenblatt. In short, Johnson has
located in the text the subversion that Greenblatt asserts is only available to
post-Elizabethans in materials outside of the plays.

The reason that Johnson is able to locate the problem within the
structure of the dramas is that he approaches it not in ideological but in
moral terms. For him, the playwright's conclusion must do justice to the
context, which encourages discrimination among his characters. Similarly,
Johnson, in judging the conclusion, feels compelled to explain the basis of his
assessment. The critic is morally obliged to make explicit his interpretation
and judgment of the work of art. What precisely is meant by interpretation
and judgment will be clarified in the next two chapters, where the principles
of Johnson's summary statements will be examined.

The moral imperative that Johnson applies to Shakespeare he also
applies to himself as a critic. Insisting that the specific problem of Falstaff's

punishment be related to the general conception, the body politic, Johnson provides particulars in the *Notes* to exemplify his generalizations in the *Preface*. On the level of literary theory, I believe that we need to follow Johnson's example. It will not do to conclude that the status quo and its opposition are left in free play in Shakespeare's Henriad, like ignorant armies of ideology. Literature and criticism create contexts that require development, modification, even contradiction of ideology. The ethical imperative insists that the particular affect the general at all levels, that the individual, the nonconformist, the Falstaffian, influence the nature of ideology, from that of the Tudor dynasty to that of modern democracy. Literature and literary analysis are thus seen not merely as a result of but as one of the forces that contribute to the hegemony of ideology.

The ethical dimension is accordingly fundamental to the procedure of this chapter. Studying theory in relation to practice reveals important new insights. The section of the *Preface* that had been taken on its own as representing traditional didacticism is understood, when related to the *Notes*, as a formulation of an ethical question. Distinguishing between didacticism and morality enables us to understand how Johnson formulated an innovative reading of *Henry IV* within the theoretical terms available to him in the eighteenth century.[25] If our analysis of Johnson's criticism can be considered metacriticism, the metacritic is morally obliged to make explicit the basis for his or her assessment and interpretation of the relationship between theory and practice.

All critics formulate themselves in terms that are limited by their historical epoch; great critics occasionally arrive at insights that point beyond the terms of their era. Literary criticism as a separate discipline rests upon such insights and must dedicate itself to a method of retrieving them. As Johnson provided quotations from the texts of others to illustrate his definitions in the *Dictionary*, so the *Notes* exemplify and clarify the generalizations of the *Preface*. This study follows in Johnson's tradition. Each chapter concludes with an axiom of literary criticism derived from Johnson's interpretation of one of Shakespeare's plays. Theory and practice are deliberately intermingled so that my principles can be evaluated in relation to my perceptions, for one final criterion of any literary critical generalization must be whether or not it helps to further an understanding of literature. Morality, the most basic and continuous element of Johnson's criticism, one linking theory and practice, becomes important for me because it also mediates between criticism and ideology.[26] Unlike didacticism, morality involves a decision about how literary meaning relates to the human predicament. The next chapter demonstrates that Johnson added a summary statement at the end of all but two of the plays to make explicit his assessment of the relation between theory and practice, to delineate precisely where abstract ideas touched the earth.

NOTES

1. See Sherbo, *Samuel Johnson*, pp. 46–60. For a more recent consideration of the *Preface*, see R. D. Stock, *Johnson and Neoclassical Dramatic Theory*. For an updated version of Sherbo's position, see Arthur Sherbo, *The Birth of Shakespeare Studies: Commentators from Rome to Boswell-Malone* (East Lansing, Mich.: Colleagues Press, 1988), especially pp. 18–26. For another recent view of Johnson and his predecessors, see Peter Seary, "The Early Editions of Shakespeare and the Judgments of Johnson," in *Johnson after Two Hundred Years*, ed. Paul Korshin (Princeton: Princeton Univ. Press, 1986), pp. 175–86. The latest book on this topic is G. F. Parker's *Johnson's Shakespeare*. Parker implies that Johnson's conception of general nature is original or at least used by Johnson in a special way (see pp. 2–8). Unfortunately, Parker does not explain how Johnson's concept is to be distinguished from those of the contemporaries and predecessors discussed by Sherbo and Stock. His claim is therefore implicit and unsubstantiated. For an assessment of Johnson's analysis of Shakespeare's use of his sources, see Karl Young, "Samuel Johnson: One Aspect," *University of Wisconsin Studies in Language and Literature* 18 (1923): 146–226. For an account of why Johnson's contribution as editor of "accidentals" has not been sufficiently appreciated, see Arthur M. Eastman, "Johnson's Shakespeare and the Laity in Textual Study," *PMLA* 65 (1950): 1112–21.

2. Jeremy Collier, *A Short View of the Immorality, and Profaneness of the English Stage* (London, 1698), p. 154.

3. Maurice Morgann, *An Essay on the Dramatic Character of Sir John Falstaff* (London, 1777), P. 410.

4. Nicholas Rowe, *The Works of Mr. William Shakespeare* (London, 1709), 1:xviii.

5. Charles Gildon, *The Works of Mr. William Shakespeare, Volume the Seventh* (London, 1725), p. 376.

6. John Nichols, ed., *Illustrations of the Literary History of the Eighteenth Century* (London, 1733), 3:379.

7. Corbyn Morris, *An Essay Towards Fixing the True Standards of Wit, Humour, Raillery, Satire, and Ridicule* (London, 1744), pp. 28–29, and edited by James L. Clifford for the Augustan Reprint Society (Los Angeles: Univ. of California Press, 1947).

8. John Upton, *Critical Observations on Shakespeare* (London, 1756), pp. 70–71. For other evidence of Johnson's awareness of the continuity of the history plays, see *Henry V* (4:383; 8:536) and *Richard III* (5:319; 8:625).

9. Arthur Sherbo finds some evidence to suggest that Samuel Johnson began work on the edition before 1745. See Sherbo, "'Sanguine Expectations': Dr. Johnson's Shakespeare," *Shakespeare Quarterly* 9 (1958): 426–28.

10. Lewis Theobald, ed., *The Works of Shakespeare* (London, 1733), 1:xviii. For the attribution to Warburton, see *SCH* 2:18.

11. E. M. W. Tillyard, "*Henry IV* and the Tudor Epic," in *Shakespeare: Henry IV Parts I and II, a Casebook*, ed. G. K. Hunter (London: Macmillan Press, 1970), p. 107. For further evidence of Johnson's understanding of the political import of these plays, see *Henry V* (4:414; 8:547; 4:444; 8:555; 4:461; 8:560; 4:479; 8:565) and *Henry VIII* (5:490; 8:657).

12. Clifford Leech, "The Unity of *2 Henry IV*," in *Twentieth-Century Interpretations of Henry IV*, Part 2, ed. David P. Young (Englewood Cliffs, NJ.: Prentice-Hall, 1968), p. 41.

13. Harold Toliver, "Workable Fictions in the Henry IV Plays," *University of Toronto*

Quarterly 53 (1983): 53–71, and Harry Levin, "Falstaff's Encore," *Shakespeare Quarterly* 32 (1981): 5–17.

14. In spite of his disapproval of the quibble, Johnson takes time elsewhere to explain Falstaff's puns, as in *Merry Wives* (2:484; 7:332), and even notes his own reliance on Falstaff's puns, in *Timon of Athens* (6:192; 8:716) and *Coriolanus* (6:499; 8:798).

15. For references in other plays to Hal's character, see *Henry V* (4:379; 7534) and *Richard II* (4:92; 8:450).

16. William Shakespeare, *The First Part of Henry IV*; ed. A. R. Humphreys (London: Methuen, 1960), p. 78.

17. Boswell, in his *Life of Johnson*, records that Johnson, in 1783, commented on this essay: "'Why, Sir, we shall have the man come forth again; and as he has proved Falstaff to be no coward, he may prove Iago to be a very good character'" (*Life of Johnson* 4:192). Probably no character is more often referred to in Johnson's *Notes* than Falstaff. On his personality, see the stricture to *The Merry Wives of Windsor*, where Johnson discusses Queen Elizabeth's delight with Falstaff and the difficulty of showing him in love (7:341). In *All's Well That Ends Well*, Johnson compares him as a coward to Parolles (3:384; 7:399). At the last appearance of Falstaff in *Henry V*, Johnson discusses the difficulty of finding future adventures that would be as entertaining as those before (4:397 8:441–42). Later in the same play, Johnson registers his sorrow at the last of the comic scenes of *Henry IV* and *Henry V* (4:474; 8:563). While recognizing the comic genius of Falstaff, Johnson continually reminds his audience that in moral terms he was below Hal (4:379; 8:534). For further evidence that Johnson stands out from his contemporaries in his concern for the theatrical spectacle of the characters, see S. P. Zitner, "Staging the Occult in *1 Henry IV*," in *Mirror Up to Shakespeare; Essays in Honour of G. R. Hibbard*, ed. J. C. Gray (Toronto: Univ. of Toronto Press, 1984), pp. 138–48.

18. See above, n. 3.

19. A. R. Humphreys, ed., *The Second Part of Henry IV*, by William Shakespeare (London: Methuen, 1966), p. 34.

20. Leech, "Unity of *2 Henry IV*," p. 38.

21. Humphreys, *Second Part of Henry IV*, p. 184.

22. Stephen Greenblatt, *Shakespearian Negotiations: The Circulation of Social Energy in Renaissance England* (Oxford: Clarendon Press, 1988), p. 38. For a British equivalent of Greenblatt's position, see Jonathan Dollimore and Alan Sinfield, "History and Ideology: The Instance of *Henry V*," in *Alternative Shakespeares*, ed. John Drakakis (London: Methuen, 1985), pp. 206–27. Like Greenblatt, Dollimore and Sinfield conclude with ambiguity: "We might conclude from this that Shakespeare was indeed wonderfully impartial on the question of politics.... Alternatively, we might conclude that the ideology which saturates his texts, and their location in history, are the most interesting things about them" (p. 227).

23. Greenblatt, *Shakespearian Negotiations*, pp. 55–57.

24. Ibid., pp. 63–65. For an example of how the new historicist position evades the constrictions of literary structure and genre, see Leonard Tennenhouse, "Strategies of State and Political Plays: *A Midsummer Night's Dream, Henry IV, Henry V, Henry VIII*," in *Political Shakespeare: New Essays in Cultural Materialism*, ed. Jonathan Dollimore and Alan Sinfield (Manchester: Manchester Univ. Press, 1985), pp. 109–28. Alternatively, Marjorie Garber stresses the importance of genre within a reader-response framework, in "'What's Past Is Prologue': Temporality and Prophecy in Shakespeare's History Plays," in *Renaissance Genres: Essays on Theory, History, and Interpretation*, ed. Barbara Kiefer Lewalski (Cambridge, Mass.: Harvard Univ. Press, 1986), pp. 301–31.

25. For some examples of Johnson's didactic notes, see *Measure for Measure* (1:377; 7:213), *The Merchant of Venice* (1:456; 7:227), and *Othello* (8:397; 8:1032–33).

26. Laclau and Mouffe, *Hegemony and Socialist Strategy*, pp. 65–75.

ABBREVIATIONS

Dictionary   Samuel Johnson. *A Dictionary of the English Language.* 4th ed. 2 vols. London, 1773.

Dryden   John Dryden. *The Works of John Dryden.* Ed. Maximilian E. Novak. Vol. 13. Berkeley: Univ. of California Press, 1984.

Garrick   David Garrick. *The Plays of David Garrick.* Ed. Harry William Pedicord and Frederick Louis Bergmann. 4 vols. Carbondale: Southern Illinois Univ. Press, 1980.

Hill and Powell   George Birkbeck Hill and L. F. Powell, eds. *Boswell's "Life of Johnson,"* by James Boswell. 6 vols. Oxford: Clarendon Press, 1934–64.

Lives   Samuel Johnson. *The Lives of the Poets.* Ed. George Birkbeck Hill. 3 vols. Oxford: Clarendon Press, 1905.

Notes   All references to Samuel Johnson, *Notes to Shakespeare*, provide first the volume and page number in the original edition (London, 1765) and then the volume and page number in the edition by Arthur Sherbo (New Haven: Yale Univ. Press, 1968).

NV   Horace Howard Furness, ed. *A New Variorum Edition of Shakespeare's "Twelfth Night."* 1901. Reprint. New York: Dover, 1964.

Preface   Samuel Johnson. *Preface to Notes to Shakespeare.* Ed. Arthur Sherbo. New Haven: Yale Univ. Press, 1968.

SCH   Brian Vickers, ed. *Shakespeare: The Critical Heritage.* London: Routledge and Kegan Paul, 1974–81. Because they represent the most readily available versions, these volumes are cited in the text. Whenever possible, notes provide information on the original sources.

Shakespeare   In any given discussion, the text of Shakespeare's play referred to is, unless otherwise indicated, that used by the editor or critic being discussed.

W   William Warburton, ed. *The Works of Shakespear.* 1747. Reprint. New York: AMS Press, 1968.

FRANÇOIS LAROQUE

Shakespeare's 'Battle of Carnival and Lent': The Falstaff Scenes Reconsidered (1 & 2 Henry IV)

In his pioneering book, Mikhail Bakhtin analyses the carnivalesque as the victory of the old world over the new, as the force which illustrates the way the principles of inversion and permutation work underneath the surface of carnival and festive misrule.[1] There 'Billingsgate', the language of the marketplace, takes precedence over the idiom of the learned, of Church and university culture. For Bakhtin, the carnivalesque is another version of the grotesque, it is the moment in the year when it is dynamically expressed in strings of abuse, in a number of comical and unexpected images; this shows how the aesthetics of the grotesque had become tied up with calendrical customs which served both to regulate and discharge the energies of popular festivity.

By creating a character like Falstaff, Shakespeare comes as close as he possibly could to Rabelais's particular style of comedy which, as we know, centres on the body and on the belly as well as on the world of the tavern and of the carnivalesque celebration of life. At the same time, the stress placed on this lower sphere is being used as a distorting mirror to reflect and undermine the upper level of court life and of the law as it is embodied by the Lord Chief Justice.

The Falstaff scenes in *1 & 2 Henry IV* provide the spectator with a dramatic counterpart of Pieter Bruegel's famous painting 'The Battle of

From *Shakespeare and Carnival: After Bakhtin*, edited by Ronald Knowles. ©1998 by Macmillan Press Ltd. Reprinted by permission.

Carnival and Lent'. As I shall show, Shakespeare's ten-act play is shaped by
an underlying opposition between those two principles. Although we can
find no proof that Shakespeare knew of Bruegel's painting nor of the
contrary (he might have seen it in the form of Flemish engravings or prints
which were widely circulated at the time), it is quite clear that a Bruegel-like
atmosphere pervades the two parts of the play.

The second scene of *1 Henry IV* presents an inverted version of the
vision of time, which is expressed in King Henry's first words at court: 'So
shaken as we are, so wan with care, / Find we a *time* for frighted peace to
pant...' (my emphasis). The problem indeed is to find a truce, a respite to the
intestine wars of the kingdom. This hope is immediately belied by
Westmoreland's news of the battle on Holy-rood day (1.1.52). In the next
scene, what we first discover is Falstaff surprised by Prince Hal turning day
into night as he lies sleeping on a bench in the afternoon:

> *Fal.* Now, Hal, what *time* of day is it, lad?
> *Prince* Thou art so fat-witted with drinking of old sack, and
> unbuttoning after supper, and sleeping upon benches after
> noon, that thou hast forgotten to demand that truly which
> thou wouldst know. What a devil hast thou to do with the time
> of the day? Unless hours were cups of sack, and minutes
> capons, and clocks the tongues of bawds, and dials the signs of
> leaping-houses, and the blessed sun himself a fair hot wench in
> flame-coloured taffeta, I see no reason why thou shouldst be so
> superfluous to demand the time of the day.
>
> (1.2.1–12; my emphasis).

Falstaff's heavy, fuddled sleep provides a powerful contrast to the breathless
tempo of war and peace ('for frighted peace to pant ...') which, like its
sleepless king, fails to come to rest. Falstaff also stands as an ironical
objective correlative to Hal, who must find something to do because of the
non-vacancy of the throne. Killing time may thus be for him nothing but a
means to kill his father by proxy. Prince Hal levels his sarcasm at the
grotesque caricature of the king represented by Falstaff, while his father
Henry laments the unworthy dissipation of the heir to the throne.

In the Prince's speech, time is seen from the point of view of various
concrete manifestations (hours, minutes, clocks and dials) and it is
emblematized in a burlesque procession with Sir John's pet sins marching by:
'cups of sack', 'capons', 'bawds', 'leaping-houses' and 'hot wench'. A similar
device to materialize time under the form of carnival pageantry appears in
the allegory of Rumour at the outset of *2 Henry IV*:

Enter Rumour painted full of tongues

Open your ears ...
Upon my tongues continual slanders ride,
The which in every language I pronounce,
Stuffing the ears of men with false reports ...
And who but Rumour, who but only I,
Make fearful musters, and prepar'd defence,
Whiles the big year, swoln with some other grief,
Is thought with child by the stern tyrant War,
And no such matter? Rumour is a pipe
Blown by surmises, jealousies, conjectures,
And of so easy and so plain a stop
That the blunt monster with uncounted heads,
The still-discordant wav'ring multitude,
Can play upon it. But what need I thus
My well-known body to anatomize
Among my household?

                                                (*Induction*, 1–22)

With its tongue-studded cloak, Rumour is a visual metonymy of the many-headed monster and the several venomous mouths that swell the body politic with the ill wind of calumny or false news and, in its final metaphor, it reveals the aesthetic principle which lies at the background of carnivalesque discourse in the play. Such concrete figuration of the abstract (time, rumour), as picturesque as it is theatrical, comes from an anatomy or dissection of the body. It is a form of comic surgery, an art which was then regarded as a ceremonial practised in the 'anatomic theatres'.[2] Such variations remind us of the anti-masque, a device consisting in using a burlesque, popular or satirical sequence to be used as a contrast or as an introduction to the more lofty theme of the masque itself.

The rest of the exchanges between the Prince and Falstaff indeed take us towards a lyrical outburst, which is reminiscent of the verbal refinements of the masque:

Fal. Marry then sweet wag, when thou art king let not us that are
    squires of the night's body be called thieves of the day's beauty:
    let us be Diana's foresters, gentlemen of the shade, minions of
    the moon; and let men say we be men of good government,
    being governed, as the sea is, by our noble and chaste mistress
    the moon, under whose countenance we steal ...

                                                            (1.2.23–9)

Besides the string of puns on 'night'/'knight', 'body'/'bawdy',
'beauty'/'booty' and the alliterative sequence, one remarks a style that
parodies Lyly's Euphuism in *Endymion* (1591), a comedy where the title-part
is a young man in love with the goddess Cynthia, the inconstant moon. The
prologue of the play presents it as 'a tale of the Man in the Moone' and one
finds in the buffooneries of the subplot a passage close to Prince Hal's first
soliloquy.[3]

In this burlesque idealization of a rather sordid situation of cony-
catcher and parasite, Shakespeare lends a euphuistic accent to his character
to suggest an association between Falstaff and Robin Hood and to make his
tavern the urban counterpart of Sherwood Forest. At the same time, the
allusion to Diana and the moon contributes to making Falstaff the champion
of carnivalesque misrule in the history plays linked to the 'monstrous
regiment of women'—by witches like Joan of Arc or amazons like Margaret
(wasn't misrule essentially regarded then as a 'rule of mis(s)?').[4] Indeed
Falstaff will later say that 'his skin hangs about him like an old lady's loose
gown' (3.3.2–3) and, in *The Merry Wives of Windsor*, he will leave Mrs Ford's
house disguised as Mother Prat, also known as 'the fat' or 'the old woman' of
Brainford (4.2.67, 69, 168). So, it would seem that, under his cloak, Falstaff
might embody the roles of both Robin Hood and Maid Marian before the
latter becomes identified with Mrs Quickly later in the play (3.3.112).
Transvestism and gender change were indeed one of the common customs
and features of carnival games. Moreover, to the popular audiences of the
Globe, the folklore linked to Robin Hood combined the conservative flavour
of 'Merry England' with the rebellion against the king's authority. An
Eastcheap tavern, like the forest of yore, seems to enjoy the privilege of a
'liberty', i.e. of a form of extraterritorial status, where the outlaws and the
merry souls could find a refuge. (Doesn't the name 'Boar's Head'
symbolically refer to hunting, the main sport and means of sustenance of the
big-hearted rebels and thieves?) So the territorial enclave gives a 'habitation
and a name' to the carnivalesque theme, itself enclosed within a parenthesis,
that of the calendary interval.

Falstaff's rebellion is first and foremost that of the belly and it is made
to look like the general leading Carnival's army against the soldiers of
famine[5] and the spare practitioners of Lent. The successive waves of assault
of the fat against the lean make up a leitmotif running through both parts of
Henry IV and they are a comic counterpoint to the real battles opposing the
rebels to the king. This is a form of popular psychomachia where the strings
of parodic litanies belong to the genre which Bakhtin calls 'praise-abuse'.[6]
Many examples of it can be found in *1 Henry IV*, as, for instance, in this
exchange between the Prince and Falstaff:

> *Prince* Why, thou clay-brained guts, thou knotty-pated fool thou
> whoreson obscene greasy tallow catch ... This sanguine
> coward, this bed presser, this horse back breaker, this huge hill
> of flesh,—
> *Falstaff* 'Sblood, you starveling, you eel-skin, you dried neat's
> tongue, you bull's pizzle, you stock-fish ... you tailor's yard,
> you sheath, you bow-case, you vile standing tuck
>
> (2.4.221–44)

In the second half of this same scene, we attend a highly theatrical rendering
of the game in a scene of a play within the play. Initially presented as a parody
of the king's rebuking his son Hal, it soon veers off in the direction of the
belly Falstaff, who is then put on trial like King Carnival on the eve of Ash
Wednesday. What should have been for Hal a rehearsal and an exorcism of
his father's angry sermonizing quickly turns into a carnivalesque show and
the condemnation of Falstaff, the Prince's punching bag:

> *Prince* Why dost thou converse with that trunk of humours, that
> bolting-hutch of beastliness, that swollen parcel of dropsies,
> that huge bombard of sack, that stuffed cloak-bag of guts, that
> roasted Manningtree ox with the pudding in his belly ...?
>
> (2.4.442–47)

The string of adjectives is the form taken up by these oral and tribal jousts,
where the totem of Falstaff is the fat ox of Manningtree fair, in Essex, or the
little boar-pig of Bartholomew Fair in London ('little tidy Bartholomew
boar-pig', *2 Henry IV*, 2.4.227), while Hal is identified with a form of dried
ling (stockfish) and with an eel's skin (if that word is used rather than 'elf-
skin', which would assimilate him to the 'changeling' mentioned by the king
in the first scene of the play [*1 Henry IV*, 1.1.85–90]).

These facetious as well as injurious appellations are complemented by
a number of pet-names which play upon patronyms as well as on the physical
appearance of the two antagonists. Thus, Hal is associated with 'egg and
butter' (1.2.21), i.e. to lean fare, in the beginning, and he becomes opposed
to the one whom Poins calls 'Sir John Sack and Sugar' (1.2.110) in the same
way as Sir John Paunch appears as the antithesis of John of Gaunt (2.2:63–4).
This brilliant pun of Falstaff's turns the bodily variations on the
carnivalesque body into the negative counterpart of the heroic dimension
since this apostrophe takes up again John of Gaunt's variations on his name
in *Richard II*, when he is about to die:

Richard How is't with aged Gaunt?
Gaunt O, how that name befits my composition!
   Old Gaunt indeed and gaunt in being old,
   Within me grief hath kept a tedious fast,
   And who abstains from meat that is not gaunt?
   For sleeping England long time have I watch'd,
   Watching brings leanness, leanness is all gaunt ...
   Gaunt am I for the grave, gaunt as a grave,
   Whose hollow womb inherits nought but bones ...
                                 (2.1.72–83)

In *2 Henry IV*, when the body appears more and more afflicted by disease and symbolizes the progressive exhaustion of the king, food is lean and it goes against the grain of Falstaff's pun which transforms 'gravy' into 'gravity' before a rather pompous Lord Chief Justice. The time of penance has arrived, even if certain champions of leanness like Shallow have now become fatter:

Falstaff I do remember him at Clement's Inn, like a man made after supper of a cheese-paring. When a' was naked, he was for all the world like a forked radish, with a head fantastically carved upon it with a knife ... I saw it and told John a Gaunt he beat his own name, for you might have thrust him and all his apparel into an eel-skin-the case of a treble hautboy was a mansion for him, a court; and now has he land and beefs.
                                 (3.2.302–22)

Doll calls Falstaff a 'muddy conger', while both, according to the Hostess, are 'as rheumatic as two dry toasts' (*2 Henry IV*, 2.4. 53, 56). Speaking of Pistol; Doll says that 'he lives upon mouldy stewed prunes and dried cakes' (2.4.142–3). Falstaff compares Poins to Prince Hal, because 'he eats conger and fennel, and drinks off candles' ends for flap-dragons' (2.4.242–3). As to the army of down-at-heel rogues whom he recruits for the battle, it only includes a bunch of pathetic starvelings with predestined names: 'Mouldy', 'Shadow', 'Feeble', 'Wart' and 'Bullcalf' (only the latter might seem worthy to join the army of King Carnival!). Life's energy has dwindled away, the 'wassail candle' is almost burnt out and Falstaff's purple piece on the praise of sherris sack, which he delivers on the eve of the battle of Gaultree forest (4.3), is like his last will and testament. This meditation on the virtues of wine that warms the blood reminds us of Rabelais's praise of the 'Dive bouteille' while it lays down the main commandments of Falstaff's carnivalesque catechism:

Good faith, this same young sober-blooded boy doth not love me, nor a man cannot make him laugh; but that's no marvel, he drinks no wine. There's never none of these demure boys come to any proof; for thin drink doth so over-cool their blood, and making many fish meals, that they fall into a kind a male green-sickness; and when they marry they get wenches. They are generally fools and cowards—which some of us should be too, but for inflammation. A good sherris-sack hath a twofold operation in it. It ascends me into the brain, dries me there all the foolish and dull and crudy vapours which environ it, makes it apprehensive, quick, forgetive, full of nimble, fiery and delectable shapes, which, delivered o'er to the voice, the tongue, which is the birth, become excellent wit. The second property of your excellent sherris is the warming of the blood ... It illumineth the face, which, as a beacon, gives warming to all the rest of this kingdom, man, to arm; and then the vital commoners, and inland petty spirits, muster me all to their captain, the heart; who, great and puffed with this retinue, doth any deed of courage; and this valour comes of sherris ... If I had a thousand sons, the first human principle I would teach them should be to forswear thin potation, and to addict themselves to sack ...

(4.3.85–124)

In this perspective, Hal, who plays the part of Falstaff's adoptive son (the phrase 'If I had a thousand sons' has here a bitterly ironic ring), uses the carnivalesque as a mask or as a cloud to hide his 'sun-like majesty' before he can rise in the full light of his glory and surprise the world with his sudden reformation in *Henry V*.[7] As a consummate actor, the Prince has understood all he could get out of his momentary eclipse from court in the 'anti-masque' of his underground life: this was a sure way of preparing his future metamorphosis and to mastermind the rebirth of the obscure changeling into a glorious sun-king, the apotheosis of the masque, where, after he has eliminated his rival Hotspur, he will keep the best role for himself.

In the last part of this essay, I shall focus on the importance of the ambivalent images of the body in the play. These serve to give a comic content to the punning association often made between carnival and cannibal.[8] This deep-seated ambivalence is part and parcel of the grotesque and it been well analysed by Neil Rhodes in *Elizabethan Grotesque*: 'The Elizabethan grotesque derives from the unstable coalescence of contrary images of the flesh: indulged, abused, purged and damned.'[9] Indeed, at the beginning of *1 Henry IV* the king's description of the horrors of the intestine strife that tears apart the kingdom evokes images of cannibalism in its presentation of war as 'butchery':

> No more the thirsty entrance of this soil
> Shall daub her lips with her own children's blood.
>   ... those opposed eyes,
> Which, like the meteors of a troubled heaven,
> All of one nature, of one substance bred,
> Did lately meet in the intestine shock
> And furious close of civil butchery,
> Shall now ... be no more oppos'd.
>
>   (1.1.5–15)

Now, this pious wish is immediately opposed by Westmoreland's atrocious news from the Welsh front:

>   the noble Mortimer ...
> Was by the rude hands of that Welshman taken
> A thousand of his people butchered,
> Upon whose dead corpse there was such misuse,
> Such beastly shameless transformation
> By those Welshwomen done, as may not be
> Without much shame retold or spoken of.
>
>   (1.1.38–46)

Hence the second Henriad opens on these images of carnage, on the scandal of bodies shamefully mutilated by furious hags. The earth is here personalized in the pathetic fallacy of line 6, which turns it into an infanticidal and cannibalistic mother, a ghoul that drinks fresh blood. This image is reinforced by Hotspur's heroic stance when he says that he is ready to shed all the precious liquid in his veins: 'Yea, on his part I'll empty all these veins, / And shed my dear blood, drop by drop in the dust ...' (1.3.131–2). The grotesque is born out of the juxtaposition of this with the quantities of sherris-sack drunk by Falstaff all along the two parts of the play! The vampiric earth is as thirsty for blood as he is of wine!

This is also present in the subterranean network of imagery which associates Falstaff's cony-catching and carnival activities with hunting: it is indeed indirectly linked to the images of 'Diana's foresters' and to the name of the 'Boar's Head' in Eastcheap.[10] Furthermore, if one thinks that the battle described by Westmoreland takes place on Holy-rood Day (14

September), one can note that the date corresponds to the opening date of the hunting season in early modern England.[11]

In this light, it is clear that the game that is being hunted in the play is no other than Falstaff himself, the big boar that will have to be chased, thus creating the comic image of a predator losing part of his tallow in the sport: '... Falstaff sweats to death, / And lards the lean earth as he walks along' (2.2.103–4). This is a subliminal introduction to the famous theme of the hunted hunter—a theme also found in *The Merry Wives of Windsor*, when Falstaff, wearing the horns of the mythical hunter, is finally identified with a deer. This is because of the expected deer/dear pun in a love comedy and also a reference to the myth of Actaeon which is here rendered in its moralizing, bourgeois version of *Ovide moralisé*.[12]

The underlying motif of the hunt in *1 & 2 Henry IV* is itself an indirect metaphor of civil war under its double appellation of 'intestine shock' and 'civil butchery' in the king's speech. One is naturally tempted to equate the adjective 'intestine' with the obsession with Falstaff's belly or 'guts', which are part and parcel of the carnivalesque preoccupation with foodstuffs and tripe. Shrove Tuesday was then regarded as the time for slaughtering cattle and Bruegel, in his 'Battle of Carnival and Lent', has painted King Carnival as a butcher straddling a wine barrel and brandishing a pike with a piglet on the spit.[13]

Shakespeare then brings carnival, tavern and hunting together on the battlefield scene when Falstaff simulates death in order to keep his body alive. The rhythm of Shrewsbury's battle is indeed quite intense and breathtaking. On the one hand we find the war tactics consisting in multiplying the images of the king (called 'counterfeits' or 'shadows') who has his arms worn by barons such as Blunt, thus giving the fiery Douglas the feeling that the king's body may grow again as fast as Hydra's heads (5.4.24). On the other hand, there is a double duel. The one opposes Hal and Hotspur and is ended by the death of the champion of a decaying chivalry while the other is a shadow combat between Douglas and Falstaff since the latter avoids the fight to fake death. This is the moment when the Prince, seeing him lying upon the earth, pronounces his death elegy:

> What, old acquaintance, could not all this flesh
> Keep in a little life? Poor Jack, farewell ...
> Death hath not struck so fat a deer today.
> Though many dearer, in this bloody fray.
> Embowell'd will I see thee by and by
> Till then in blood by noble Percy lie.
>
>   (5.4.101–9)

Falstaff rises at once, indignant at the words he has just heard: 'Embowelled? If thou embowel me today, I'll give / you leave to powder me and eat me tomorrow' (5.4.110–11). On the one hand, we find war with its codes, tricks and honour, on the other the hunt and its ritual. Falstaff, like the deer before the quarry, must be embowelled. His body becomes food in the ironical anti-phrase, which he mentally addresses to the Prince as already suggested earlier in the burlesque scene of the bottle used as a pistol:

> Well, if Percy be alive, I'll pierce him. If he do come in my way, so: if he do not, if I come in his willingly, let him make a carbonado of me
>
> (5.3.56–8)

So, Falstaff is once again turned into the 'Manningtree ox with the pudding in his belly' (*1 Henry IV*, 2.1.446–7), fat carnival food to feast his friends. Besides those discrete allusions to cannibalism, echoed by Pistol's slip when he evokes in front of the Hostess and Bardolph 'Caesars and ... Cannibals' instead of Hannibals (1.4.163), he becomes, in the phrase of Michael Bristol, 'a clownish paraphrase of the political doctrine of *dignitas non moritur*: the king's mystical identity or dignity never dies.'[14]

In the last analysis, whether it presents us with Douglas's frustration in his inability to kill the king during the battle, since he can only attack his make-believe counterparts ('counterfeits') or duplications of himself ('shadows'), or whether it is the question of Falstaff's fake death, the comedy of the grotesque lies in the multiplication of trompe-l'oeil images and in the physical impossibility of seizing the reality of the identity or of the state of the adversary's body (either alive or dead).

Parallel to these *ad infinitum* duplications, the tension between the macabre and the culinary or between horror and festivity remains the dominant factor. Before the battle, Falstaff had cynically called his lean and hungry troops 'food for powder' (*1 Henry IV*, 4.2.65–6). At the heroic level, Percy's last words before he dies are a real macabre exemplum, a form of *Vanitas* in which human flesh is nothing but food for worms:

> *Hotspur* O, I could prophesy
>   But that the earthly and cold hand of death
>   Lies on my tongue: no, Percy thou art dust,
>   And food for—[*Dies.*]
> *Prince* For worms, brave Percy.
>
> (*1 Henry IV*, 5.4.82–6)

At this juncture, we are made to understand the fundamental complementarity of tavern life and battleground, of Carnival exuberance and Lenten restriction or negativity: they are the two sides of the same coin. On the one hand, there is the slaughtering of cattle at Martinmas and the pigs butchered in Carnival time with vast amounts of wine or sherris sack being drunk to fill Falstaff's hungry belly and bottomless throat; on the other, we find the butchery of civil war that fattens the worms and offers fresh drink to a vampiric earth. The recurring images of molten grease or lard in the various Falstaff scenes are the grotesque counterpart of the blood shed by the victims of the war. The libations in honour of Bacchus and the price paid for sacrifices to the god of war, Mars, all look like almost reversible elements in the carnivalesque vision of body and body politic where battle and banquet, hunting party and hearty eating are progressively woven into one another's patterns in successive networks of analogies.

The world of appetite, as illustrated by Falstaff's cynical sponging on the Hostess, leads to ruin as the latter bitterly complains to the Lord Chief Justice: 'He hath eaten me out of house and home, he hath put all my substance into that fat belly of his' (*2 Henry IV*, 2.1.72–3). The voracity of the carnivalesque body, emblematized by a gaping mouth and a swollen belly ('embossed', 'blown', etc.), provides an objective correlative of the idea of uncontrollable expense. It is also at the origin of a movement of expansion and excess illustrated by the puns on Falstaff's belt (see, for instance, the pun on 'waste' and 'waist' in *2 Henry IV* 2.2.39–42).[15] Falstaff is an apostle of extravagance like Lear with his hundred knights. This anticipates the whole trend of sickness imagery which announces both the end of carnival and of Falstaff himself. These become more and more important in *2 Henry IV*, so that Falstaff's banishment at the end can be read as a 'farewell to the flesh' or *Carnivale*, one of the supposed etymologies for the word carnival. At the beginning of *2 Henry IV*, Falstaff is anxious about the state of his urine, he complains of the various evils that plague him (gout and the pox) or of the weight of his belly ('my womb, my womb, my womb undoes me', 4.3.22–3). But these metaphors, as everything else in this play of mirrors and structural correspondences, overlap on the higher spheres, as Falstaff's diseases are also the symptom of the evil that is eating away into the body politic. Indeed, the king's body is itself being wasted by disease:

> *King* Then you perceive the body of our kingdom
> How foul it is, what rank diseases grow,
> And with what danger, near the heart of it.
> (*2 Henry IV*, 3.1.38–40)

In the Falstaff scenes of *1 & 2 Henry IV*, the battle of Carnival and Lent serves as a comic duplication of the opposition between the worlds of court and battle on the one hand, and of the festive life of the tavern on the other. The dominant patterns of imagery in these scenes find their justification and coherence in carnival and popular culture which pits the fat against the lean in a series of comic verbal assaults. There is a pendulum effect from one pole to the next which one may observe at work in the two Falstaff plays.

In this world of shadows, the more than substantial body of Falstaff becomes the metaphor of the avatars of the body heroic and politic in a world which, because of the crisis of traditional values, has now been possessed by a sense of relativity. In this murky world, the royal son/sun has been obscured by clouds and the heir to the throne, Prince Hal has decided to wear the mask of a reveller and boon companion, money and the body have become the yardsticks of all things. The size of Falstaff's body is certainly partly due to a capacity for caricatural and carnival enlargement and excess, but it also stands for the triumph of life at the expense of tragic sacrifice.

Carnival, like the king, never dies.

NOTES

All Shakespeare references are to the current Arden editions: *1 & 2 Henry IV*, ed. A.R. Humphreys; *Richard II*, ed. Peter Ure; and *The Merry Wives of Windsor*, ed. H.J. Oliver.

1. Mikhail Bakhtin, *Rabelais and His World* (1965), trans. Hélène Iswolsky (Bloomington: Indiana University Press, 1984).

2. See Marie-Christine Pouchelle, *Corps et chirurgie à l'apogée du Moyen Age* (Paris: Flammarion, 1985).

3. *Sir Tophas* [a bragging soldier] ... love is a lord of misrule, and keepeth Christmas in my corps.
Epithon [page to Sir Tophas] No doubt there is good chere: what dishes of delight cloth his lordship feast you with withal?
Top. First, with a great platter of plum-porridge of pleasure, wherein is stued the mutton of distrust.
Ep. Excellent love lap.
Top. Then commeth a pye of patience, a hen of honey, a goose of gall, a capon of care, and many other viands; some sweet, and some sowre.... (V.2)
The Dramatic Works of John Lyly, ed. F.W. Fairholt, (2 vols, London, 1892) I, pp. 69–70

4. See my article 'La notion de "Misrule" a l'époque élisabéthaine: la fête comme monde à l'envers et comme contre-temps' in *L'image du monde renversé et ses representations littéraires et para-littéraires de la fin du XVIe siècle au milieu du XVIIe*, ed. Jean Lafond et Augustin Redondo (Paris: Vrin, 1979), p. 167.

5. Indeed Falstaff says of Shallow 'a was the very genius of famine', *2 Henry IV*, 3.2.307–8.

6. *Rabelais*, p. 419. But the analysis of the concept is found earlier in the book: 'Praise and abuse are, so to speak, the two sides of the same coin. If the right side is praise, the wrong side is abuse, and vice versa. The billingsgate idiom is a two-faced Janus. The praise

... is ironic and ambivalent. It is on the brink of abuse; the one leads to the other, and it is impossible to draw the line between them' (p. 165).

7. See Kristen Poole, 'Saints Alive! Falstaff, Martin Marprelate, and the Staging of Puritanism', *Shakespeare Quarterly* 46 (Spring 1995), p. 73: '*Henry IV, Part I* ... is largely driven by Hal's flirtation ... with border between authority and subversion, orthodoxy and heresy. Like the anti-Martinists, Hal enters into the terms of carnival subversion, represented and embodied by Falstaff, while still maintaining his position of authority.'

8. In this connection, see Le Roy Ladurie's *Carnival in Romans*, p. 198 and my own comments on these analyses in *Shakespeare's Festive World* (Cambridge: Cambridge University Press, 1991, repr. 1994), p. 274.

9. *Elizabethan Grotesque* (London, Routledge & Kegan Paul, 1980), p. 4.

10. As P.E. Jones reminds us in his book *The Butchers of London* (London: Secker and Warburg, 1976), pp. 77–8, Eastcheap was the butchers' headquarters in London and a boar's head was the emblem of the Butchers' Guild of Saint Luke. I am grateful to Richard Wilson for calling my attention to this in his paper ' "A Brute Part": *Julius Caesar* and the Rites of Violence' (forthcoming in *Cahiers Élisabéthains*).

11. On this see Richard Marienstras's *Le proche et le lontain* (translated as *New Perspectives on the Shakespearean World*, Cambridge University Press, 1985), Paris, Éditions de Minuit, 1981, pp. 61–2. When reading this, we realize that the time which corresponds to the symbolic calendar of *1 & 2 Henry IV* follows closely the calendar of doe hunting which went from Holy-rood Day to Candlemas (2 February), i.e. to the first possible date before Shrove Tuesday (St Blaise's Day on 3 February).

12. See my article 'Ovidian Transformations and Folk Festivities in *A Midsummer Night's Dream, The Merry Wives of Windsor* and *As You Like It*', *Cahiers Élisabéthains* No. 25 (April 1984), pp. 27–9. Let us note, incidentally, that Falstaff, earlier on in this comedy, had expressed a feeling of nausea at the image of a 'barrow of butcher's offal' (*Merry Wives*, 3.5.5).

13. See Claude Gaignebet, 'Le combat de carnaval et de carême de P. Bruegel (1559)', *Annales*, No. 2, March/April 1972, p. 336.

14. *Carnival and Theater: Plebeian Culture and the Structure of Authority in Renaissance England* (New York & London, Methuen, 1985), p. 183.

15. See Poole, p. 74: 'Within the plays themselves, Falstaff assumes a voice and role similar to that of Martin Marprelate, becoming a swelling carnival force that threatens to consume Hal's "princely privilege"....'

Character Profile

Sir John Falstaff, we are told repeatedly, is corpulent and aging. When he first appears in *Henry IV, Part One*, he is about sixty years old, with white hair. This man, "as fat as butter," revels in sensual pursuits such as eating, drinking, and sex. But, curiously, for Falstaff the pleasure of joking and inciting laughter in a roomful of his friends is even more delightful than corporeal satisfaction. He is remarkably witty and the ultimate master of language and puns, endowed with a quick brain that seems will never be outsmarted.

One of the earliest samplings of Falstaff's deftness is his account of the robbery on the road. He relates how he and his friends are attacked and then bravely fight against two men, then changes it to four men, increasingly exaggerating the number of attackers. With each embellishment, he is questioned yet continues, delighting in the hyperbole. Finally, Prince Hal calls Falstaff "this sanguine coward, this bed-presser, this horseback-breaker, this huge hill of flesh," and explains that he and his cohort Poins had disguised themselves and that they are the men who actually robbed Falstaff and his group. The prince and Poins, therefore, know the truth—namely that Falstaff and his men fled like cowards from only two robbers.

Because the prince has revealed the truth, he believes Falstaff is trapped and will have to sheepishly admit that he wildly fabricated the story. But Falstaff refuses to be outwitted. Instead, he explains that he did not fight, since he saw through the disguises and recognized the prince and Poins. "Was it for me to kill the heir apparent?" Falstaff asks. "Should I turn upon the true prince? Why thou knowest I am as valiant as Hercules, but beware instinct. The lion will not touch the true prince." Unruffled by the trick, Falstaff adds, "But, by the Lord, lads, I am glad you have the money."

This episode demonstrates Falstaff's charm, skill, and ability to turn any situation in his favor. Indeed, he is much more than the traditional comic sidekick but rather has been compared to characters as complex as Hamlet and Don Quixote. Falstaff exists in his own world and draws us into it, a world of near total freedom. In this world, usual societal constraints no longer exist. Falstaff makes us question ideas as diverse as honor, religion, honesty, and patriotism. These concepts are addressed in outrageous ways, such as on the battlefield when Hal asks for Falstaff's gun and finds in its holster a bottle of sack instead. And these concepts sometimes are questioned verbally, pondered by Falstaff's intellect: "What is honor? A word. What is in that word honor? What is that honor? Air—a trim reckoning! Who hath it? He that died a Wednesday. Doth he feel it? No. Doth he hear it? No. 'Tis insensible then? Yea, to the dead. But will it not live with the living? No...."

Indeed, Falstaff was appreciated by many theater enthusiasts in his time. Tradition has it that Queen Elizabeth found him so enchanting that she requested that Shakespeare write a play where Falstaff falls in love. This play Shakespeare supposedly dashed off, in between the two parts of *Henry IV* possibly, resulting in the comedy *The Merry Wives of Windsor*, where Falstaff, however, is nothing of the man he is in the Henry plays. Here he is tricked, insulted, repentant, and hardly a gifted wit. The queen's request, apparently, seemed impossible for Shakespeare to satisfy with the true Falstaff.

Falstaff is appreciated for his wit, intellect, clear vision, and the fantastical fun world he creates in the *Henry* plays. At the same time, he has flaws (other than his overindulgences) that hasten his downfall, the most fatal being his lack of understanding of his relationship with Hal. Whereas in *Henry IV, Part 1* Falstaff and the prince are almost always together making merry, in *Henry IV, Part 2* they almost never are together. Also, in *Part 2* Falstaff's more seamy side appears stronger. He is still dependent on the monetary resources of Hostess Quickly and others, but now she brings a lawsuit against him. Similarly, powerful characters who previously had little or no contact with Falstaff—the Chief-Justice and Hal's younger brother John—do not appreciate Falstaff's wit. Falstaff defies the Chief-Justice; he also appears a worn-out lecher.

At the very end of *Henry IV, Part 2*, news is heard that Prince Hal is soon to be crowned king. Upon learning this, Falstaff prepares to go see Hal. "I know the young king is sick for me," he says. "Let us take any man's horses; the laws of England are at my commandment. Happy are they which have been my friends; and woe unto my Lord Chief-Justice!" Falstaff sets off immediately, stealing the nearest horse and riding with friends on the long trek. His words show his excitement and anticipation, yet they also show his grave flaw. Falstaff believes that he will gain great benefits from the new king and does not anticipate or prepare himself for a different scenario.

Upon arriving in the city, Falstaff addresses the new king in his ceremonial procession. The new king completely rejects Falstaff, publically and cruelly. His first words to Falstaff are cutting, for they erase their past relationship: "I know thee not, old man." He continues to scorn Falstaff, belittling him and focusing on his physical flaws.

The king banishes Falstaff, as he says he has done with his other "misleaders," telling Falstaff he cannot come within ten miles of him. Yet only moments later, the king sends Chief-Justice after Falstaff and has him thrown in jail. The last words Falstaff says on stage, in this his final play, are "My Lord, my Lord,—." This may be the only time he has not been able to save himself with his words, indeed perhaps the only time he has been kept from speaking at all.

In *Henry V* we hear Hostess Quickly at the tavern in Eastcheap exclaim that Falstaff is ill (although we do not actually see him at any point in this play). The scene changes, holding our suspense, and then in the scene after this, it is announced that Falstaff is dead:

> Pistol: … Boy, bristle thy courage up;—for Falstaff he is dead,
>   And we must yearn therefore.
> Bardolph: Would I were with him, wheresome'er he is, either in
>   heaven or in hell!
> Hostess: Nay, sure, he's not in hell.…

It seems quite fitting that the announcement comes in Falstaff's favorite tavern and that Bardolph, one of Falstaff's old servants, would wonder whether Falstaff is in heaven or hell, indicative of the ambiguity surrounding the character. Bardolph is a minor character, but his words are true, selfless, and affectionate, a great contrast to so much that has been said and done by the king's court in the *Henry IV* plays and, so, a great tribute after all.

Contributors

HAROLD BLOOM is Sterling Professor of the Humanities at Yale University and Henry W. and Albert A. Berg Professor of English at the New York University Graduate School. He is the author of over 20 books, including *Shelley's Mythmaking* (1959), *The Visionary Company* (1961), *Blake's Apocalypse* (1963), *Yeats* (1970), *A Map of Misreading* (1975), *Kabbalah and Criticism* (1975), *Agon: Toward a Theory of Revisionism* (1982), *The American Religion* (1992), *The Western Canon* (1994), and *Omens of Millennium: The Gnosis of Angels, Dreams, and Resurrection* (1996). *The Anxiety of Influence* (1973) sets forth Professor Bloom's provocative theory of the literary relationships between the great writers and their predecessors. His most recent books include *Shakespeare: The Invention of the Human* (1998), a 1998 National Book Award finalist, *How to Read and Why* (2000), *Genius: A Mosaic of One Hundred Exemplary Creative Minds* (2002), and *Hamlet: Poem Unlimited* (2003). In 1999, Professor Bloom received the prestigious American Academy of Arts and Letters Gold Medal for Criticism, and in 2002 he received the Catalonia International Prize.

WILLIAM HAZLITT was an essayist, critic of literature, drama, and art, and a philosopher. His books include *English Drama and Stage Under Tudor and Stuart Princes*, *Studies in Jocular Literature*, and *Spirit of the Age*. His essays, lectures, and other writing have been collected in various volumes.

A.C. BRADLEY was Professor of Poetry at the University of Oxford. His renowned book *Shakespearean Tragedy* remains a key source for scholars. He also is the author of *The Reaction Against Tennyson* and *Commentary on Tennyson's "In Memoriam."*

HAROLD C. GODDARD was head of the department of English at Swarthmore College from 1909 to 1946. He published work on Shakespeare, as well as other titles such as *Blake's Fourfold Vision* and *Chaucer's Legend of Good Women.*

KENNETH TYNAN was a highly influential theater critic who wrote for *The Observer, The New Yorker,* and the *Evening Standard.* He was a consultant for the National Theatre from 1962–1971 and authored numerous books on theater.

LEO SALINGAR has been a fellow at Trinity College of Cambridge University. He is the author of *Dramatic Form in Shakespeare and the Jacobeans.*

E. TALBOT DONALDSON was Distinguished Professor of English Emeritus at Indiana University and also taught at Yale. He was a founding editor of *The Norton Anthology of English Literature.* His books include *Chaucer's Poetry: An Anthology for the Modern Reader* and *Speaking of Chaucer.* He also translated *Beowulf.*

NORTHROP FRYE was University Professor at the University of Toronto and also Professor of English in Victoria College at the University of Toronto for many years. He wrote numerous books, including the seminal work *Anatomy of Criticism.*

WILLIAM EMPSON was an English critic and poet who taught at Sheffield University in Britain. His book *Seven Types of Ambiguity* is viewed by many as a classic of modern literary criticism. He also wrote books of poetry and other works, such as *The Strength of Shakespeare's Shrew, Milton's God,* and *Some Versions of Pastoral.*

PAUL M. CUBETA is College Professor Emeritus of Humanities at Middlebury College, where he also had been Director of the Bread Loaf School of English. He wrote *Modern Drama for Analysis* and edited *Twentieth Century Interpretations of* Richard II.

EDWARD TOMARKEN has taught at Miami University. He is the editor of *As You Like It from 1600 to the Present* and the author of books on Samuel Johnson.

FRANÇOIS LAROQUE has been Professor of English Renaissance Studies at the University of Sorbonne Nouvelle. He is the author of *The Age of Shakespeare, Shakespeare's Festive World*, and *Shakespeare: Court, Crowd and Playhouse*. He edited a *History of English Literature, 1550–1996* and Marlowe's *Doctor Faustus*.

Bibliography

Abrams, Richard. "Rumor's Reign in *2 Henry IV*: The Scope of a Personification," *English Literary Renaissance* 16, no. 3 (Autumn 1986): pp. 467–95.

Amirthanayagam, David P. "'I Know Thee Not, Old Man': The Renunciation of Falstaff." In Breyfogle, Todd, ed. *Literary Imagination, Ancient and Modern: Essays in Honor of David Grene*. Chicago: University of Chicago Press, 1999.

Barber, C.L. *Shakespeare's Festive Comedy*. Princeton, NJ: Princeton University Press, 1959.

Barish, Jonas. "Hall, Falstaff, *Henry V*, and Prose," *Connotations* 2, no. 3 (1992): pp. 263–68.

Barton, Anne. "Falstaff and the Comic Community." In Erickson, Peter and Kahn, Coppélia. *Shakespeare's "Rough Magic": Renaissance Essays in Honor of C.L. Barber*. Newark, DE: University of Delaware Press; London: Associated University Presses, 1985, pp. 131–48.

Battenhouse, R. "Falstaff as Parodist and Perhaps Holy Fool," *PMLA* 90 (1975): pp. 32–52.

Bloom, Harold. *Shakespeare: The Invention of the Human*. New York: Riverhead Books, 1998.

Bradby, Anne, ed. *Shakespeare Criticism, 1919–1935*. London: Oxford University Press, 1936.

Brooks, Douglas A. "Sir John Oldcastle and the Construction of Shakespeare's Authorship," *SEL: Studies in English Literature, 1500–1900*, 38, no. 2 (Spring 1998): pp. 333–61.

Brown, John Russell. "The Interpretation of Shakespeare's Comedies: 1900 1953," *Shakespeare Survey* 8 (1955).

Bueler, Lois E. "Falstaff in the Eye of the Beholder," *Essays in Literature* 1, no. 1 (1973): pp. 1–12. Chambers, E.K. *William Shakespeare: A Study of Facts and Problems*. 2 vols. London: Oxford University Press, 1930.

Charlton, H. B. "Falstaff," *Shakespearian Comedy*, 4th ed. London: Methuen and Co., Ltd., 1938.

Dean, Leonard F., ed. *Shakespeare: Modern Essays in Criticism*. NY: Oxford University Press, 1957.

Desai, Rupin W. *Sir John Falstaff, Knight*. Fennimore, WI: Westbury Association, 1975.

Efron, Arthur. "War Is the Health of the State: An Anarchist Reading of *Henry IV, Part One*," *Works and Days: Essays in the Socio-Historical Dimensions of Literature and the Arts* 10, no. 1 (Spring 1992): pp. 7–75.

Everett, Barbara. "The Fatness of Falstaff: Shakespeare and Character," *Proceedings of the British Academy* 76 (1990): pp. 109–28.

Freedman, Barbara. "Falstaff's Punishment: Buffoonery as Defensive Posture in *The Merry Wives of Windsor*," *Shakespeare Studies* 14 (1981): pp. 163–74.

Galvin, John. "Pickwick on the Wrong Side of the Door," *Dickens Studies Annual: Essays on Victorian Fiction* 22 (1993): pp. 1–20.

Goodman, Alice. "Falstaff and Socrates," *English: The Journal of the English Association* 34, no. 149 (Summer 1985): pp. 97–112.

Grady, Hugh. "Falstaff: Subjectivity between the Carnival and the Aesthetic," *Modern Language Review* 96, no. 3 (July 2001): pp. 609–23.

Greenfield, Matthew. "*1 Henry IV*: Metatheatrical Britain." In Baker, David J. and Maley, Willy, eds. *British Identities and English Renaissance Literature*. Cambridge: Cambridge University Press, 2002.

Greenfield, Thelma N. "Falstaff: Shakespeare's Cosmic (Comic) Representation." In Teague, Frances. *Acting Funny: Comic Theory and*

Practice in Shakespeare's Plays. Rutherford, NJ: Fairleigh Dickinson University Press; London: Associated University Press, 1994, pp. 142–52.

Hall, Jonathan. "The Evacuations of Falstaff." In Knowles, Ronald, ed. *Shakespeare and Carnival: After Bakhtin*. London: Macmillan; New York: St. Martin's Press, 1998, pp. 123–51.

Harbage, Alfred, ed. *Shakespeare: The Tragedies. A Collection of Critical Essays*. Englewood Cliffs, NJ: Prentice-Hall, 1964.

Hardin, Richard F. "Honor Revenged: Falstaff's Fortunes and *The Merry Wives of Windsor*," *Essays in Literature* 5 (1978): pp. 143–52.

Hartwig, Joan. "Falstaff's Parodic Nexus for the Second Tetralogy," *The Shakespeare Yearbook* 1 (Spring 1990): pp. 28–36.

Hembold, Anita. "King of the Revels or King of the Rebels?: Sir John Falstaff Revisited," *Upstart Crow* 16 (1996): pp. 70–91.

Hemingway, Samuel B. "On Behalf of That Falstaff," *Shakespeare Quarterly* 3 (1952): pp. 307–11.

Hinley, Jan Lawson. "Comic Scapegoats and the Falstaff of *The Merry Wives of Windsor*," *Shakespeare Studies* 15 (1982): pp. 37–54.

Hunter, Robert G. "Shakespeare's Comic Sense as It Strikes Us Today: Falstaff and the Protestant Ethic." In Bevington, David; Halio, Jay L.; Muir, Kenneth and Mack, Maynar. *Shakespeare, Pattern of Excelling Nature: Shakespeare Criticism in Honor of America's Bicentennial from The International Shakespeare Association Congress, Washington, D. C., April 1976*. Newark, Delaware: University of Delaware Press; London: Associated University Presses, 1976, pp. 125–32.

Jonassen, Frederick B. "The Meaning of Falstaff's Allusion to the Jack-a-Lent in *The Merry Wives of Windsor*," *Studies in Philology* 88, no. 1 (Winter 1991): pp. 4–68.

Kaiser, Walter. *Praisers of Folly*. Cambridge, Mass.: Harvard University Press, 1963.

Kernan, Alvin B. "*The Henriad*: Shakespeare's Major History Plays," *Yale Review* 59 (Autumn 1969): pp. 3–32.

Kirschbaum, Leo. *Character and Characterization in Shakespeare*. Detroit: Wayne State University Press, 1962.

Lee, Chiu Chin-jung. "Falstaff-Hal Relationship: Role Dynamics," *Studies in Language and Literature* 5 (October 1992): pp. 123–43.

Leslie, Nancy T. "The Worthy Wife and the Virtuous Knight: Survival of the Wittiest," In Donaldson, E. Talbot and Kollmann, Judith J. *Chaucerian Shakespeare: Adaptation and Transformation.* Detroit: Publications for Michigan Consortium for Medieval and Early Modern Studies, 1983, pp. 25–41.

Levin, Harry. "Falstaff's Encore," *Shakespeare Quarterly* 32, no. 1 (Spring 1981): pp. 5–17.

Levin, Lawrence L. "Hotspur, Falstaff, and the Emblem of Wrath in *1 Henry IV*," *Shakespeare Studies* 10 (1977): pp. 43–65.

Murai, Kazuhiko. "Falstaff's False Stuff: An Essay on the Dramatic Language of Sir John Falstaff," *Shakespeare Studies* 27 (1989): pp. 21–45.

Nahm, Milton C. "Falstaff, Incongruity and the Comic: An Essay in Aesthetic Criticism," *The Personalist* 49 (1968): pp. 289–321.

Orkin, Martin R. "Sir John Falstaff's Taste for Proverbs in *Henry IV, Part 1*," *English Studies* 65, no. 5 (October 1984): pp. 392–404.

Ornstein, Robert. *A Kingdom for a Stage.* Cambridge, Mass.: Harvard University Press, 1972.

Parten, Anne. "Falstaff's Horns: Masculine Inadequacy and Feminine Mirth in *The Merry Wives of Windsor*," *Studies in Philology* 82, no. 2 (Spring 1985): pp. 184–99.

Prior, Moody E. "Comic Theory and the Rejection of Falstaff," *Shakespeare Studies* 9 (1976): pp. 159–72.

Ridler, Anne Bradby, ed. *Shakespeare Criticism, 1935–1960.* New York and London: Oxford University Press, 1963.

Roberts, Jeanne A. "Falstaff in Windsor Forest: Villain or Victim?" *Shakespeare Quarterly* 26 (1975): pp. 8–15.

———. "The Windsor Falstaff," *Papers on Language and Literature* 9 (1973): pp. 202–230.

Ross, Charles Stanley. "Shakespeare's *Merry Wives* and the Law of Fraudulent Conveyance," *Renaissance Drama* 25 (1994): pp. 145–69.

Rothschild, Herbert B., Jr. "Falstaff and the Picaresque Tradition," *Modern Language Review* 68 (1973): pp. 14–21.

Scoufos, Alice L. "The 'Martyrdom' of Falstaff," *Shakespeare Studies* 2 (1966): pp. 174–91.

Siegel, Paul N. "Falstaff and His Social Milieu." In Rudich, Norma. *Weapons of Criticism: Marxism in America and the Literary Tradition*. Palo Alto, CA: Ramparts Press, 1976, pp. 163–72.

Smith, D. Nichol, ed. *Shakespeare Criticism*. New York: Oxford University Press, 1916.

Smith, Stan. "The Hunchback and the Mirror: Auden, Shakespeare and the Politics of Narcissus," *Miscelánea: A Journal of English and American Studies* 18 (1997): pp. 281–98.

Somerset, J.A.B. "Falstaff, the Prince, and the Pattern of *2 Henry IV*," *Shakespeare Survey* 30 (1977): pp. 35–45.

Spiekerman, Tim. "The Education of Hal: *Henry IV*, Parts One and Two." In Alulis, Joseph and Sullivan, Vickie. *Shakespeare's Political Pageant: Essays in Literature and Politics*. Lanham, MD: Rowman and Littlefield, 1996, pp. 103–124.

Spivak, Bernard. "Falstaff and the Psychomachia," *Shakespeare Quarterly* 8 (1957): pp. 449–59.

Steadman, John M. "Falstaff as Actaeon: A Dramatic Emblem," *Shakespeare Quarterly* 14 (1963): pp. 231–44.

Tiffany, Grace. "Falstaff False Staff: 'Jonsonian' Asexuality in *The Merry Wives of Windsor*," *Comparative Drama* 26, no. 3 (Fall 1992): pp. 254–70.

———. "Shakespeare's Dionysian Prince: Drama, Politics, and the 'Athenian' History Play," *Renaissance Quarterly* 52, no. 2 (Summer 1999): pp. 366–83.

Tillyard, E. M. W. *Shakespeare's History Plays*. London: Chatto and Windus, 1944; New York: Macmillan Co., 1946.

Toliver, Harold E. "Falstaff, the Prince, and the History Play," *Shakespeare Quarterly* 16 (1965): pp. 63–80.

Traversi, D. A. *Shakespeare: from* Richard III *to* Henry V. Stanford: Stanford University Press, 1957; London: Hollis & Carter, 1958.

Wilson, John Dover. *The Fortunes of Falstaff*. London: Cambridge University Press, 1943.

Whittier, Gayl. "Falstaff as a Welshwoman: Uncomic Androgyny," *Ball State University Forum* 20, no. 3 (1979): pp. 23–35.

Womersley, David. "Why Is Falstaff Fat?" *Review of English Studies: A Quarterly Journal of English Literature and the English Language* 47, no. 185 (February 1996): pp. 1–22.

Yoder, Audrey. *Animal Analogy in Shakespeare's Character Portrayal.* New York: Columbia University Press, 1947.

Acknowledgments

"*Henry IV*" by William Hazlitt. From *Characters of Shakespeare's Plays*: 148–158. First printed in 1817; printed in 1916 as part of The World's Classics series. Reprinted by permission.

"The Rejection of Falstaff" by A. C. Bradley. From *Oxford Lectures on Poetry*: 247–275. ©1909 by Macmillan and Co., Ltd. Reprinted by permission.

"*Henry IV, Part I; Henry IV, Part II*" by Harold C. Goddard. From *The Meaning of Shakespeare*: 175–190. ©1951 by the University of Chicago Press. Reprinted by permission.

"The Old Vic '*Henry IV*,' Parts 1 and 2, at the New Theatre" by Kenneth Tynan. From *He That Plays the King*: 48–53. © 1950 by Longmans, Green and Co. Reprinted by permission.

"Falstaff and the Life of Shadows" by Leo Salingar. From *Shakespearean Comedy*, edited by Maurice Charney: 185–205. ©1980 by New York Literary Forum. Reprinted by permission.

"Love and Laughter: *Troilus and Criseyde, Romeo and Juliet*, the Wife of Bath, and Falstaff" by E. Talbot Donaldson. From *The Swan at the Well: Shakespeare Reading Chaucer*: 119–140. ©1985 by Yale University. Reprinted by permission.

"The Bolingbroke Plays (*Richard II, Henry IV*)" by Northrop Frye. From *Northrop Frye on Shakespeare*, edited by Robert Sandler: 51–81. ©1986 by Northrop Frye. Reprinted by permission.

"Falstaff" by William Empson. From *Essays on Shakespeare*, edited by David B. Pirie: 29–78. ©1986 by William Empson. Reprinted by permission.

"Falstaff and the Art of Dying" by Paul M. Cubeta. From *Studies in English Literature, 1500–1900* 27, no. 2 (Spring 1987): 197–212. ©1987 by William Marsh Rice University. Reprinted by permission.

"*Morality in Henry IV*" by Edward Tomarken. From *Samuel Johnson on Shakespeare: The Discipline of Criticism*: 14–34. ©1991 by the University of Georgia Press. Reprinted by permission.

"Shakespeare's 'Battle of Carnival and Lent': The Falstaff Scenes Reconsidered (*1 & 2 Henry IV*)" by François Laroque. From *Shakespeare and Carnival: After Bakhtin*, edited by Ronald Knowles: 83–96. ©1998 by Macmillan Press Ltd. Reprinted by permission.

Index

Index